THE MEANING OF WORK

THE MEANING
OF WORK

Papers on Work Organization
and the Design of Jobs

Lisl Klein

KARNAC

First published in 2008 by
Karnac Books Ltd
118 Finchley Road, London NW3 5HT

British Library Cataloguing in Publication Data

A C.I.P. for this book is available from the British Library

ISBN: 978 1 85575 348 8

Edited, designed and produced by The Studio Publishing Services Ltd
www.publishingservicesuk.co.uk
e-mail: studio@publishingservicesuk.co.uk

Printed in Great Britain

www.karnacbooks.com

CONTENTS

ACKNOWLEDGEMENTS

Many people have helped in the production of this book. First of all, of course, there are all those people who were part of the action research projects which are reported in Part III, and without whom there would be no book; anything I am able to say on the subject is due to them.

I am grateful to the trustees and to my colleagues in the Bayswater Institute for allowing me the time to put the book together, and for their patience. They were not always pleased about how long it was taking, but they were always gracious.

Juliet Merrifield and Ann Scott helped with the original sorting and selection of material, turning the varied output of forty years' work into raw material that might be made coherent; Chris Chism coped with innumerable problems around the computer and its vagaries.

I am particularly grateful to a number of people who have commented on parts or all of the text. Some of the people involved in the action research projects have checked and commented on drafts of the chapters about the work they were involved in: Dr. Günter Keil, formerly of the Federal Ministry of Research and Technology in Germany, checked Chapter Seven; John Marks, former Chairman of the Trebor Group Ltd., checked Chapter Eight; David Leonard, of Taylor Woodrow (now Taylor Wimpey plc), as well as Ronald Mackay, of the European Commission, checked Chapter Eleven.

Two trustees of the Bayswater Institute, Brian Shackel and Sylvia Shimmin, discussed and commented on an early draft of the whole. The book has been a long time in the making, and both these good friends have since then died. Loretta Bellman also read and commented on the early draft. More recently, Stephen Overell and Malcolm Ballantine have taken the time to read and make helpful comments on the complete draft. And particularly Ken Eason, at the time the Director of the Institute, took trouble with it and made some very thoughtful suggestions. He also reminded me of a piece of work which I had forgotten to include. The additional chapter this led to (Chapter Ten) should, incidentally, reduce the impression that the early action research was only about manufacturing!

In respect of previously published material, acknowledgements are due to the following.

The British Management Data Foundation, for permission to reproduce, in Chapter Fourteen, a paper published in *The Management of Automation*, 1980.

Cambridge University Press, for permission to reproduce, in Chapter Two, an extract from the Introduction to my book, *New Forms of Work Organisation* (1976), and in Chapters Eight and Nine, extracts from the book *Putting Social Science to Work: The Ground between Theory and Use Explored through Case Studies in Organisations* (Klein & Eason, 1991).

Elsevier Ltd, for permission to reprint the article "Luddism for the twenty-first century", which was published 2001 in the *International Journal of Human–Computer Studies, 55*: pp 727–737; and to Colin Davies, of Corus, for permission to reproduce the figures in that article.

The Fabian Society, for permission to reproduce extracts from my pamphlet, "The meaning of work", published in 1963 as Fabian Tract 349.

The Institution of Engineering and Technology, for permission to reproduce an article, "The production engineer's role in industrial relations", published in the journal *Production Engineer, 57*(12): December 1978.

Springer-Verlag, London, for permission to reproduce a chapter, "On the collaboration between social scientists and engineers", from the book *Designing Human-centered Technology: A Cross-disciplinary Project in Computer-aided Manufacturing* (Rosenbrock, 1989).

Taylor and Francis, for permission to reproduce a chapter, "Some problems of theory and method", from the book *Satisfactions in Work Design: Ergonomics and Other Approaches* (Sell & Shipley, 1979).

ABOUT THE AUTHOR

Lisl Klein came to England at the age of ten; since graduating she has alternated between working in industry and in academic settings. Her industrial experience included a year on the shop-floor and, after training in personnel management, two-and-a-half years as a factory personnel officer. She then moved into research in industrial sociology, with early projects on the human implications of work study and the behavioural consequences of management control systems.

Research in organization and work organization led to a concern for the use and application of the social sciences, and she became Social Sciences Adviser to the Esso Petroleum Company from 1965–1970, and a senior member of the Tavistock Institute of Human Relations from 1981–1989.

In 1990 she founded the Bayswater Institute, was its first Director, and is now Research Director.

Her published works include: *Multiproducts Ltd. A Case Study in the Social Effects of Rationalised Production* (London, HMSO, 1964); *New Forms of Work Organisation* (Cambridge University Press, 1976), also published in German; *A Social Scientist in Industry* (London, Gower, 1976), also published in German; *Working with*

Organisations: Papers to Celebrate the 80th Birthday of Harold Bridger (editor) (London, Tavistock Institute of Human Relations, 1989); *Putting Social Science to Work: The Ground Between Theory and Use Explored through Case Studies in Organisations* (with Ken Eason) (Cambridge University Press, 1991; *Working Across the Gap: The Practice of Social Science in Organizations* (London, Karnac, 2005).

FIGURES AND TABLES

PREFACE

This is the second volume of papers about the two topics that have preoccupied me now for more than forty years. It is companion to the earlier book about the practice of social science in organizations, which was published under the title *Working Across the Gap* (Karnac, 2005). Chronologically, my interest in work, what it means and how it is organized came first, and how this came about will be part of the story.

The two topics are both separate and joint. While the work I have done on organization has by no means always been about job design and the organization of work, the converse does not apply: issues of work organization cannot be separated out from other issues of organization; working with them gets one into the methodological questions of using the social sciences; and many engagements with organizations in any case have more than one focus. The two topics are still linked in ways that make any separation artificial, and it has sometimes been difficult to decide where a piece of work better belongs; to some extent the allocation has been arbitrary.

Although the twin interests of work organization and the use of the social sciences have been with me consistently over time, the work reported here was done from different institutional bases. I should perhaps explain what these were, since they are sometimes mentioned in the text:

After leaving college I did information and library work for two years, and then worked as a general factory hand for a pharmaceutical company. It will be relevant to say more about this later, since that was where the interest in work satisfaction began. As a result of that experience, I decided to train in personnel management, and worked for three years as personnel officer in one of the Metal Box Company's factories.

Then came some eight years of research: in the Department of Scientific and Industrial Research I took part in a research project on the human implications of work study, towards the end supervised by Joan Woodward and located at Imperial College. I then joined her there to work on research about the behavioural consequences of management control systems (having in between spent some time at the London School of Economics to get better qualified).

By the mid-1960s, industry was becoming interested in the use of the social sciences. Esso Petroleum Company created an experimental post of Social Sciences Adviser, and, at the end of my part in the control systems research, I moved there, holding this post for five years and engaging in a range of projects exploring the use of different kinds of social science. I then joined the Tavistock Institute, where I worked for nineteen years, and in 1990 founded the Bayswater Institute, which I directed for its first twelve years. In both institutes I have been engaged in a mix of research, action research, and consultancy.

All of these bases have contributed illustrations and experiences that feature in these papers. The two research projects in Part II were based in the DSIR and the Bayswater Institute. The five action research projects were based in the Tavistock Institute and the Bayswater Institute.

About this book

I find, on looking back, that the impulse about the importance of work in human life has taken me in a number of directions: to research; to action research and therefore the methodologies of action research; to getting involved in job design and from there also to working with engineers and questions of technology design; to attempts to teach and proselytize, including some attempts at political influence.

These are broadly the threads in the chapters that follow. After a historical introduction describing the context in which they arose, they are arranged in sections:

- Section I contains three papers that make the case; as it were, setting out the stall.
- Section II contains accounts of two pieces of research, separated by forty years.
- Section III brings together a number of action research and consultancy activities.
- Section IV contains a group of papers about relating to, and working with, other professions which influence the design of jobs—production engineers, ergonomists, engineering designers.
- And finally . . . The last chapter gives some reflections on these experiences, particularly on their implications for institutions and policy.

The thematic arrangement of a collection of papers means that some repetition is inevitable; I have done my best to keep it to a minimum.

CHAPTER ONE

Introduction: the context

A perspective on work organization in the twentieth and early twenty-first centuries

I n 2006, the winner of the Best Actress award in the Hollywood Oscars said, "I just want to matter and live a good life and make work that means something to somebody." In 2003, a young woman who had just landed an exciting, well-paid job that she had very much wanted, was already looking beyond it and said, "It will look good on my CV afterwards." In 1944, a German refugee servant girl could see nothing beyond her situation and found comfort in a hymn, "Lord of the pots and dishes". In their very different circumstances, and with their very different perspectives, all of them were looking for meaning in their work.

Work has always been central to human existence, though its content as well as its meaning for individuals and their societies continue to change and evolve as historical, technical, and economic circumstances change. In this chapter I present some of the background to the papers in this volume, which arose at various times during the second half of the twentieth century and the beginning of the twenty-first century. It is, of course, impossible to be comprehensive, and it would be foolish to try. I provide some indications of context where I know about it. That means that the more detailed historical background tends to have a European and

British focus. It also means that I need to give some of my own background, to explain both why this has been such a preoccupation—not as an interesting topic for academic study, but as a vital aspect of human and social life—and how the papers arose.

There are topics under discussion today that do not feature in this collection, such as outsourcing or "portfolio working". On the other hand, it is too fashionable to say that everything is different now. Jean-Paul Sartre's dictum that there is nothing new under the sun is largely true. There are exceptions: information technology is—was—a truly new development, but the human dilemmas of adjusting to it and working with it and designing it, in their many variants, are essentially the same as they were for earlier technologies. We persuade ourselves that they are new only through not knowing what went before. I try to address this question at the end of the chapter.

Technology? Politics? Science? Psychology?

At the beginning of the twentieth century, the conditions of work were a political issue in Europe. On the one hand there were the interests of "capital"—that is, the owners of capital—and on the other hand countervailing forces had developed, through both trade union movements and political parties, to represent the interests of working people, or "labour". The technical developments of the industrial revolution had mainly served to support the interests of capital, by reducing labour costs in both the quantity of human work that went into a product and in the level of skill required. Most obviously, mechanization meant that fewer people were needed to produce the same amount of output, and in many industries women and children could now do the work that had previously been done by men, who were more highly paid. Unemployment and the fear of unemployment, as well as the lowering of living standards, led to sporadic outbreaks of rebellion against the introduction of machinery (see Chapter Four); the poverty and privation that resulted from early industrialization are well documented, both in scholarly work and in some of the well-known literature of the time.

In the wake of these technical developments, the work that resulted from mechanization came to be studied, analysed, and broken down to its smallest components so that it could be further simplified—and therefore reduced in skill content and variability (and cost)—and so that the people who did it were, as far as possible, interchangeable and easily replaced. The originator of this approach was Frederick Winslow Taylor (1856–1915), widely described as the "father of scientific management".

Taylor was an engineer, and greatly enthused about scientific methods: the excitement of the Victorian age about the marvels of science and their contribution to human welfare carried over on to a scientific approach to people at work. These were the reductive scientific methods of mechanical engineering, which understood a system in terms of its individual parts and aimed to analyse complex things into their simplest constituents. Taylor believed that workpeople should be selected according to the level of the task they were doing, and that this should not include elements that were more appropriate for the attention of more intelligent and better educated managers. He considered that the methods and improvements in a job that were developed over time by experienced workpeople, perhaps with the help of their supervisors, were, in fact, inefficient and allowed management to avoid their responsibilities, which were the thinking, planning, and controlling part of operations. Having persuaded management to take up these responsibilities, one needed first to improve scientifically the equipment or machines being used; then select scientifically the workpeople involved; then simplify and improve their physical movements through method study; then train the people in the improved methods; and then follow this by detailed study with a stop-watch to arrive at the time in which that work should be performed:

> The idea, then, of taking one man after another and training him under a competent teacher into new working habits until he continually and habitually works in accordance with scientific laws, which have been developed by someone else, is directly antagonistic to the old idea that each workman can best regulate his own way of doing the work. And besides this, the man suited to handling pig iron is too stupid properly to train himself. Thus it will be seen that with the ordinary types of management the development of scientific knowledge to replace rule of thumb, the scientific selection of the men, and inducing the men to work in accordance with these

scientific principles are entirely out of the question. And this because the philosophy of the old management puts the entire responsibility upon the workmen, while the philosophy of the new places a great part of it upon the management. . . . Every single act of every workman can be reduced to a science. [Taylor 1911, pp. 63–64]

In this way, workpeople would be relieved of the burden of thinking and planning. Enormous improvements in productivity could be—and indeed were—obtained, which in turn meant that wages could be substantially increased. This in turn would mean that industrial conflict would be eliminated and replaced by harmony, mutual goodwill, and co-operation.

Taylor did not set out to reduce people to the lowest possible level of skill and initiative, but that was the effect of his way of thinking and system. Its influence has been pervasive throughout the industrialized world, and continues to be so. Therefore, it clearly taps into a need to rationalize, measure and control, which is more deeply ingrained, and therefore more widespread, than would otherwise be effected by the work of one man. It is, in fact, remarkable how both Taylorism and its counterpart, the "human relations movement", seem to last. The thread of Taylorism is a constant, interweaving with different technologies as they succeed each other, but always re-emerging. Currently, it can most clearly be seen in the organization of call centres, and in the continuing "industrialization" of many tasks previously considered to be "professional"; that is, needing skill, experience, and judgement (for example, the design of power stations, see Chapter Eleven). Fifty years ago, its manifestation was in the techniques of work study, although people's response to these was not what Taylor would have expected.

Already, quite early on, scientific management was causing unease, even in the USA. As early as 1915 there appeared a detailed critique based on an investigation of scientific management in its relation to labour, made for the United States Commission on Industrial Relations. It does not directly confront the question of individual satisfaction or development through work, but it includes criticism of unsubstantiated claims to "science", of poorly trained practitioners jumping on to the bandwagon set in motion by more responsible workers in the field, of over-simplifying and lumping together methods that in fact vary considerably. And it discusses the effects of these techniques, which are more than one would expect: that the economic effects are very great, that the social effects are not the beneficial ones claimed but are, in fact, frequently harmful, and that ways must be sought to retain the first while reversing the harm done by the second (Hoxie, 1915).

In the long run, however, such expressions of unease had little impact, and, while Taylorism has been seen by many as the logical expression of American capitalism, it had scarcely less influence on the organization of work in the Soviet Union. In the newly established Soviet Union there were vigorous debates about Taylorism and scientific management. I was once told by an elderly Russian émigré that, in 1917 or 1918, students at Moscow University had rioted against Taylorism. In an effort to check this and to document it, I discovered a wealth of literature about the debates concerning Taylorism that took place in the early years of the Soviet Union:

Throughout the 1920s there was controversy, essentially between two factions. They were not debating for or against Taylorism, but about different versions of it: on the one hand there were those who interpreted the scientific organization of work along very strictly Tayloristic, or "technicist" lines, the chief proponent of which was Alexei Gastev, Director of the Central Labour Institute. Gastev was a poet. It will sound very paradoxical to modern ears that it was the very uniformity and harmony of rationalized work, produced by mechanization and standardization, and resulting in "a most exact molecular analysis of the new production" (Bailes, 1977, p. 5) which appealed to him as creating the culture of the new proletariat, equally standardized and mechanized.

On the other hand, critics in the "Moscow Group of Communists actively interested in Scientific Management", centred in the Council on Scientific Management of the Commissariat of Workers' and Peasants' Inspection, took a broader, more systemic line, emphasizing the need to modify Taylorism with industrial psychology and to instil scientific management with more concern for the individual worker (*ibid.*). However, expression of the subjective experience of the individual worker—what we would call "job satisfaction"—does not feature on either side of this debate (any more than it does in the studies of the UK's Industrial Health Research Board being conducted at about the same time). The issue was how best to heave a huge and largely agricultural population into the industrial age while at the same time retaining the ideals of communism.

Lenin himself expressed contradictory views about Taylorism, but some writers think it is more the case that he saw the inherent contradictions:

> Although some analysts draw a sharp distinction between Lenin's pre-1917 censure and subsequent espousal, it seems more accurate to say that Lenin echoed a dual note towards Taylorism from the start. As early as 1914 he contended that Taylorism was at once a way of extracting the last ounce of sweat from the worker and of securing "an enormous gain in labour productivity". Of particular interest is Lenin's suggestion that Taylorism was not entirely successful because it was "confined to each factory" and ignored the "distribution of labour in society as a whole". In other words, it was not so much the inherent methods and principles of Taylorism that Lenin rejected as their use and application . . . The proposition which emerges from Lenin's discussion of Taylorism is that capitalist methods could be employed to build socialism. [Sochor, 1981, pp. 247–248]

Lenin himself wrote:

> The possibility of socialism will be determined by our success in combining Soviet rule and Soviet organisation or management with the latest progressive measures of capitalism. We must introduce in Russia the study and teaching of the Taylor system and its systematic trial and adoption. [cited in Bell, 1956, p. 41]

The kind of issues being debated in the Soviet Union were:

- whether work was separate from the rest of life, or part of it;
- whether the scientific organization of work meant only the physical movements and skills needed for a task or included elements of psychology;
- whether the search for increased productivity benefits should focus on the factory units or the society as a whole;
- a fragmented, piecemeal approach of distinguishing between "preparatory" (i.e., managerial) work and "actual" work, vs a more comprehensive, systemic approach;

- the contradiction inherent in maximum exploitation of the worker while promising maximum economizing of worker strength and upgrading of worker skills;
- the function of time in organizing work—the need to instil some feeling for time in peasants with no experience of industrial work, vs "chronometric barbarism";
- the conflict between improving material welfare and deferring individual gain in favour of broader social benefits.

These issues are not unlike the discussions in professional books and journals that I was to encounter when I did research on the "Human implications of work study" during the 1950s (see Chapter Five). The difference is that in Britain they were professional discussions conducted in the work study and psychological literature and conferences, while in the Soviet Union they were public policy debates, conducted in central conferences and the party journal *Pravda*. The difference is not between whether these methods benefited "capital" or "labour", but whether these were questions for professional or political debate.

It is a cultural difference, and I find myself on both sides of it. I need to say something about that, and about how I come to be engaged in this subject area. Although I had not been aware of this history, which I have only just discovered, there must have been something of this way of thinking in my own background, and so it is necessary to say something here about where I come from— literally as well as figuratively.

The personal context

I have never understood why the enormously important topic of the nature of work, which takes up a large part of most people's lives and influences them and their societies in myriad ways, has never been on anyone's political agenda in this country. Almost my first publication was a Fabian Society pamphlet, "The meaning of work" (see Chapter Three), but this was at first rejected by the Fabian Society Executive as "not being political enough" and only a considerable fight, and the support of its then Secretary, Shirley Williams, got that decision overturned. Some time later, I developed some ideas for policy on the topic of the nature of work. I made a number of attempts, between 1970 and 2000, to get it on to a policy agenda, with both the Labour and the Social Democratic parties. But it was not in line with the prevailing culture of what constitutes politics in this country.

What had mainly concerned the trade unions and politicians of the left in Europe in the first half of the twentieth century was not so much the content and psychological meaning of work as its basic conditions: its availability and the problems of unemployment; pay and other rewards; hours and working conditions; physical dangers and health hazards. These were urgent and difficult issues, representing clear conflicts of interest that permeated upwards from the shop floor to the political and international arena. Over time, and with many difficulties that are too easily forgotten, improvements were achieved—through trade union action, law and regulation, and through custom and practice.

In this historical development, the Czechoslovakia into which I was born between the wars was on a par with other industrialized nations, perhaps a bit more progressive than some. The most important influence in my early life was an aunt, Fanni Blatny, who was a social-democratic member of parliament in the first Czechoslovak government of President Masaryk. Born in 1873, she had become a socialist as a very young woman, horrified by the poverty, inequalities, and working conditions in our part of the country, which was at that time part of the Austro-Hungarian Empire. She and I were very close, and as a child I liked nothing better than to listen to her stories of family and history. She was not academic, but in 1937 she and a colleague, Alfred Kleinberg, published a book detailing the working and living conditions of women in the Sudeten–German region at the end of the nineteenth and beginning of the twentieth century. They called it *Das Denkmal der unbekannten Proletarierin* (*Memorial to the Unknown Woman Worker*) (Kleinberg & Blatny, 1937) and it is my most prized possession. She collected the accounts of numerous women and their families and the conditions in which they lived and worked, and Kleinberg put them into historical and economic perspective. There was no Charles Dickens or Mrs Gaskell to popularize knowledge of these conditions: a four-year-old is told by her mother that if she works hard at the lace-making she can have maize gruel to eat instead of maize soup, the gruel having more kernels in it than the soup. A domestic servant writes the saddest of letters to her sister before taking her own life; she can see no other way out from the unremitting overwork and ill-treatment. In such conditions of grinding poverty, and of the ill-health and early mortality that came with it, women were awakened to political organization. A fourteen-year old girl working in a grocery shop tries to persuade her boss the shopkeeper to give credit to women whose husbands were out of work. She is angrily asked, "Have you been infected by the Reds as well?"

As an adolescent in England during the Second World War, I again listened avidly to the political reminiscences and discussions, this time of the international group of social-democratic émigrés who collected around my aunt. But by the time I entered the world of work myself, the circumstances of post Second World War Britain had shifted and the values I had absorbed from my family's influence found a different expression. Largely because of changes brought about during the war and relatively full employment, basic working conditions were not desperate in the way they had been. The priorities of the post-war government of Clement Attlee were social security, the establishment of a National Health Service, and the nationalization of key industries. There was concern that people should have some say in the policies and practices of the workplace, and some of the newly nationalized industries set up groundbreaking systems of joint consultation. But, in the fierce debates of that time about nationalization, it seemed to me that whatever the arguments about public ownership, a person's day-to-day experience of work would not be much affected by who owned the plant or the business, even where joint consultation was a feature. Whatever economic or political reasons there might be to bring this or that industry into public ownership, a short-cycle repetitive job would remain a short-cycle repetitive job. And this day-to-day experience might be more important in the life of the men and women involved than the broader issues.

This view had been fuelled by my own early work experiences. The reasons why some work was stultifying, and some exciting, turned out not to be what one might expect (I have already touched on some of this in my earlier volume (Klein, 2005)): I left university with a degree in modern languages and applied for the first job vacancy sent by the University Appointments Board. I became assistant to the Information Officer of an association of specialist libraries. The job consisted of endlessly filing correspondence about enquiries. It led later to a junior job in the library of the Royal Institute of International Affairs at Chatham House. But this work had nothing to do with international affairs; this time it consisted of endlessly writing catalogue cards. I was wretchedly bored and miserable, and eventually started running mysterious temperatures for which no cause could be found. Once I had a fever for so long that they wrote from Chatham House to say that they were sorry, but they could not keep the job open any longer. Then I started to get better. Surprise, surprise.

So once again I had to find work. This time I went to the local labour exchange and was sent to a small local pharmaceutical company, where they made wheat-germ extract and vitamin pills. I became a factory hand, some of the time working in the addressograph department, where envelopes were addressed and stuffed by hand with advertising materials, and some of the time packing pills. To do this you held the handle of a wooden board that had twenty indentations. You dug it into a heap of pills and brushed off the surplus. In this way you had twenty pills, which you poured into a bottle. I started to enjoy myself.

Getting the hang of the job took about ten minutes. After that it became automatic, and one sat round a table with a group of very pleasant women, chatting all day. The subjects were very like those one had chatted about at college. The language may have been a bit different, but the essentials, both topics and ways of thinking about them, were the same—family, friends, men, local intrigues, national news. There was a young man who came into the department three or four times a day with packaging materials, bringing empty cartons and taking away full ones. He had been brought up a Christian but was losing his faith, and three or four times a day the threads of this discussion were picked up: was there a God, how did one know if there was a God, if there was a God why did he let disasters happen? Just like at university. Other visits could enliven the day: someone making a collection for a wreath or the children's Christmas party, someone selling nylon parachute material that had probably fallen off the back of a lorry. And always these visitors from other departments brought interesting bits of news and gossip. Other excitements occurred when the river-barge housing the personnel department sank with all the records, which happened fairly regularly.

After three or four weeks, instead of leaving as I had intended, I changed to working full-time. I stayed for nearly a year, and really had to force myself to think about moving on. People were saying to my mother, "You make sacrifices to let her go to university and look at her, £5 a week in a factory", and I, too, began to think that I should probably not let this way of life go on for ever. However, I certainly did not regard it as an "experiment", as people since then have sometimes tried to suggest. It was real, and I was a real part of it, not an observer.

The paradox was striking: why was it that I had been bored and unhappy working in a prestigious library and enjoyed working on the shop-floor in a factory? The answer lies in the details, and I have ever since been impatient with judgements and generalizations about people's work if the details have not been examined. For instance, an important element of the pill-packing and envelope-stuffing was that it was automatic and required no attention. That was why we could talk and think about other things, develop friendships, and get involved in each other's lives. If the work had required some attention without being intrinsically very interesting, as perhaps work with a sewing machine, it might have been quite different. An important element of the library work had been that there was virtually no connection between the catalogue cards and the books they represented, let alone the whole organization.

I was reminded of this years later, in the 1970s, when I was doing some work for the National Economic Development Office. In a factory making electrical equipment I came across a woman who was assembling the back half of an electric iron. She had been doing it for fourteen years, and longed to know how the front half was made, but did not have the opportunity to find out. What a waste of her interest and intelligence and potential.

Research? Advocacy? Action?

So then there is the question of what can be done about it.

Marie Jahoda was a friend, mentor and colleague for many years. One of the many things I learned from her is a way of clarifying and managing the boundary between research and political values: you can express values and political views in how you select topics for research, and you can express them in what you do with the findings afterwards—but absolutely not in between. It is the "détour via detachment". Confusion about this has, unfortunately, dogged much of what happened in the social science world in the second half of the twentieth century.

In Britain, publicly funded research on work organization began during the First World War and tended to focus on particular aspects, such as fatigue. Its early development is briefly described in the Introduction to *Working Across the Gap* (Klein, 2005). At the same time there were some studies and discussions of job satisfaction in a more philosophical framework, or of particular occupations, particularly in continental Europe. In Germany, the psychologist Kurt Lewin was fascinated with the experience of people in their work and saw a contribution of psychology in complementing scientific management by attention to "job satisfaction" and the relation of individuals to the job they most wanted to do. From today's perspective, it is significant that his paper on this is published in a political journal, *Practical Socialism* (Lewin, 1920). A Belgian psychologist produced a book titled *Joy in Work* (de Man, 1927).[1]

Politicians and trade unionists were, in the main, preoccupied with the problems of unemployment. However, a ground-breaking study of the effects of long-term unemployment on the population of Marienthal, a village in Austria which depended on one main industrial employer, vividly and convincingly made the connection between work and the quality of life (Jahoda, Lazarsfeld, & Zeisel, 1933; English translation, 1971).

The Second World War solved the problem of mass unemployment in this country, and the early post-war years were also a time of relatively full employment. From the 1950s, public preoccupation shifted to productivity. Sometimes linked with the search for productivity and sometimes separately from it, there also developed a growing interest in the nature of work. Work-related research was boosted by funding which became available under the Conditional Aid scheme that was part of the Marshall Plan. Some studies were of particular aspects of work such as shift work, the effect of ageing on skill, or financial incentives. But there also began at this time a research-based concern for the whole work role in its organizational context. My own first involvement in research was within the Conditional Aid programme, and also involved the whole work role (see Chapter Five). It demonstrated the short-term impact on both production operators and management created by the introduction of work-study techniques—the Tayloristic administrative equivalent of mechanization—and the kind of long-term adaptation and adjustments that both operators and the organization made to them.

Best-known and most influential among the post-war studies is the work which the then newly-formed Tavistock Institute did in coal mining. In essence, there were two findings, both accompanied by conceptual developments: the capacity of miners to organize themselves around their work without supervision, and that there was more than one way of organizing round a given technology (Trist & Bamforth, 1951, Trist, Higgin, Murray, & Pollock, 1963). In documenting how groups of miners organized themselves around the tasks involved in coal-getting, and how changes in technology both affected these modes of organization and could in turn be accommodated, the researchers pointed to the interdependence between what they called the technical system and the social system, and generated the concept of the work system as a "sociotechnical system". The second finding is signalled in the title of the book that resulted from these studies, *Organizational Choice*.

I take the term "sociotechnical" to refer to the interdependence between *the technical and social elements* of a work system, rather than between "the technical system" and "the social system". It seems to me contradictory to continue to think in terms of two distinct systems at all, once this interdependence has been laid open and one is thinking in terms of the work system as a whole.

While this basic *concept* of interdependence between the social and the technical remains constant, it seems in subsequent developments to have become identified with a particular *solution*, that of the autonomous work group, so that the solution has also come to be regarded as constant. The self-regulating work groups that the Tavistock researchers discovered with such excitement in the Haighmoor coalfield in South Yorkshire (Trist, 1981) came to be regarded as the model for work redesign, including in situations where this configuration was not necessarily appropriate and where other solutions needed to be found.

An obvious reason for this was that the autonomous or semi-autonomous work group at shop-floor level, by putting decision-making at the level of the primary work group, resolved that part of the problem of industrial democracy that is left untouched by systems of electing representatives to decision-making roles, which were being developed at that time in various forms in Europe (Emery & Thorsrud, 1969). However, workplace democracy is not the same thing as creating meaningful work or designing satisfactory jobs, and this double meaning has lent confusion to many of the later developments. Recently, I believe I have found another reason why such a high value was put on autonomous work groups: Eric Trist records how the self-regulating groups discovered with such excitement at the coal face exhibited some of the same characteristics as the leaderless groups involved in the work of the psychoanalyst Wilfred Bion on group dynamics (Trist & Murray, 1993). The excitement of discerning major coherence between apparently disparate elements of the Tavistock Institute's work must have been at least as great as the discovery of the self-regulating groups themselves; it may well explain why the autonomous work group almost became an article of religion in parts of the field.

To say that the social and technical aspects of a work system are interdependent was to put the concept at a very high level of generality. The originators of the sociotechnical idea went on to work with it in a number of settings that acquired status as the classics in this field, and in each of them conceptualization continued. However, little was done to make the concepts operational for use by others. In a paper published in 1976, Albert Cherns formulated some principles of sociotechnical design, reconsidering and revising them later (Cherns, 1976, 1987). Throughout he is limiting the discussion to work organization design and is not referring to technology design. They are, however, formulated in a way that takes account of complexity and the varied and changing environment.

During the 1970s, work organization came to the forefront of public attention in Europe, much influenced by the publicity given to developments in the Volvo car company. A new production plant at Kalmar was designed on the principle of a sociotechnical system, with the basic production units being semi-autonomous work groups; it attracted both a great deal of attention and a good deal of controversy (Lindholm & Norstedt, 1975).

On the ground there was by then already a great deal going on. In 1972 I was commissioned by the Kommission für Wirtschaftlichen und Sozialen Wandel (KWSW; Commision for Economic and Technical Change), set up in Germany by Chancellor Willy Brandt, to produce a state-of-the-art report on developments in work organization in Europe. It was an opportunity to catch up with what was happening in the field, and it became clear that there were by then some hundreds of experiments in train (Klein, 1975, 1976a) (see Chapter Two).

The movement to improve the quality of working life was also percolating into policy making. The following are a few brief indications: in Sweden, employers paid a levy into a Work Environment Fund, which funded research and action research into questions of the working environment, while at the same time the definition of the work environment was broadened to include the "psychosocial environment". In Norway, workers gained the right by law to jobs conforming to sociotechnical principles such as the opportunity to continue learning. In France, the Agence Nationale pour l'Amélioration des Conditions du Travail (ANACT) was established and continues to operate within the Ministry of Work, Social Cohesion and Housing; in Britain, a Work Research Unit was set up within the Department of Employment. It was later moved into ACAS (the Advisory, Conciliation and Arbitration Service) and eventually disbanded. Currently, the Health and Safety Executive is trying to extend the area it covers by propagating "management standards" on work-related stress.

The role of the trade unions in these activities has varied greatly. In Britain, the trade unions found it difficult to engage with the issue of job design and redesign. When I gave evidence about work satisfaction to the steering group that set up the Work Research Unit, one of its trade union members said, "That's all very well, but you have to realize that we have other worries." I could only respond by asking him to name one day in the previous thirty years when he would not have had other worries. There were three main reasons for their concerns: one was the ever-present anxiety about unemployment and concentration on the number of jobs rather than their content. A second was the fact that redesigning work roles could bring with it demarcation problems between different unions. And the third reason was anxiety about "job satisfaction" being used by employers as a way of undermining the ties of workpeople to their unions; there were rumours that this had been the case in the application of Herzberg's ideas about "job enrichment" in the United States (Herzberg, Mausner, & Snyderman, 1959).

These are indeed real issues, and there were real grounds for ambivalence: in Germany, a young trade union official once said to me: "You mustn't do away with mass-production assembly lines; the mass-production assembly line is the basis for collective organisation!" (Several years later, when he had risen to a top position in the German trade union movement, he hotly denied having said this.)

In the UK, the Trades Union Congress set up a working party which discussed these matters, and eventually the then General Secretary, Len Murray, dealt with the problem by writing a letter to all general secretaries of individual unions, in which he said that the TUC would support job design activities where new plant was being built and new jobs created, but would not support them with regard to existing jobs. I found this letter very useful when I was working on the design of a new plant in a strongly unionized company (see Chapter Nine).

With the emphasis on autonomy in work came emphasis on participative processes of design, in which those who are affected by the organization of work play a part in its design and development. The common view is that "design groups should be representative of all direct users of the system" (Mumford, 2003). Desirable as this clearly is, such participative design processes generally mean that what is happening is redesign or reorganization, not new design. In the situation of designing a new work system, the people likely to be working in it cannot be drawn into the process because, by definition, they and their experience do not exist yet.

I have three times been involved in the design of new plant or equipment, with different degrees of "newness" from the point of view of the nature of the jobs involved.

1. In the design of a new confectionery plant (Chapter Eight), the technology in the new plant was not to be very different from that in an old plant, which was to close down, and experience of the operators in the old plant contributed to the design. It was very generous of them to contribute it, because it was for

the benefit of others, not themselves. Those who were eventually to work in the new plant could not be involved—they were not recruited until two years later, when the plant was up.

2. In the design of a high-speed canning plant (Chapter Nine) the technology was to be very different from that in the old plant, which was to close down, so that the experience of the operators in the old plant was not very relevant, even if they had been willing to contribute it. The operators who would work in the new plant, again, were not in place yet. There were, on the other hand, other activities already going on at the new site, so that there were trade union representatives who could be consulted to some extent. But neither they nor, indeed, the engineers as yet had experience of the new technology.

3. The development of a flexible manufacturing system, designed so that the operator should be in control of the process, was happening in a university engineering department (Chapter Fifteen). Again, relevant operators were not available to consult—would, indeed, not appear for several years if the experiment was successful. However, operators from a nearby car manufacturer could be invited in for comment. So caution is needed in the generalized advocacy of "participative methods of design".

My work on two of the above projects was much influenced by what I was learning in Germany at the time. Although the German government came later to this field than, for instance, the Scandinavian countries (a board member of the KWSW asked, characteristically, "Is it true that everyone else is cooking with wine and only we are cooking with water?"), when they did, it was more systematic and on a larger scale than elsewhere:

In 1974 the German government launched a major programme to "humanize life at work". I cannot remotely claim that this was a consequence of my study of new forms of work organization for the Brandt Commission. Rather, they both came from the same common impulse, in which the German metalworkers' union (IG Metall) had played a major part. But I think the study may have influenced the people who set up the programme and who at that stage had no experience of the topic. I then worked on that programme for seven years, until 1981 (see Chapter Seven).

By that time, the tide of enthusiasm throughout Europe was beginning to wane a little. One of the German civil servants I encountered was to write later how the industrialized nations "had just begun to permit themselves the luxury of talking about the quality of life", before they were hit by the Arab oil embargo.

The coming of information technology

The coming of information technology (IT) brought a considerable challenge to ideas of sociotechnical design. Very quickly the essential designing of software got locked into the suppliers and vendors of equipment, with purchasers buying equipment "off-the-shelf". Sociotechnical design attention mainly focused on the systems within which the technology was being implemented and the process of implementation, rather than the technology itself.

One person who specialized in this was Enid Mumford, who was a member of the International Council for the Quality of Working Life (see p. 20), and who turned her attention to participative methods for the management of change in IT systems. Entering the increasingly popular framework of structured methodologies and acronyms, she devised the ETHICS method for implementation (Effective Technical and Human Implementation of Computer-based Systems). (See, for example, Mumford & Weir, 1979; Mumford, 2003.)

In a more comprehensive way, the HUSAT (Human Sciences and Advanced Technology) research institute was founded in Loughborough University in 1970 for research into human factors and information technology, and became the largest such centre in Europe (see, for example, Shackel, 2000). From this base Ken Eason carried out research on the human and organizational issues surrounding the implementation of information technology, using a sociotechnical systems framework. As a result he developed, among others, what have become known as user-centred approaches to the design of sociotechnical systems (Eason, 1988, 2002).

His position is that the difference between sociotechnical approaches in the age of IT, compared with those around earlier forms of mechanization, is largely a matter of degree:

IT is an extremely flexible technology—it can be used to micro-manage the work of a call centre operator (even putting their "script" on the display) or, in the form of a general purpose PC, it can be the most sophisticated tool for the support of intellectual work that has so far been devised. It creates issues of both techni-cal and organisational choice, with very significant consequences for the nature of work. As the opportunities for choice grow, so do the issues about who is exercising it. Opportunities for local work design are, in fact, very big; they are a matter of systems specifica-tion rather than software design—applications are configurable, but are not often seen that way. [Eason, personal communication]

The papers in the present collection that are explicitly concerned with IT include the one, already mentioned, where a rare attempt was made to design manufacturing technology incorporating IT, including software design, so that the human operator should stay in control (Chapter Fifteen). My own contribution here was rather limited, as I was in the early stages of trying to understand IT. A second paper arose from evaluation research on the implementa-tion of computers in hospitals (Chapter Six), and a third describes an attempt to contribute to the development and implementation of advanced technologies in the construction industry from a human and organizational perspective (Chapter Eleven).

Information technology has had major effects on the boundaries within organizations, and has therefore also affected the frames of reference within which organizations are studied. In the past, the work of social scientists in relation to industrial organization tended to come under two distinct headings. The first was con-cerned with the workplace, work organization at the level of the production process, and the primary work group. The second was concerned with the wider organization and its environment, and thus involved such things as the relationship between marketing and production, centralization and decentralization, different types of control system, and so forth.

With the coming of advanced manufacturing technology (AMT), and particularly computer-integrated manufacturing (CIM), the distinction and boundary between sociotechnical theory and organization theory becomes a disadvantage. Some profession-als have responded to this by widening old definitions: for exam-ple, expanding the word "sociotechnical" to encompass other aspects of structure. This carries the danger of fudging the fact that "technical" actually has a meaning, and that choices in technology design have to be made. I prefer to regard the organization as an open *sociostructural* system in which technology is one of the structural factors. As the story of Chapter Eleven demonstrates, IT also plays a major part in the relations between organizations.

A new millennium—all change!

From about 1980 there can be detected the beginnings of a paradigm shift, from the relatively simple and manageable—in the sense of being able to understand what was happening—to the unmanageably diverse and complex. One indication of this can be seen in the organization of those who were concerned with research, development, and action in the field of work organization.

In the early days of sociotechnical thinking, the Tavistock researchers and a few other colleagues formed a body they called the International Council for the Quality of Working Life, to propagate the ideas. The small size, and the centralized and self-appointed nature of this body became less and less tenable, and at a large international conference on the Quality of Working Life in Toronto in 1981 it dissolved itself. Instead, a body that was more representative of what was happening in the field world-wide was elected; I was appointed its secretary. It became immediately obvious, however, that institutionalizing this way of thinking into something like a body of practitioners was an impossible undertaking. For one thing, there were no funds. Even to get the now democratically elected international committee together for a meeting would have cost about £20,000. And to get a membership to provide funds through subscriptions meant that criteria for membership would have to be agreed, procedures and records established, etc., the whole institutional paraphernalia. There seemed no feasible compromise between a centralised élite and an unwieldy bureaucracy. The idea was abandoned, although some people were left disappointed and felt that the cause had been damaged.

This diffuseness and complexity affecting the professionals engaged with the world of work mirrors in a small way what was happening in the world of work itself. Information technology not only continued the process of progressive automation; it facilitated massive changes in patterns of work, including, for instance, where and when it is carried out. (A recent example, being rolled out across London but intended to cover the UK, is the "slivers-of-time" system, made possible by new web technology: individuals list any spare hours they would like to sell and local employers buy them.) In addition, there were structural, political, and market changes adding up to the phenomenon of "globalization", which were partly enabled by IT and partly independent of it.

The situation appears to have led to the condition that Fred Emery and Eric Trist classified as "turbulent". In a landmark paper they introduced, or rather re-introduced, the concept of the causal texture of the environment of organizations, classifying those conditions as turbulent where the environment itself, and not only the behaviour of specified elements in it, creates the conditions within which organizations function (Emery & Trist, 1965). Trist later elaborated on the thinking behind this concept: because of the increasing complexity and interdependence of factors in the macro-social environment, which raised the level of uncertainty, the wider contextual environment was undergoing a phase change from a disturbed–reactive to a turbulent field. The world was moving towards being on a continuous change gradient. It had gone beyond the stable state (Schön, 1971), and was in "permanent white water" (Vaill, 1982).

> It can be said that we are always in transition, though just to say this leaves out the large question of the speed of various transitional processes which can vary enormously. This formulation in terms of varying speeds yields in my view a more useful perspective than creating a dichotomy of steady states versus transition. [Trist, 1989, p. 51]

A detour via some recent literature

One effect of the emerging turbulence was that the world of work appears to have come rather suddenly to the attention of management writers and sociologists, in a way that had not previously been the case. Something about this literature needs to be included here, but it is different from that which I have drawn on before, in that these writers were observers and commentators of the scene, rather than being engaged with it.

Stephen Overell has contributed an overview of some of this literature (personal communication). He finds that in the 1990s a somewhat feverish atmosphere set in, with commentators jostling for their opinions to be part of the "consensus regarding change" at work. He attributes this spate of turbulent and sometimes apocalyptic writing to the prospect of a new millennium, and talks of "the millennial fixation with change": a new millennium—new everything! Drawing on this overview, some salient features of the writings of that period are described as follows.

The end of "the job" and rise of the "micropreneur".

More people would become self-employed. Much smaller organizations than before would co-ordinate the work of temporary staff, free agents, "micropreneurs", and subcontractors, who themselves would become "portfolio workers", stringing together their working lives doing different things for different employers. Charles Handy (1994) wrote: "Before very long, having a proper job inside an organisation will be a minority occupation", and "What was a way of life for most of us will have disappeared. Organisations will still be critically important in the world, but as organisers not employers".

William Bridges, in *Jobshift: How to Prosper in a World without Jobs* (1994), predicted the end of the concept of "the job": "What is disappearing today is not just a certain number of jobs, but the very thing itself—the job" (p. 1). The title of a book by Jeremy Rifkind is *The End of Work* (1995). Ulrich Beck (2000) foresaw the ending of "the work-based society". He created a new label for this revolution, describing it as the "Brazilianization" of the West. This referred to the way that only a minority of Brazilians perform full-time work within the established understanding of "a job". Working *"á la brasilienne"* involved the majority of the population scraping together a precarious living in craft activities, personal services, and small retailing—a multi-activity, nomadic style of work—taking on the risks that were previously carried centrally. This phenomenon was now migrating to the industrialized world: "For a majority of people, even in the apparently prosperous middle layers, their basic existence and lifeworld will be marked by endemic insecurity. More and more individuals are encouraged to perform as 'me&co', selling themselves on the marketplace" (p. 3).

However, the declining rule of paid work contained optimistic possibilities, provided we were prepared to shed our attachment to old-style stable jobs:

> The antithesis of the work society is not free time or a leisure society, which remain negatively imprisoned in the value imperialism of work. It is the new self-active, self-aware, political civil society—"the do-it-yourself culture"—which is developing, testing and implementing a dense new concept of the political. [ibid., p. 7]

André Gorz, in *Reclaiming Work: Beyond the Wage-based Society* (1999), also contended that into the shoes of the Fordist wageworker was stepping a new character: the jobber, the freelancer, the one-person enterprise. This new kind of person understood work to be fundamentally discontinuous; his/her difficulty was how to derive a continuous income from discontinuous work. Nevertheless, self-employment could be the "springboard for self-affirmation";

> The society in which everyone could hope to have a place and a future marked out for him/her—the work-based society, in which he/she could hope to have security and usefulness—is dead . . . We are a society of phantom work, spectrally surviving the extinction of that work by virtue of the obsessive, reactive invocations of those who continue to see work-based society as the only possible society and who can imagine no other future than the return of the past. [ibid., p. 57]

We shall see later how over-dramatic and apocryphal much of this forecasting was. In a more reflective way, Richard Sennett considered the consequences of some of the changes that were happening. He argued that the constant emphasis on "flexibility" was rupturing the narrative of people's lives and the coherence that comes with it. In *The Corrosion of Character* (1998), he argued that the aspects of work that had gone to build "character" were being eaten away:

The uncertainties of flexibility; the absence of deeply rooted trust and commitment; the superficiality of teamwork; most of all the spectre of failing to make something of oneself in the world, to "get a life" through one's work. All these conditions impel people to look for some other scene of attachment and depth. [*ibid.*, p. 138]

In contrast to these predictions, an Economic and Social Research Council (ESRC) study, *Managing to Change?* (White, Hill, Mills, & Smeaton, 2004), based on evidence from managers of 200 workplaces, found that organizations expanding grades actually outnumbered those engaged in de-layering by two to one. Careers and long-term relationships were popular—employers appeared to have become persuaded of the value of retaining staff because doing so provides the best answer to unpredictable demand: training employees to undertake a variety of roles is the path to "intelligent flexibility". Standard employment was expected to increase faster than flexible employment.

Solid objects vs the "thin air economy"

Manufacturing in the UK today employs far fewer people than before: only about eleven per cent of the workforce is today employed in manufacturing (though rather more if one counts those in the assorted manufacturing supply chains). This does not, of course, mean that manufacturing is in decline, but that the location in which things are made has changed—to China, Brazil, Turkey, India, etc. Even UK jobs in the manufacturing sector are often in research and development, brand building, management, etc. It is a truism to say that "services" predominate, though that includes a wide range of work.

The labels to describe work now are revealing—post-Fordist work, the knowledge economy, dematerialization, "weightlessness". Charles Leadbeater wrote, in *Living on Thin Air* (1999),

These days, most people in most advanced economies produce nothing that can be weighed: communications, software, advertising, financial services. They trade, write, design, talk, spin and create; rarely do they make anything. The assets they work with are as ephemeral as their output. [p. 18]

Some of this is not as "new" as all that. The label of a "knowledge economy" was invented by Peter Drucker in the 1960s (Drucker, 1969). Before that, there were sociologists who noted that many of the then rising middle classes made their living not by making things but by manipulating people and data, notably C. Wright Mills (1951), and William H. Whyte (1956). Moreover, it has been noted that some writers carried away by the weightless, post "thing" rhetoric seem to be deleting the human factor from work altogether, living in an abstract world of computer networks, brands, and virtual reality. In an entertaining demolition of some of this rhetoric, Ursula Huws (2003) pointed out that often in the knowledge economy, at the end of the immensely complex production process, there was some solid object: for example, Nike is a global brand, but where would it be without shoes?

Nevertheless, it is clearly true that computers now do quite a lot of work traditionally done by humans, and that this has consequences. According to *The New Division of Labor* (2004) by Frank Levy and Richard Murnane, if a job involves following a set of "if-then-do" rules, then it is programmable, and a candidate for either computer substitution or off-shoring. The loss of these jobs leaves a growing division between those who can and those who cannot earn a good living in the computerized economy. The skills most important to the future, as nations move up the value chain, would be in two areas: "expert thinking"—advanced problem solving and pattern recognition, and "complex communication"—human interactions involving persuasion, collaboration and negotiation. The effect of advancing IT in factories and offices would be that more of the jobs humans do would revolve around interpersonal interactions and sophisticated intellectual work.

It is therefore not surprising that the biggest growth has been in jobs that require significant education—managers, professionals, technical and administrative staff. Low-skills service jobs have also grown, but not at the speed of higher-level jobs; hence rising social polarization. Levy and Murnane write:

> Between 1969 and 1999 the number of adults employed as service workers [in America] grew from 11.6 per cent to 13.9 per cent of the adult workforce, but managers, administrators, professional workers and technicians taken together—the highest paid categories— grew from 23 per cent to 33 per cent. [p. 44]

Outsourcing and fragmentation

Charles Handy also predicted the rise of outsourcing, more and more activities being contracted out to specialists.

Some functions, for instance that of corporate lawyers, have traditionally been drawn in from outside organizations. There is little doubt that this is now happening with more and more functions. Many things are now outsourced, and BPO (Business Process Outsourcing) has become a recognizable business in its own right, applying to "professional" activities such as human resources, accounting and payroll, and to administrative ones that can be handled in call centres. This kind of arrangement between organizations can create considerable ambiguity for individuals: when a worker employed by one company is working for that company's client, who, if anyone, is responsible? Who directs the work of outsourced workers—the external service contractor who supplied the labour or the client who pays for it?

It is a legal and psychological grey area that is felt very acutely, for instance, in the event of accidents. In less serious ways, this ambiguity is now experienced by very many people around the world. Such arrangements mean that the traditional two-way employment relationship may be being superseded by something more akin to a triangle. In effect, many employees now have a number of people in some kind of employment authority over them. A book on "multi-employer networks" *Fragmenting Work* (Marchington, Grimshaw, Rubery, & Wilmott, 2004), argues that "It is often unclear where one organisation ends and another begins"—outsourcing can create a "psychological limbo" in which employees are uncertain who they are really working for.

The book relates the story of a baggage handling agency working on contract for airlines. One airline wanted the agent's staff to wear its uniform. And they plied them with HR initiatives such as performance-related pay and bonding exercises, although none was an employee of the airline. Other tensions arise when "retained" and "transferred" (i.e., outsourced) staff work alongside each other in the same office and one group gets a performance bonus, or other benefits, while the other does not. The nature of their work is determined to a great extent by the state of the relationship between employer and client. Sometimes, the worker may now be expected to identify with the aims and values of one organization in their capacity as employee and another set of aims and values in their capacity of providing a service to a client.

The "work–life" balance

The inverted commas here indicate that I have some difficulty with this phrase, now in common use. A balance between work on the one hand and home and family on the other, yes. But life? As if work was not a part of life, and as if much of what happens at home—maintaining it, cooking, cleaning, gardening, caring for children or the ill, or the old—did not involve work.

Spurred originally by the particular concerns of women in managing the integration of work and personal life, but applying no less to the lives of men, much of the discussion in the literature here is about demographic changes and about patterns of working rather than about the actual content of tasks. However, there are situations where changes in the pattern (time, location, combination with other tasks, employer) are so important a feature of the work experience that they in fact constitute a change in the content of work for the person doing the job and not only for the observer; the pattern becomes the content. Most of this wave of studies analyses and reflects on recent or current changes or predicts future ones. Very little of it actually engages with the changes. An exception is the work of Lotte Bailyn, who has taken the work–life boundary to be subject to analysis and design (Bailyn, 1993; Rapoport, Bailyn, Fletcher, & Pruitt, 2002).

So—where are we now?

As we saw, Stephen Overell attributes the feverish atmosphere and turbulent writing of recent times to the excitement associated with the turning of the millennium.

Now that things have calmed down a bit, perhaps one can look at them more coolly. In 1998, the ESRC launched a large programme on "The future of work", encompassing some twenty-seven research projects. Two of the objectives were to:

Replace speculation with a rigorous empirical and conceptual mapping of present changes in the character of paid employment and the shifting boundaries between paid and unpaid work; and situate contemporary patterns of work in historical context and expose points of continuity and change.

Michael Moynagh and Richard Worsley have made some of the programme's research findings available in a book, *Working in the Twenty-first Century* (2005). Backed with a wealth of statistical and other empirical data, the following are some of the trends they see:

- Good and bad jobs have polarised as the number of middling jobs has declined, creating an "hour-glass" shaped society (p. 3).
- Globalisation will tend to increase this polarisation. How far Britain moves up the value chain will influence whether middling jobs drift towards the top or bottom of the glass (p. 3).
- There are more jobs in Britain, and more people in employment, than ever before . . . Total employment fell from a peak in 1979 to a low in 1983, hit another peak in 1990, declined considerably till 1994 and has risen since to a record 28.4 million (p. 11).
- The demand for "new economy" skills will grow . . . [but] "old economy" skills will remain important too . . . The key skill of "communication" may be extended to "emotional literacy" (pp. 28–29).
- There has been no clear trend to self-employment since the mid 1990s, nor to employment in micro-companies (which can feel similar to self-employment) (p. 85).
- Individualised work may not replace the corporate workplace as quickly as some have thought (p. 85).
- One job per person has stayed the norm, permanent full-time employment remains dominant, workers are not moving more often from one employer to another and the "career"—as a way of viewing work—has triumphed. The content of jobs has changed more than their duration (p. 93).
- Workers will want stable employment for financial reasons, while employers will want the same to aid the accumulation of knowledge, hang on to key staff and manage change more easily (p. 93).
- The "contingent" workforce is unlikely to grow at the expense of permanent employment. Change will continue to occur

more in job content than in the frequency of movement between jobs (p. 93).

- Working mainly from home is likely to expand in remoter parts of Britain. Working from home for some of the time will continue to spread mainly among managerial and professional staff (p. 101).
- For many people, work and leisure will be less distinct, managing time will be a key issue, new forms of management control will be developed and more workers will have greater discretion over when they travel . . . (p. 101).
- The expansion of specifically home-working will be eclipsed by the continued expansion of mobile work—people who travel as part of their job (p. 109).
- Automation has re-engineered processes, boundaries have been blurred within organisations, collaborative networks have spread, dis-aggregation and re-aggregation have become commonplace, but the elimination of hierarchies may have reached a limit (p. 111).
- Some of today's forms of organisation will remain, alongside many new ones. Outsourcing will be more limited than many expect. Decentralisation will spread, but vertical organisations will still exist (p. 111).

I said at the beginning of this chapter that I would try to address the question of what is new. It seems that it is more sensible to think in terms of evolution than revolution: some things change quickly, some more slowly. Some are claimed to be changing, by commentators hungry for novelty. (The wish for novelty and drama, incidentally, seems to have some endemic character in the social sciences. In about 1978 I was waiting for a train in the London Underground. As the train drew in, a young colleague got out of the carriage I was about to get into. In the few moments it took us to pass, he said, "Well, 1976 was Job Design Year. What's next?")

And some things do not change at all but get forgotten and rediscovered—or not. Like Taylorism, some of the interdependencies produced by new technical developments are universal: in a study of vocational training in the light of technical change, carried out for the European Productivity Agency at the end of the 1950s, David King documented a number of breakdowns in chemical plants and investigated the training that the operators involved had received. He wrote of the difference according to whether an operator had been merely trained to respond to signals, and did so automatically, or whether he understood what lay behind the signals; for instance, knew what it meant if there was blue smoke coming from somewhere, and was able to take remedial action before there was a breakdown; and he calculated the waste which resulted from the more limited kind of training (King, 1960). In Richard Sennett's book (1998) there is the story of a bakery that he revisited after twenty years. The bakery workers now did not know how to bake, were not in physical contact with dough or bread, but pushed buttons in a Windows programme designed by others. This made them "flexible" in a new and spurious way—"baking, shoe-making, printing, you name it, I've got the skills," joked one of the women.

Waste featured here, too:

> To deal with the computerised batches which misfire, it's easier now to chuck out the spoiled loaves, reprogram the computer, and start all over. In the old days, I saw very few waste scraps in the shop; now each day the huge plastic trash cans of the bakery are filled with mounds of blackened loaves. [Sennett, 1998, p. 68–69]

The difference between the two situations is that waste in the bakery had no doubt been factored in. But the implications for the human operators and their relationship to the task are remarkably similar, nearly forty years later. Why, oh why do we have to keep discovering the same things?

Sennett is not alone among the recent writers to conclude that what is important now is for people to find meaning in their work.

Which is where we came in.

Note

1. I am indebted to Stephen Overell for drawing my attention to the publi-cations of the Arno Press on these topics. A list of their titles, between 1881 and 1977, can be found in Appendix I.

SECTION I
MAKING THE CASE

The papers in this section set out the case for paying attention to the organization of work. They span forty years.

The first comes from the Introduction to a book, *New Forms of Work Organisation*, written for the German Government's Commission for Economic and Social Change. In 1971 the German Chancellor, Herr Willy Brandt, set up this Commission to help the government towards an informed social policy: on the basis of existing knowledge and commissioned research, it was to advise the government on action in the field of social, economic, and educational policy that would facilitate the process of technical and social change in such a way that they would serve the interests of the population, within the framework of a market economy. They divided the topic into themes, and commissioned reports to summarize what was already known about those themes. One of them was to review theoretical developments and European experience in new forms of work organization. When the contract for that study arrived, it was Project No. 56—a staggering perspective on the scale of effort that was being put in, compared with what was happening in this country. The study was carried out in 1973. The story of the Commission is written up in Klein and Eason, 1991.

The second paper is an extract from a Fabian Society pamphlet, which was published ten years earlier, based on a Fabian Lecture. I was fresh from working in industry on the shop floor and as a factory personnel officer. It was unusual for Fabians to have industrial experience, and I wanted to get them interested in the topic. Shirley Williams had recently become Secretary of the Fabian Society; she heard the lecture and encouraged me to turn it into a Fabian pamphlet, but the Fabian Executive at first turned it down because they considered it to be "not political enough". It was eventually published in 1963, and reprinted in 1964 and 1971.

The third paper is the most recent. It was given at an anniversary symposium in 2000, and is more light-hearted than the others; but it also sets out the case from a broader historical perspective rather than an individual one.

CHAPTER TWO

The function of work in human life

The book *New Forms of Work Organisation* was published in German in 1975 and in English in 1976. The piece reproduced here was part of the Introduction, and was an attempt to set the issues out at a general level.

* * *

Issues of human welfare can be ranged along a continuum: from those most internal to individuals—concerned with their most personal needs and development in life—to those which are external to them—concerned with political and social organization in the world around them. The way in which work is organized has relevance at many points on this continuum.

At the individual, personal level, work is a main means of achieving economic viability and adult status in the Western world, of expressing and developing the personality, and of relating to society. At an intermediate level, the way in which people spend their working lives—that is most of their waking lives—helps to shape their perceptions and attitudes and therefore in turn has cultural and social consequences. At the level of the wider society, the forms taken by the division of labour have led to structural and class alignments, to the creation of political "worker" or "labour" parties in a number of European countries, and to the development of trade union movements with varying degrees of political as well as economic power. In the future, it is likely to become the subject of international politics as well, first because of the development of multi-national employers, and second because, in a variety of ways, the more prosperous nations are exporting some of their tasks to the less prosperous nations.

At any one of these levels enough is known now to tackle the problems, if not entirely to solve them. Some of the most important questions, therefore, now arise from the difficulty of relating the different levels to each other, since solutions at one level can conflict with solutions at another.

Consequences for individuals

To begin, then, with the individual. Psychoanalysts do not all take the same view about whether the importance of work in human life has direct biological origins or derived cultural ones. Some attribute it to a primary biological drive to master the environment; others to a more socio-cultural force, the pleasure that is gained from achievement. This includes both the achievement of the immediate and direct consequences of performing a task, and the achievement of independence, freedom, and security (Neff, 1965).

Whatever the answer to this dilemma, i.e., whatever the basic origins of the importance of work, Freud saw the function of work as providing one of man's main links with reality:

> Laying a stress upon importance of work has a greater effect than any other technique of living in the direction of binding the individual more closely to reality; in his work he is at least securely attached to a part of reality, the human community. Work is no less valuable for the opportunity it and the human relations connected with it provide for a very considerable charge of libidinal component impulses . . . than because it is indispensable for subsistence and justifies existence in a society. The daily work of earning a livelihood affords particular satisfaction when it has been selected by free choice, i.e. when through sublimation it enables use to be made of the existing inclinations, of instinctual impulses that have

retained their strength, or are more intense than usual for constitutional reasons. [Freud, 1930a]

This view is substantiated by studies of the unemployed and by the problems experienced by people after retirement. The nature of the link with reality is discussed by Jahoda (1966), who suggests a number of dimensions: first, work strengthens the experience of the passing of time, people without work tending to lose a sense of time; second, work "encourages the continuous action necessary to maintain objective knowledge of reality", since ordinary persons need to experience the consequences of their actions and to put their subjective knowledge of reality continuously to the test; third, work permits the pleasurable experience of competence; fourth, work adds to the individual's store of conventional knowledge, particularly knowledge of interdependence with others in common purposes; fifth, work permits the enrichment of the world of immediate experience, and it permits the mutual reinforcement of pleasure and reality principles as regulators of adult behaviour.

Among the scenarios for the future that are currently being discussed is one which predicts the disappearance of work. This not only seems rather unrealistic, but it also raises the prospect of immense personal, and therefore social, difficulties. The transition to an absence of work would be, at the very least, extremely difficult to make and would produce many casualties. If scarcity is no longer the dominant driving force and there is spare capacity (Higgin, 1973), it would seem better to devote this capacity to modifying work so that in fact it has more of the characteristics that are helpful to people in their development.

Among social, as distinct from clinical, researchers, there now exists a very large body of research about work satisfaction among various kinds of working populations, generally expressed in such statistics as labour turnover or absence rates, or in responses to interviews or questionnaires. One contribution by Frederick Herzberg and his colleagues (1959) makes the distinction between extrinsic or "hygiene" factors in the work situation, and intrinsic or "motivating" factors. Faced with conflicting evidence from the literature on the subject, the research workers asked their respondents to describe times when they had been particularly happy in their work situation and times when they had been particularly unhappy. A large number of these incidents were collected and analysed, and the following pattern emerged from the analysis.

When people talked of times when they were dissatisfied, the reasons fell into these groups:

company policy and administration;
supervision (technical);
salary;
interpersonal relations (supervisory);
working conditions.

On the other hand, when people talked of times when they had been happy, the reasons fell into different groups. These were:

achievement;
recognition for achievement;
the work itself;
responsibility.

The first time this enquiry was made was among a group of middle-management people, accountants and engineers. It has since been repeated among a variety of jobs, at many levels, and in a number of different countries, and the main findings still hold good.

The important thing about these findings is that the two lists are different. They represent not opposite ends of the same scale, but different scales. The things that lead to positive satisfaction and the things that cause dissatisfaction are different in kind, and not merely different in the way people feel about them. This explains a good deal of management (and perhaps government) heartache: it means that, however much is done to remove grievances or to improve working conditions in any particular situation, nothing has necessarily been done thereby to create positive satisfaction. At best, the result will be what has been called a mood of "dull contentment". It also means that in any situation both questions need to be asked. (It must be remembered, incidentally, that an important function of money is as a symbol of achievement and recognition for achievement.)

However, social researchers also have their disagreements. There is a good deal of consensus about what characteristics of jobs people like or dislike, but some disagreement about whether all populations exhibit these needs to the same degree, given that their experiences outside the work situation vary—in other words, about how far it is possible to generalize about human needs in work. One group of researchers has found differences between sub-cultures, specifically between workers in rural or town surroundings and those in urban or city surroundings (Turner & Lawrence, 1965). This has been interpreted (Hulin & Blood, 1968) as showing a closeness to traditional middle-class values regarding work and achievement in the small-town factories in the sample, and an alienation from such values in the urban setting. Another group of researchers claims that while the workers in their study held views about the characteristics of their work which were very similar to those found elsewhere (particularly disliking monotony, pace, lack of autonomy, and lack of opportunity to use skill), the fact that they actually remained in these jobs showed that they brought an economic, instrumental orientation to the work and that its intrinsic characteristics were not very important to them (Goldthorpe, Lockwood, Bechhofer, & Platt, 1968).

Clearly, the part played in all this by adaptation on the one hand and by perception—which may be a form of adaptation—on the other has not yet been adequately charted. Clearly, too, differences in research findings are to some extent a function of differences in research methods. Sometimes the complexity and dynamics of a situation are better illustrated by a single case than by a number of surveys. A maintenance mechanic in a chemical process firm was being interviewed. It was an unstructured interview, during which no specific questions were asked, and for about two hours he talked freely about his job. At first, he took a fairly instrumental line: "All I'm interested in is the money. This firm pays well, and that's the only reason I stop here. What a working man wants from his job is the pay packet, and don't let anybody kid you about other fancy notions."

Half an hour later he was talking about the firm, and discussed various things that he thought were wrong with it. The interviewer said nothing, but the mechanic seemed to think that he was being inconsistent, because he stopped himself. Then he said, "Well, you see, when you get a bit older, and the kids are off your hands, and you've paid for the house, and your wife's got a washing machine—you don't need money so much any more and you find you start noticing the firm. And by God it can annoy you!"

Half an hour after that he said, "You know—what I really like is when the machine goes wrong and I'm the one who knows how to put it right."

It would be foolish to argue about which of these was his "real" attitude: they were all real. Like the skins of an onion, most of these attitudes exist in most people, and the question is which of them gets tapped. It explains, too, why such conflicting evidence is thrown up by a good deal of research: the view one would take of this man's attitude would depend on when the interview was closed.

The present state of knowledge about work satisfaction therefore suggests two observations. In the first place, in a general sense knowledge about the subject is incomplete, especially if the model of knowledge being used is that of engineering science. Human motivation will continue to provide material for doctoral theses for a long time. In themselves, attempts to draw up simple mechanical guidelines on how to deal with it deny the dynamic nature of the subject. In the absence of "definitive" and "complete" knowledge, therefore, ideas about psychological health are to some extent value-laden and will remain so, and choices have to be made. However, a good deal of understanding and experience exists about the consequences of such choices.

Second, in any specific situation one must take steps to explore the history, tradition, needs, and values of the people in the situation. The theoretician is left with a number of unknowns about human needs; the practitioner in a particular situation, however, has the means of finding out.

Consequences for culture

The current intense interest in job design has focused very much on the effect of present forms of work organization on the need satisfactions of individuals. It must be pointed out, however, that important effects can be seen at other behavioural levels. The way in which work is organized influences how people see and experience their surroundings; and the ways in which they experience and respond to things add up to strong and well-rooted cultures. These in turn then have consequences for society. This conclusion is based on research on the implications of rationalized production systems, (described in Chapter Five). Perhaps most importantly, the study highlights that a distinction needs to be made between short-term consequences—which may lead to protest—and long-term adaptations to changes in work organization, which cumulatively add up to cultural change.

Organizational contexts

If the organization of work is interpreted in a rather wider frame of reference, then account needs to be taken of the relationships between the task an organization sets itself, the means it selects to carry out that task (Lupton, 1963),[1] and the human and social situations that result. A number of studies in the past fifteen years have suggested that there are some patterns and regularities in such relationships, that circumstances can be described in which some kinds of organization are more effective than others, and that degrees of freedom to choose can be made explicit. Research has shown links between the forms, relationships, and problems to be found in an organization, sometimes even the characteristics of its industrial relations, and such structural factors as the kind of market in which a firm operates (Burns & Stalker, 1961; Lawrence & Lorsch, 1967; Lupton, 1963), the technology it uses (Woodward, 1965), the control systems it installs (Woodward, 1970), and its size (Pugh, Hickson, Hinings, & Turner, 1969).

Again, the knowledge produced by such studies is not "definitive" or "conclusive". There is need for a great deal more research based on detailed observation of what happens in real, not hypothetical, organizations. What this field of study has produced already, however, is guidelines for diagnosis. When a situation is examined with these relationships in mind and from the point of view of the interaction between structure and behaviour, there frequently emerges a new understanding of the situation that can serve as a basis for future action. Stresses and incompatibilities may become apparent which permit restructuring the situation or, if restructuring is not possible or acceptable, which at least make it clear why certain problems continue to recur.

Methods of organizational diagnosis need to go far beyond the conventional sociological tools of questionnaire and interview. Observation methods, tracer methods (tracing a product or other key unit through everything that happens to it in the organization and analysing the work roles of all the people involved), activity sampling, analysis of documents, and depth analysis of roles all have a place in the equipment of applied social science. The main problems that are uncovered in this way may not in the first instance—or even at all—be those connected with tasks at the lowest level of the enterprise. But the systemic relationship between situations at different levels will become explicit, and strategies for change and development can be selected on a basis of knowledge.

If I have so far approached the question of re-designing the work at the lowest level of the enterprise with some caution, and in the context of other kinds of organizational diagnosis, it is because the case is too important to risk damaging it by over-simplifying or over-stating it. Many tasks, particularly in industrial organizations and particularly at subordinate levels in these organizations, are unsatisfactory from the point of view of the personal needs, development, and even health of those who have to carry them out. This problem is at last attracting attention and there is much concern with reform. However, if reform is not carried out with an understanding of organizational contexts, the new structures will not work or will not last. Second, if the enthusiasm of reformers leads them to over-emphasize one factor in the situation (such as participation) at the expense of others (such as money, or security, or the needs of others than shop-floor operators) the next generation of reformers or researchers will pull down the whole edifice, including the valuable parts of it. It is throwing out the baby with the bathwater, and in the field of applied social science there is already some experience of it. The excitement of a new discovery, particularly discovery of a way of righting something experienced as wrong, carries within it the seeds of its own destruction if it leads to exaggeration. F. W. Taylor himself, after all, the arch-priest and nowadays perhaps the arch-villain of "scientific management", was only over-reacting to obvious inefficiencies that he witnessed— workers deciding how to produce a part guided only by their own skill and past experience, and holding their knowledge as trade secrets, with no concern for any wider systemic needs.

Enthusiasm that is not rooted in reality or, more usually, that is based on a partial view of reality, takes on the characteristics of an ideology, and there are many ideologies current in industry today: for management by objectives, or MBO, for management information systems, or MIS, etc. There must not be another fad called participative job design, or PJD. The nature of work is too important.

Note

1. Lupton's research is mainly concerned with shop-floor response to incentives, but he shows incidentally that this response appears to differ in different market situations.

CHAPTER THREE

The meaning of work

This chapter consists of some extracts from *The Meaning of Work* (Fabian Tract no. 349). It was almost my first publication, and the content was very much influenced by my own life experience: I had been miserable and bored in my first job in a library and enjoyed the flavour and comradeship of life in a factory, packing pills, and the liveliness of working as a personnel officer in a Metal Box Company factory in London's Bermondsey. The factory manager I quote yelling across the yard was my manager there, Mr Clift. One of the two women described working in a wartime jobbing factory in Blackfriars was my mother.

The text, published in 1963, shows some signs of the times, for instance in the assumptions it makes about the division of labour between men and women and the use of "he" to mean both. There is a reference to the liner *Queen Mary*, which has long since gone out of commission. On the other hand, the question raised about whether it is necessary for economic growth to be at the fastest possible rate could not be more up to date: currently (2007) it features strongly in the fight to prevent Burberry from moving their production from the Rhondda Valley to China. And the question "Why must all clerical work be done in Central London between nine and five . . ." seems prophetic.

* * *

The ingredients of work

There is a widespread misconception in middle-class intellectual circles that all industrial work is dull. One has only to hear *The Critics* [an arts programme] on the BBC, on the rare occasions when industrial life or factory work come into their discussions, to sample some of the strange beliefs that are held about them. They would be very surprised to see factory workers pitying social scientists for the dull lives that *they* must have—yet this is a common experience for sociologists and psychologists working in industry. As one girl in a factory put it to a research worker, "Don't you get bored, just interviewing people all day?"

The same research worker was one day watching a girl whose job was to put the little bits of cork into the tops of toothpaste tubes. In her turn she asked the girl, "Don't you get bored, doing that all day?", and the girl looked up in complete surprise and said, "Oh, no! They come up different every time!" So the first thing is to look at this question without preconceptions, and to be careful in the judgements one makes.

There is a great deal of pleasure to be got out of factory life. This shows, presumably, the great capacity of people to adapt themselves and get something out of any environment. It might be objected that they should not have to, that they are rationalizing a situation that would otherwise be intolerable. But then, anyone who finds his work interesting or enjoyable may be doing that. In any job, much of the beauty or ugliness is in the eye of the beholder. For instance, it is usually thought that a lawyer has a varied and interesting job, and he certainly has one of the most highly esteemed jobs in our society. In fact what he does is to process particular cases through a set of known rules and precedents—a routine which, when put like that, does not sound very exciting and which a computer might well be able to do more cheaply.

It all depends how you look at it. In a large organization even a manager, with a highly responsible administrative and co-ordinating job, and big decisions to make, may still be only part of a bigger pattern. A foreman, in charge of two hundred people in a very large firm, recognized this when he said, "It pays you to be a cog, even if it's a big cog." And this is true. Anyone who, if he comes to work on a Monday morning full of a new idea, cannot pursue it, either because it must be referred to Head Office, or because someone else in the organization might be upset, or because it means creating a difficult precedent, is, however senior his position, only a bigger cog. So we may all be kidding ourselves.

In considering the question of the actual content of work, I want, first of all, to state the obvious and get it out of the way. It goes without saying that the first thing that matters about work is to have it. Any discussion about intrinsic work satisfaction has to presuppose that there are no fears of large-scale unemployment, and becomes nonsense if there are such fears. The next thing, still before the intrinsic satisfaction of work matters very much, is to be adequately paid for it. To leave wages out of such a discussion is to beg another very big question. Nevertheless, I want to discuss the question of work as if basic security and basic living standards can be taken for granted. It is hard to know whether this is justified. One moment we seem to be on the brink of disaster and, with shoulders to wheels and noses to grindstones, are exhorted to pant along behind the industrious Germans, Japanese, Russians, Americans, and Uncle Tom Cobley; the next we are apparently affluent to the point of demoralization. So, leaving the economic argument out of account, I am going to give us the benefit of the doubt. After all, unions now include shorter hours and longer holidays in their claims, which suggests that they are beginning to feel secure about the basic necessities and to look beyond them. And even when demands *are* for money, more cash often represents something other than purchasing power: it may be compensation for boredom, it may be an indication of how well one has got on as compared with others, or a measure of one's bargaining strength. The new needs, which arise when basic needs are satisfied, are complicated and difficult to define. We do not know how to demand satisfaction in work, so we continue to demand money.

There are, then, two possible next steps: one is to do away with work as far as possible, to increase leisure and get satisfaction from leisure activities. But it does not seem likely that the bulk of work can ever be done away with, and this way out is, in a sense, an admission of defeat. If the affluent society now gives us some economic leeway, it would seem at least as important to take a look at the nature of work itself, to see where its satisfactions lie and whether they can be increased.

Certainly, whichever way you look at it, work satisfaction is a very slippery topic. Almost everything that can be said about it can also be contradicted; for instance, mining is by most standards a terrible job—dangerous, dirty, unpleasant, unhealthy. But because it has existed for a long time, because traditions have grown up round it, because there are social compensations for the arduousness and the danger, miners will fight hard for the right to do it. Joint consultation is supposed to stimulate a sense of participation; on the other hand nobody ever seems to get a sense of participation from it, and many people do not want a sense of participation. Again, everybody wants more money, but many are prepared to take less money for a job that gives them a sense of purpose and self-fulfilment.

The reason for these, and similar, contradictions is that satisfaction in work does not lie along merely one dimension. Many factors go to make it up, and I want next to list some of them to show how complex a subject this is. They can be divided, rather arbitrarily, into three groups: those which lie in the nature of the job itself, those which are social, and those which lie in the circumstances surrounding the job. The things that contribute to satisfaction or dissatisfaction at work apply to any job, and this should be borne in mind when we look at them in more detail, although I shall do so mainly in relation to industrial work.

The job itself

The first group consists of those experiences which are intrinsic in the operation itself: *first of all, the physical experiences*—the strain, or lack of it, degrees of comfort, dirt, noise, colour, ease or difficulty of operation experienced in the course of the job. (Under "strain", one could include the effort involved in getting to work, although this is not part of "the job itself". Your view of a job can be very much coloured by how far from home it is and how easy or difficult to get to.)

In this connection, it is important whether a job has within it the opportunity, or the excuse, to move about occasionally. In a firm where the effects of work study were being investigated, the main change that was made was that people had loads of work brought to them, instead of having to go and fetch them for themselves. Instead of experiencing this as a relief, they resented it very much, because fetching their own work had given them the opportunity to move around occasionally, have a change of scene and an occasional chat. (And, incidentally, some of them had devised ways of picking and choosing jobs, of being ready just when a good job was coming up, and didn't like having this interfered with.) But there are also good physiological reasons for changing position occasionally. The repeated use of certain muscles, even in light work such as typing, contributes to a feeling of monotony, which is very often really a feeling of fatigue. However, the relationship between boredom and fatigue is a complicated one: a typist may feel she is bored when she is really mildly fatigued; but she *may* also become fatigued more quickly when she is bored.

Then there is the feel of the stuff you are handling; the pleasure of handling nice shiny pieces; the pleasure of handling efficient tools, or the constant frustration of having to use tools that are inadequate or have not been properly maintained. All contribute to your overall feeling about the job.

Another big factor in giving meaning to work is having your own machine or set of tools, and being responsible for them. One may find, say, a press operator developing a very strong attachment to his own particular machine, getting intensely resentful if he is moved somewhere else, or if the nightshift leaves his machine in a mess. People set up relationships with tools and machines, and even with their own geographical position in the shop or office, which can be very important to them. Pin-ups, rows of boxes cordoning off somebody's "own" corner, traditions about where to put the Christmas decorations, all demonstrate and strengthen this relationship.

Variations in batches. There is often a difference in materials or components that the outsider cannot spot but that can have great meaning to the people handling them. When the factory manager yells across the yard for three more boxes of four and a halfs, this can really mean something to everyone involved: the people who made them, the people who have handled them in the stores, the people who load them on to the lorry. Four and a halfs are different, and if you haven't handled them yourself you don't know. Where a job is repetitive, people may introduce their own variations, and may later defend those variations as being essential and inherent in the job; conversely, if there is too much variety, and too many decisions to make, they may "switch off". This is where the eye of the beholder is so important that it is impossible to generalize: there may be interest and variety in different pieces of cork, while all arithmetic classes look alike to the disgruntled teacher, and all post-operative cases look alike to the tired nurse.

Variation in speed. Variation in speed can make piecework attractive. On many piecework jobs it is possible to bash away hard for a couple of hours and then take ten minutes off to have a cigarette or a chat, without incurring the wrath of the foreman, because in quite a big way one is one's own boss. This may even be possible on a conveyor belt. There have been experiments in letting groups of people decide the speed of their own belt, and they have usually varied it at different times of the day.

Having one's own particular knacks and ways of doing things; the extra twist or pressure which is not laid down in the method but which you know makes all the difference; the jig you rigged up yourself; the extra carbon copy which saves you looking through the files. This is important in all kinds of jobs, clerical and administrative jobs particularly lending themselves to people developing their own routines and systems. Sometimes, these are highly inefficient in terms of the whole organization, but people cling to them possessively, and will find good reasons for retaining them because this is what makes a job *your* job, One of the dangers of work study is that it may determine methods too precisely and take away the opportunity to develop small tricks.

This leads to what is perhaps the most important factor in this group: the satisfaction that the job gives is perhaps most closely related to the opportunity it provides to develop and use skills. Self-expression, development, fulfilment, whatever you want to call it, has much to do with using skills and developing skills; for most people, also, with having their skills and progress appreciated. Both work that is too easy and work that is too difficult are frustrating, so that there are two sides to the equation: what talents (official and unofficial ones) the job enables a person to use or to develop, and whether he has been selected and trained to be able to meet its demands. There is real pleasure to be got from having and beating an attainable target, and real misery in having a target which is always just out of reach.

Both sides of this equation can also go wrong at management level, and indeed in professional and other non-industrial jobs.

There are plenty of graduates in industry kicking their heels and feeling that they are not being used, who were recruited for reasons related to prestige and not the needs of the job; at the same time, many managers suffer from strain and pressure, because at middle-management level targets tend to be unlimited or undefined. If managers were allowed to have a sense of achievement more often, their subordinates would probably feel the benefit too.

The coercion there is in a job. This is, of course, why employment can never provide all the satisfaction of a hobby—once one has taken on a job one is no longer free not to do it. Within this limit, however, there may be many degrees of freedom and flexibility. There are probably many jobs where flexibility could be greater if one thought about it, where work could be taken home or done at unusual hours. Why must all clerical work be done in Central London between nine and five, for instance?

Coercion may also come from sources outside the job. How you feel about a job or a career depends a lot on whether you chose it yourself or were pushed into it, either through some form of positive pressure, or lack of opportunity to train for something else, or simply through not knowing what else was available. There is a lot we do not know yet about the range of choice that is actually open to people. It can be surprisingly limited. There was a man whose firm moved from one side of London to the other, so that to get to work he had to go through London every day on his motor-cycle. He found this very tiring and began to develop various symptoms of strain. When he went to his doctor about them, the doctor asked whether he could not perhaps change his job—and it simply had not occurred to him! This kind of thing may be quite wide-spread and needs to be examined. It is not necessarily always good to stay in a job for fifty years and earn a gold watch. We need more effective vocational guidance, and not only for school leavers. Many people do not realize until they are quite a bit older that something is wrong with their choice of job. The Labour Exchange interview would seem to be the obvious opportunity for more positive guidance.

Social contacts

The second big group of factors affecting work satisfaction consists of social factors: whether the nature of the job itself brings you into contact with others, or contact only takes place in spite of the job; whether these contacts are only with people at your own level of the organization, or with those at other levels as well; whether geographically you are alone or in a group; what opportunity there is to gossip. Gossip can be a big source of satisfaction on jobs that are so routine that they require no attention, and for this reason women often enjoy routine jobs. On the other hand, if there is a lot of noise, or people are too far away from each other to talk, the situation is very different. A sewing machine, for instance, or a power press, isolates the operator socially and takes just enough constant vigilance to prevent him or her attending to anything else—but without absorbing the attention.

Then there is ganging up with your mates against something or somebody. This is a great source of pleasure, and it ranges from huddles in the cloakroom, through the solidarity-creating trade union activities, to extreme militancy at the other end of the scale. The need for an opportunity to oppose is important, and I shall come back to it. Related to this category are also such assertions of independence as fiddling the management, beating down the time study man, sitting in the canteen for a while after the bell has gone. All of them assert one's independence vis-à-vis "them", and all of them may give a special satisfaction when done in company. They are things that people put into the work situation themselves, bits of freedom and pleasure that people find for themselves which are not designed into the job.

There are many other relationships that may combine to give a job its unique flavour, either in the direction of pleasure or of misery: how you get on with your supervisor; the ritual slap-and-tickle with the girl on the tea trolley; the long-standing vendetta with a particular inspector; the exchange of insults with the canteen staff; the weekly transactions with the chap who runs the football pool or lottery, or with the woman who has a supply of cheap cigarettes or nylon parachutes; and many others.

The circumstances of the job

Into the third group I have put a number of factors that lie in the circumstances surrounding the job, some of them in the policies of the employer. There is *the social esteem of the product*: one may be proud of driving rivets into the *Queen Mary* and indifferent about doing it for domestic hot water tanks; one may feel ashamed to work an adding machine in a tax office and boast about doing it for a film or television company. To complicate matters, the social evaluation of occupations changes. Many girls fifty years ago would have been proud to be allowed to work as bank clerks and ashamed to model clothes; now this merely sounds quaint.

Then there is *the prestige attached to your particular position within some hierarchy*: since the whole of our culture is competitive, people may derive pleasure or misery from quite small differences between their own position and someone else's. The attainment of a carpet in the office, or the right to a particular parking space, or the key to Top People's lavatories may be greatly valued. Wages and salaries are also important here. Above certain levels, money is often valued mainly as an indicator of status.

Whether you accept the aims of the organization you work for; knowing where your job fits into the whole; knowing what goes on in the firm; feeling that you are making something valuable; feeling that what you do matters. In a dirty old factory in Blackfriars during the war, a job came in one day that consisted of painting a large quantity of metal "Ds"—the letter D stamped out in metal. These were put on to trays, sprayed with paint, and dried, and two women had the job of turning them over so that they could be painted on the other side. Hour after hour, and day after day they turned these things over, and were at screaming point with boredom when, by chance, the foreman, who was walking through the shop, said that these "Ds" were for labelling drinking water for the troops fighting on the second front in Normandy. Obviously, this changed the whole meaning of the job; they were doing something of national importance and began to enjoy it.

Whether you can feel that what you do is effective: cleaning something, for example, can be quite a satisfying experience in itself. What makes washing dirty dishes a drudgery is the knowledge that the effect will only last a few hours, and the job will have to be done over and over again, three times a day for ever. There is a world of difference between spring-cleaning, say, in the country, and spring cleaning in a dirty back street in Kings Cross, where the best that you can hope for is that the effect will last for a week.

A knowledge of results. This can come in various ways—it can be obvious from the job itself, it can be due to an understanding boss keeping you informed about your own progress, as well as the progress of the firm and its products, it can take the form of various ways of target-setting against which you can measure your own achievements.

The more progressive managements are aware of the type of factor included in this group and some, though not enough, go a long way in their attempts to meet it. The bigger the organization, the more difficult this may be. For this reason some of the prestige advertising of the larger companies is aimed at arousing pride in their employees quite as much as at their customers. On the same lines, joint consultation, various training schemes, and particularly induction training where new recruits may be shown the whole factory, the whole product and the uses to which it is put, are all aimed at increasing people's knowledge of, and therefore participation and satisfaction in, what is going on. The position here is a bit tricky. On the one hand it is still necessary to press for more of this kind of activity, because many managements are still not even aware of the need; on the other hand a high level of this sort of activity tends to lull managements (and unions?) into a false sense of finality, of "now the workers ought to be happy". It covers, after all, only one aspect of life at work, and a rather debatable one at that. I shall come back to this later.

These are some of the factors that go to make work satisfying or unsatisfying. There are probably many others that have been left out, and their various combinations and permutations are innumerable. Add to this the fact that in different situations they have different orders of priority, and it becomes clear that the problem is not a simple one. It is just not possible to generalize; one has to look at a lot of jobs in very great detail. There is no way round this.

Combining the ingredients

Probably the most useful way of looking at jobs is under different technical conditions, to see how these may influence the possible frustrations and satisfactions that have been listed.

If one looks first of all at a craft job, say that of a tailor making suits one at a time, there is very little mechanization, and there is very little sub-division of work. This job has built into it a lot of the satisfactions listed. The tailor is using skill, he is using knowledge of materials and techniques, and he is also developing skill; it is a job on which he can improve. He can easily assess results or the customer makes him very quickly aware of results, and he can use this information to improve his performance next time. He knows, obviously, what it is for, and where the different parts fit in. He has to know this as part of the job. He has a variety of tasks. Within an overall time limit he plans the work himself and co-ordinates the different parts of it. He has a choice of methods and he can develop his own special knacks. In other words, many of the important satisfactions that were listed are built into the demands of the job and do not have to be inserted by deliberate policy.

Mechanization

As mechanization develops, and bigger quantities are produced, work gets broken down into component parts. In the production of very large batches, one man is likely to see only one component of a product, and to perform only one operation on that component, and that one operation repeatedly. This could be called a horizontal sub-division of work, but at the same time there has also been a vertical sub-division. He is not performing the whole work content of his one operation: someone else has planned it, has specified the material to be used, the tools, the methods, sometimes quite precisely the movements he has to make, and the time he has to take; someone else has prepared the work for him, and someone else inspects it. In other words, all the control, planning and decision-making functions have been removed from the job itself and transferred either to the machine or to higher management. He does not need to know where things fit in, though a progressive management may tell him; he does not need to develop skills that he thinks up himself, in fact he will be a more satisfactory worker if he does not.

In the production of smallish batches, there is often still a good deal of scope for people to compensate for this, to take back for themselves little bits of freedom, to acquire little bits of skill, though it may not be the kind of skill the management wants them to have. The average engineering workshop is a marvellous arena for all kinds of small fiddles and manipulations, which are all signs, it would seem, of people asserting themselves against the system, introducing satisfactions for themselves, many of them of the social kind.

Mass production

It is in the real mass-production situation that the least opportunity for anything of this sort lies. When work is highly machine-paced, or on a conveyor belt, so that the operator has no control over the flow of work or over anything else, the situation arises that Charlie Chaplin depicted in *Modern Times*—a robot forever tightening a screw on a moving belt—with a minimum of decisions to make, or skill to use, in the course of the work.

Many people think of this as the typical industrial job. It is not; in this country there are not as many of these jobs as one thinks. For one thing, the ratio of clerical, administrative, and technical workers to manual workers has been changing. Between 1900 and 1956 it changed from 1:12 to 1:4 in manufacturing industry alone. For another, only a fairly small proportion of manufacturing firms are actually engaged on mass production. Third, even in a mass production firm, not everyone is on the assembly line.

But what is life like for those who do have this kind of job? In a study of assembly-line production of motor cars, the American sociologists Walker and Guest found that people were very concerned to try to find small ways of varying conditions, and that most of the men disliked intensely the pace, the repetitiveness, and the lack of opportunity to develop skills (Walker & Guest, 1952). The effect of this situation seemed to extend beyond their working lives, since the men's wives made comments to the effect that their husbands seemed to lose interest in out-of-work activities such as sport, or local affairs, or the church, since they began their current jobs.

I mentioned at the beginning that people are very adaptable. Now, in this situation, if a man's ability to grow as a person, make decisions and take responsibility shrink to fit the opportunities that are normally available to him, so that he becomes what we call apathetic, who is to say that this is not a healthy adaptation to his environment? Or if, unable to adapt in this way, he becomes militant instead, this too need not be unhealthy for him and should not surprise. The only thing that would be surprising is if the technical environment in which a man spends his days did not have some influence on him.

Automation

So far we have looked at what happens to work under increasing mechanization of production. When mechanization develops still further, there comes the situation of process industry and automation.

It gives a false picture to lump all automatic processes together, first because there are different kinds, and second because automation is a matter of degree and there are many stages before that of the fully automatic factory. The skills required from workers on these processes therefore vary greatly. In general, an automatic process may be organized so that the operator *monitors* the process, having a "push-button" type of job, where only one course of action is open to him and he behaves in many ways like the mass-production operator; or it may be set up so that the operator *controls* the process, in which case new and important skills may be required from him (Crossman, 1960).

In some cases of automation, therefore, fundamental changes have taken place in work content for those people who are still employed on the process. (I have ignored here the problems of those who are no longer employed.)

In mass production the operator is, quite correctly, called a machine hand. On an ordinary machine tool he puts in the piece, starts the machine, the machine cuts, he stops the machine, takes the piece out. On an automatic machine tool the machine itself does all that, the machine hand is eliminated and what is required is a very highly skilled setter to set the machine and control it. Similarly, in process work—chemicals, oil, etc.—what is required from the worker is to control the process—to watch for changes, spot faults, weigh up their importance and decide on action.

What has happened to the role of the operator? In a craft job we saw him doing the whole job: planning it, carrying it out, checking it, and modifying what he did next time according to the results he achieved. In a mass-production job, he only performs the operating part of this cycle—all the planning, deciding, inspecting, and adapting is done by other people or by machine. Now, with a high degree of automation, the operating part is done mechanically too, and the operator may once more be doing a whole job—but the job, this time, is to control a complicated piece of apparatus.

In many ways his role now resembles that of a craftsman again. For instance, he has to have information—it is not a matter of being nice to him and telling him what the process is about, he *has* to know. Because the equipment used is so expensive, and the rate of output so high, the cost of even short breakdowns on automatic plant is extremely high. It is therefore very important that the people working the plant should be able to recognize faults or impending faults and know what to do about them. This is not always realized. In several cases of breakdown that were investigated as part of a study of training needs for automation (King, 1960), managers acknowledged that a higher degree of training of their operators could have saved very large sums. In one case

> the manager concerned estimated that the financial loss involved amounted to £150,000 over the year [from quality variations]. He was convinced that more highly trained operators could reduce this figure by possibly as much as £50,000. This would result from sounder on-the-spot decisions based on a more skilful analysis of the factors involved. [*ibid.*]

The operator therefore needs to have skills. They are usually different skills—instead of dexterity and manipulative skill he now has to develop more intellectual abilities, to perceive, think, and make decisions.

In addition, other things seem to happen to his job: he has very often become the key point in a communication system. He has direct access to people at a very senior level because the information that he has is very important. He has direct access to maintenance people because he is in charge of very expensive equipment. For economic reasons the machinery in a highly mechanized factory usually runs throughout the twenty-four-hour period so that there are shifts of operators on continuous duty. The foremen and maintenance men, however, are often only on duty during a normal working day so that the operator, in addition to his routine controls, forms the chief link of communication between the machine and the foreman and maintenance staff. This leads to a free exchange of views, and, as a result, a group or team often develops spontaneously and grade barriers tend to break down, with the so-called unskilled operator being regarded as a responsible person and, apparently, beginning to take up attitudes which elsewhere are characteristic of management rather than of labour.

The requirements of the task are so obvious to everyone that unusual attitudes do seem to develop. For example, in a chemical process plant investigated in one particular study (Woodward, 1958), it was found that the evening shift came on regularly half an hour early so as to enable the day-shift to go off in time to have a drink before closing time on their way home. It did not occur to anyone to leave the plant unattended. Relationships also seem to improve when they are dictated by the obvious needs of the situation, which everyone understands.

One more point can be made about automation: it is that at this level of mechanization we are still at the development stage. It is in some cases still possible to choose between alternative ways of designing and setting up the process, before vast sums are irrevocably invested in equipment.

To sum up, in a rather over-simplified way: as mechanization advances it first tends to separate out all the processes that a man has been performing, does them by machine, and puts in men as adjuncts to the machine. At a later stage it tends to put them together again in a more complex machine and may put in men as controllers of the machine. The demands on the people are different at each stage and the response is different at each stage.

It is thought that through understanding the firm, its economic position and its products, workers will also come to understand that there are not really two sides in industry, that everyone is really working for the same goal.

But how true is this, in fact? Isn't it merely a question of perspective? In the long term it may be true that, if the company goes bankrupt, both the manager and the worker are out of work. But on the whole this is a very long-term and theoretical point of view and the manager, in any case, has greater safeguards. In the shorter term, there are not only two sides but there are many sides in industry, and their short-term interests are often opposed. For one thing there are functional clashes: the operator is up against the inspector, the production foreman is up against the sales manager, the research engineer is up against the production manager. And then there are economic clashes: when it comes to dividing the cake there are still different interests to be represented (again, not only two, but many). Further, efficiency is a management goal, only in a remote sense is it a worker goal. It is much more real, in the short term, that the boss wants you to work hard and you don't feel like working hard; that he wants you to get to work at five to eight and you want to get there at ten past. This is a very real divergence of interests. Somewhere along the line between the immediate experience of the job and a global view of the firm, the national interest, and world interest, everyone ceases to "show understanding" when this goes against his own interest. The narrower the job, the nearer home this limit is likely to be put.

Industrial organizations generally have a number of goals, and some of them are incompatible. In that case the behaviour of the firm, if not its explicit policy, will show what the priorities are. Even purely economic goals are not simple, since short-term profitability often conflicts with long-term profitability. All the time different goals have to be evaluated and assigned their measure of priority, and being a good employer is often one of them. The *Harvard Business Review* once made an interesting analysis of the surprising way in which large firms in fact do *not* maximize profits but pursue other goals (Anthony, 1960). Even allowing for the fact that only an economically efficient firm can afford to do this at all, and that there will be some element of hoping for a long-term payoff in terms of worker loyalty, there is no doubt that there exists a genuine paternalistic wish, however motivated, to do something that will benefit employees, to do the "right thing". This could mean deliberately abandoning a technique of management practice or of production engineering because one does not like its effects. It is a new and strange idea in technology, and one that could not have been feasible until technology was so far advanced that there were alternative ways of achieving the same effects. But in the field of warfare we are beginning to get used to the idea of refraining from using the most efficient techniques for social reasons, so why not in the field of production engineering?

Technically, there is probably very little that could not be done in the way of reorganizing work so as to abolish those aspects of work that might be demonstrated as harmful to the people doing them, though this would require more research and clearer knowledge. The question is whether anyone is prepared to afford it—either to slow down the rate of production so as to introduce more freedom and flexibility, or to invest in automatic machinery where the market may not warrant the investment. (This blithely assumes, of course, that the optimum economic decisions on these things are always made now—which is by no means the case.) It is argued that people doing dull work also want the high standard of living that dull work produces. Of course they do—but is it essential for the standard of living to rise *at the fastest technically possible rates?* Ask the question at a time of slump, and people will throw tomatoes. Ask it during a time of boom, and many will agree that it is worth asking. Therefore, it is difficult to ask until the economy shows more signs of being under control.

The fact remains: the working environment is a large part of most people's lives. People have great powers of adaptation, and most of them can make some sort of adaptation to most kinds of work situation. What sort of adaptation they make will depend partly on their personality structure and partly on the work situation. We now know quite a lot about responses to the work situation; what we have not fully recognized is the amount of choice we have in the sort of work situations we create for each other.

CHAPTER FOUR

Luddism for the twenty-first century

This was a keynote speech at the thirtieth birthday symposium of HUSAT, the Human Sciences and Advanced Technology Research Institute at Loughborough University, in 2000. Because of HUSAT's location in the Midlands, and because of the nature of the occasion, a reference to Luddism seemed appropriate. It turned out to be more relevant than at first suspected (Klein, 2001).

I introduced my speech by saying that I hoped the audience would not mind if I began with something of a history lesson, as I thought that if I was going to talk about Luddism, I ought to find out what it is.

The history of Luddism

Machines being introduced into textile manufacture at the turn of the eighteenth century could do the work of men, certainly more quickly and often more accurately and predictably. And machinery could be tended by women and children, who cost less than men. But Luddite machine-breaking activity was only one of several kinds of disturbance and rebellion in the years of the Regency. It was a period of minor rebellions and risings of the poor and desperate, one of the most disturbed and riotous in English history. In 1812 there were not only food riots but waves of collective direct action to control food prices—that is, people refusing to pay the prices asked and paying only the prices which they considered fair, described by Hobsbawm as collective bargaining by riot (Hobsbawm, 1952). This was happening in places as far apart as Falmouth, Bristol, Sheffield, Nottingham, Bolton, and Carlisle. In May that year the Prime Minister, Spencer Percival, was assassinated in the lobby of the House of Commons.

Of Luddism itself there were one major and three minor waves. The major wave was that of 1811–1812, which was started in the lace and hosiery trades of the counties of Nottingham, Leicester, and Derby and spread among the croppers and cotton weavers of Yorkshire, Cheshire, and Lancashire. It owed its origins to the disastrous state of trade and bad harvests of 1809–1812; it was not machinery itself or by itself that provoked the riots, but the economic context. And not all machines—some of these men were already using quite sophisticated weaving looms—but "machinery hurtful to Commonality"; that is, which had to be installed in factories and thus broke up the local, community way of working and living. And all these disturbances, whether of framework knitters or shearers, whether of machine wreckers or food rioters, had a common origin in the widespread distress of England's manufacturing districts during the closing stages and aftermath of the Napoleonic wars, including the sudden closure of the American market.

The machine breaking was of two types, the type directed against employers to force them to make wage concessions, and that directed against the use of machinery as such; and sometimes these overlapped with the food riots.

Luddite anger was first felt in Nottingham and its surrounding towns. In addition to the high prices and depressed wages common throughout the industrial counties just then, Nottingham weavers —mostly of stockings and mittens, called stockingers—faced competition from a new wide-frame machine that produced shoddy cloth but could turn out six times as much as a normal machine. "Cut-up" stockings, as these were called, were a particular bone of contention. They led to shoddy work as well as calling for unskilled labour at lower wages. Moreover, all around there were factories arising. In Derbyshire 100 cotton and eleven wool factories and in Loughborough a new lace-making factory were showing what the future held for people who were used to working at home in small, interdependent communities.

The first outbreak of machine breaking occurred in February 1811 at Arnold, a small town near Nottingham, where "cut-ups" were being manufactured on the wider frames. Framework knitters broke into the workshop of the hosiers concerned and disabled their frames by removing the jack wires. It served as signal to the neighbouring districts and meetings began to take place, among them a rally of stockingers in the marketplace of Nottingham. A further riot followed at Arnold, and by early April, when the arrival of military put a stop to the disturbances, over 200 frames had been destroyed.

The first attack on textile machines by men who used the name "General Ludd" and called themselves his followers, was on the night of 4th November 1811 in the village of Bulwell, four miles north of Nottingham, when a small band of men gathered in the darkness and marched to the home of a master weaver called Hollingsworth. They posted a guard, forced their way in, and destroyed a half-dozen weaving machines.

The name Ludd itself is said to derive from a certain Ned Ludlam, a Leicester stockinger's apprentice who, when reprimanded, lost his temper and smashed his master's frames with a hammer. But this may not be accurate and there are other explanations of the origin of the name.

Almost nightly for three months, the Luddite armies would train and march and smash and disappear. At least 1,100 knitting machines were broken in that time, despite the presence of increased constabulary and the dispatch of soldiers to keep order. Both sides sent petitions to Parliament. The most striking outcome was that Parliament passed a law making the destruction of a machine a capital offence, punishable by hanging.

At the March Assizes ten men arrested for Luddism were prosecuted and seven of them convicted and sent to Australia—transportation rather than hanging because the offences had been committed before the act was passed.

It was a message that apparently had an effect in Nottingham, because the riots decreased sharply. By the spring of 1812, rioting in the lace and hosiery districts had virtually ended.

But the movement shifted to the cotton industries of Manchester and the woollen industries of Yorkshire. At the Lancashire Assizes in May 1812, eight Luddites were hanged and thirteen sentenced to transportation; at Chester, of fifteen sentenced to death, four were hanged and a total of seventeen transported. By July, Luddism in the cotton districts was virtually ended.

Like the framework knitters of the Midlands and the weavers of the north-western counties, the Yorkshire shearmen were suffering from the effects of poor harvests and trade depression; and like them they resorted to machine breaking to protect their livelihood. Some of the disturbances in Yorkshire were more violent than elsewhere, with some deaths on both sides. During the summer and autumn of 1812 some 100 prisoners were taken and lodged in York castle. Of these, sixty-four came up for trial in January 1813. Half were acquitted, seven were transported for seven years, and seventeen were hanged. But the movement had burned itself out. There were minor waves in the winter of 1812–1813, the summer and early autumn of 1814, and the summer and autumn of 1816. And that was more or less the end.

There were some practical outcomes: wages in some places were raised, some machinery was discarded by manufacturers (the Nottingham hosiers gave up making "cut-ups", at least temporarily), several factories moved out of the Midlands, and a national organization for poor relief was established. In some places, new machinery was not introduced for fear of a Luddite reaction. At the height of the disturbances in the summer of 1812, there had been more than 12,000 troops stationed in the Luddite districts between Leicester and York, and the machinery and property destroyed is considered to have amounted to a value (at that time) of over £100,000. But overall the movement failed, the introduction of machinery was not halted (Darvall, 1934; Rudé, 1964).

Luddism today

And yet Luddism has left its mark, more so than I had realized. I have discovered that a light-hearted suggestion for a lecture title turns out to touch on important contemporary matters much more seriously than I realized at the time I first made it.

Consider: the Luddites were a small movement of distressed textile workers who created disturbances in the early part of the nineteenth century. They gained some concessions and were heavily punished. By 1817 it was all over.

And yet, last September, when I first started playing with ideas about this talk, there were on the Internet 1,157 web sites referring to Luddism. Last week, using the same search engine, there were 1,628. Using a different search engine there were over 4000, and using "Best of the Web" there were over twelve and a half thousand! Talk about Pandora's box!

Among the sources I have used for the historical material is an article called "The Achievements of General Ludd" by Kirkpatrick Sale, published only last year (Sale, 1999). Sale is described, or describes himself, I'm not sure which, as a neo-Luddite leader. He writes and campaigns, and early last year he took a sledgehammer to a computer on a public platform in New York.

That symbolic gesture by a man who, as far as one can tell, is middle-class and quite prosperous, seems to me to be very far removed from, I would even say a mockery of, the breaking of machines that are destroying their livelihood and way of life by men who are hungry and desperate.

However: what are you to do if you feel uneasy about current developments? You can't even get together with others of a like mind, as the Luddites did, without making use of the very technology that causes your discomfort; it is only via the Internet that people who feel like this can meet. We are isolated with our frustrations. It is this helplessness in the face of forces one cannot influence that seems to me to be the main characteristic of the situation of today and the reason for the amazing groundswell of opinion that I unwittingly tapped into. Sale's gesture, however melodramatic and unsuitable, is a symptom of a wider unease, particularly expressed in the United States. The Internet now is full of Luddite links and information, there are neo-Luddite manifestos, articles and books, a Luddite Reader, a New Luddite Society, Luddites On-Line, Luddite Industries, the Luddite Book Review, Luddite T-shirts. One talk cannot do justice to this extraordinary phenomenon. I would suggest to university colleagues that there are some solid PhDs here.

Luddism may have failed, but it has left us the great legacy of reflecting on these issues and not accepting all technology as if it came, inexorably, from God. If anxiety about new technology now does not touch a vital nerve, why would the name of this small provincial movement still be so alive? We may laugh it off—I too first proposed the title of this lecture half in joke—but that will not do. And once one is sensitized to this, it is surprising how often the term is currently used here too, in newspaper articles, sometimes half-apologetically by a journalist expressing his or her own unease, and in other writings. I started collecting newspaper cuttings, and the file grew very quickly.

The writing is by no means all critical. One "Neo-Luddite Manifesto" says,

> We see the personal computer as a great emancipator. Within each computer is the power to fulfil the dream. . . . Like those Luddites who spun garments in their cottages, we present unique creations to a community of intellect from our own homes. We have come full-circle . . .

But for some "neo-Luddites" the demand is to overthrow not just particular technologies but all the tools and chemicals of industrialization, in fact industrialism as a whole, especially in its Western capitalist form. This, unfortunately, makes it easy to ridicule and dismiss criticism in an equally sweeping, wholesale way and use the word as a term of abuse. Microsoft's lawyers declared in Washington that the anti-trust case was "a return of the Luddites, reactionaries who went around smashing machines with sledgehammers . . ." Intermediate positions, with judgements made on particular issues, are always the most difficult to take, because they mean the hard work of engaging with details and operational realities; and that is really the banner that I would like to hoist.

Respecting operational realities

So, let me come down to some particulars. The Bayswater Institute was engaged for about six years around the introduction of computers in hospitals. For three of these years we were involved in evaluation research around the Electronic Patient Record, spending a week at a time in each of four hospital wards in two hospitals and carrying out tracer studies of consultant ward rounds in a third. We did not do a systematic attitude survey, but some patterns became clear.

The people who were most single-mindedly in favour of computerization were those who talked of what it would be able to achieve in the future, untrammelled by operational considerations. Clearly, it held out the promise of research, trend analysis, protocols, intranational and international comparisons. We did not come across anyone who rejected the idea of computers wholesale; the vast majority of the people we encountered were struggling with the everyday operational realities of using the systems. A nurse deduces the value system underlying the computer when she says "I can go home without changing a dressing, but I can't go home without doing my computing". She is not making a Luddite, or a political, point, she is telling the simple truth. If she is late going home, she can delegate changing a dressing to a colleague, she can even phone in from home and point out that it remains to be done. She cannot similarly delegate inputting to the computer the information she has collected in her head or on the bits of paper on which she has scribbled in the course of her shift, since it is, of course, impossible to go back and forth to the terminal to input as she goes. And this structural fact conveys a sense of the value systems of the powers that be. Most felt that, overall, though the problems were often considerable, the advantages probably outweighed the disadvantages.

What I find troubling is that the global, high-level optimism appears to win much more respect from policy makers and development funders than the day-to-day operational struggle, which in fact is often denigrated. Let me tell you a story.

One of the best known theoreticians of the Tavistock Institute was Philip (later David) Herbst. By the time I joined the Institute in 1971 he had left to live in Norway, but he was really a citizen of the world, turning up now in India, now in Gibraltar, now in Israel, now in Algeria. In the mid-1980s, after a long absence, he turned up in London, wanting to reconnect with old friends and colleagues. It happened that there was a small flat available in the house I was living in, and I got this for him, so for some weeks we were living under the same roof.

David was eager to re-establish old links, and I suggested we might give a joint party. Wonderful! But, he said, we really needed two parties—no, three, there was this category of person and that category of person (categories, a higher level of abstraction than people)—no, what we really needed was four parties. I managed to negotiate this down to two.

The first party was for Tavistock colleagues and went well. We then started to plan for the second party and, as the list of people to invite got longer and longer, I realized that I would not be able to cope and suggested that we should get a caterer to provide the food. David agreed, but then came the question of drinks. I didn't have enough glasses. The caterer said we could hire glasses from him at 10p per glass, and forty glasses at 10p each did not seem so terrible. David, however, saw it as money wasted. If I were to buy cheap glasses, he said, it would not cost much more, and then I would have the glasses, whereas hiring them was throwing money away.

This became a big argument. From his point of view, buying was more economical than hiring. From my point of view, I didn't need forty glasses; I didn't have room to store them; in order to find and buy them I would have to take half a day off work, losing half a day's income; and I would have to bring them home in a taxi, I couldn't carry forty glasses on a bus—David himself was not a person who did such practical things. The taxi fare alone would wipe out the economic advantage. None of this made any impact, the argument went on for several solid, exhausting hours and remained unresolved. There was no way the operational realities could be brought to bear on the theoretical concept.

The problem was eventually solved because we found a caterer who let us borrow glasses for no charge. But my view of high-level theory has been permanently affected.

Some current issues in information technology

Policy makers urge, and funders encourage, novelty and rapid implementation, and they are not too troubled about the fact that these are incompatible—which everyone in this room knows. I hope.

It's not as if technology hubris should not by now be tempered by caution. It is almost too easy to catalogue disasters of recent years in Britain alone: the London Stock Exchange, the London Ambulance Service, examination results in Scotland, five million wrong records in the Inland Revenue, the Air Traffic Control Centre at Swanwick, the wrong kind of dust in the equipment when votes in the London mayoral elections were being counted, the Passport Agency, the SERPS pension debacle . . . And these are the major ones that affect large numbers together, not the minor ones that affect large numbers separately.

And then there are the potential disasters that did not happen but nevertheless cost a lot: the fraud-free benefit swipe card that was recently abandoned. The Millennium Bug? Question: when does avoiding disaster itself amount to disaster? Perhaps when the costs involved are greater than intelligent and patient development would have cost in the first place. How do you rebel against a system designer who cannot handle complexity?

Grand visions of the future come so trippingly off the tongue—not just e-commerce, but e-democracy, e-health-care, e-everything, e-sex, I shouldn't wonder. Don't laugh, we are already in a situation where if people talk to each other it is regarded as a failure in communication.

It is, of course, impossibly difficult to think in terms of a balance of gains and losses, especially as those who lose in the short term are often a different population from those who may gain in the long term. The Luddites experienced loss of livelihood and threat to the cohesion of their communities. I am not competent to assess the balance of employment lost and gained and employment relocated within the global economy as a result of information technology. And of course I am aware of the positive effects. But here a few other effects I see:

- A loss of contact with the direct human and physical environment.
- Homogeneity—with this loss of direct contact with different kinds of environment comes a loss of variety. Whether you are an architect, a lathe operator, a nurse, a researcher, a journalist, you spend much of your working life staring at a screen.
- The sacrifice of content to form. This alone is an enormous topic. In a binary world, what happens to nuance and complexity?

- Dependency—when it goes wrong, there is often no alternative way of proceeding, you are completely stuck. (I owe this item to Ronald Mackay.)
- Conformity—you have to obey. How many people in this audience regularly move to a place marked "start" when what they want to do is finish? How many mind? How many used to mind but have stopped minding? That is the problem. Stopping minding may be a psychologically healthy response to a situation you cannot alter. It is common to totalitarian environments.
- New forms of class division and the resultant exclusion and snobbery. The digitally challenged are not necessarily inferior human beings. They may be slow to keep up with new developments because of age, but then age is not necessarily an indication of inferiority. They may also, dare I say it, simply be interested in other things. It is worth noting the prejudiced use of language here, with adjectives like "progressive" and "obsolete" judging when they appear to be describing.

That brings me to the argument that IT is, after all, only a tool. Well, yes, but it is a tool the nature of whose evolution means that it is a constant preoccupation. It is a tool you never master, because it keeps changing and it distracts, both in terms of the costs and the time involved, from the task that it is intended to serve. I thought it might be my own lack of expertise that makes this such a problem for me, and discussed it with the highly expert manager of an IT project we are in. He said that it is even worse for him, because he is obliged to keep in touch with new developments—"You are always having to learn new systems . . . if you find something you like and stick with it, you accidentally become a reactionary." Interesting use of the term "reactionary".

Information technology, centralization, and control

In case you think that this is merely the complaint of a semi-computer-literate old fogey, let me introduce you to some work of Colin Davies, a highly IT-literate metallurgist from the Swinden Technology Centre of Corus (which used to be British Steel). I have his permission to show a few slides extracted from a presentation about standards. He postulates some characteristics of modern business that I imagine few would argue with.

Organizations come together in partnerships, consortia, etc. (Figure 1). They tend to be involved in more than one such partnership, so one of many problems is what to do when people use different computer systems. Colin postulates three solutions and says that most people seem to go for one of the first two (Figure 2).

But point-to-point translators are costly—where T is a translator and S is a system, twenty translators are needed for five systems (Figure 3).

However, it's worse than that, because each manufacturer produces upgrades, they come out about once every six months, they don't all come out at the same time, and each organization has to get its people up to speed on the changes. Also, some data is

---

Characteristics of modern business

- Partnerships, alliances, consortia, virtual enterprises
  Companies come together in projects as equal partners, not as sub-contractors

- Dynamic environment
  Composition of partnerships, etc., constantly changing

- Heavy reliance on computer systems
  Accountancy, project management, engineering, and communication
  Computer systems develop rapidly, and become obsolete rapidly

- Life cycle management
  Commitment to the product lasts longer than the system that created it

---

Figure 1. Typical business situation today.

How can data be managed in this environment?

- Point-to-point translators between different systems?

- Member-companies agree to use a common system?

- Neutral format for data?

Figure 2. Possible solutions.

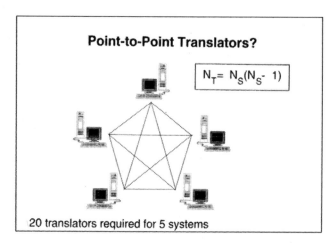

Figure 3.   Point-to-point translators?

usually lost in translation; it is generally not dramatic, but some "richness" can be lost. All this is bad enough if you are only involved in one partnership. If you are involved in more than one . . . So the usual decision is to invest in a common system, but whose? (See Figure 4.)

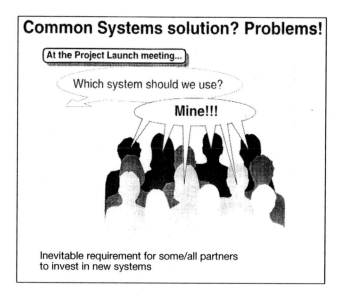

Figure 4.   Common system—whose?

Moreover, if anyone else joins the consortium they are forced to conform, the manufacturer has not had to do anything to get the new customer. If a new and better system comes on the market the cost of everyone changing is horrendous, there is a huge disincentive to go over to the better system. So the manufacturer knows he does not have to produce the best possible system, only one that is just good enough.

And resolving that problem still leaves many more—see Figure 5.

And so on, and so on, and so on. It is a prescription for the Tower of Babel.

It is a characteristic of this tool that its enormous potential is best realized if there is agreement between parties. Here is a different example, from a keynote speech about medical education at a conference on healthcare computing. The speaker began with a logical argument, that there is now so much medical knowledge that you cannot hope to get it all into the heads of medical students during the five years of their training; it would be better to collect

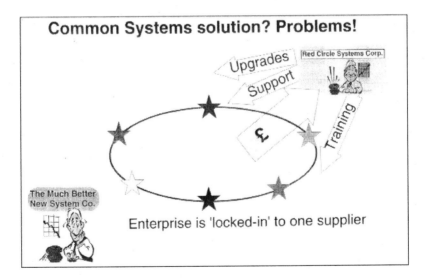

Figure 5.   Yet more problems.

Note: Both company names in this figure are clearly fictional. Since the time when the figure was first drawn, there is now a company with the name "Red Circle Technologies Ltd"; no reference to this company was or is intended.

the best available knowledge into protocols and teach how to use those. You would also then not need the highest calibre of student. Moreover, medical knowledge is not uniformly relevant. When a patient presents with, say, abdominal pain, it could be caused by 100 possible conditions, three of which account for 95% of cases (I am inventing these figures). The doctor may well not have encountered at least some of the other ninety-seven; it would be safer for him to work through a protocol which systematically guides him in eliminating them.

So far, so very persuasive. Then comes the question of how to get all medical education and qualifications changed—you cannot have some medical schools teaching this way and others not. They have to be persuaded, said the speaker. And if there are some professors of medicine who do not agree? They have to be sacked. Of course, at this point he lost the audience. But this is also an example of the disparity between vision and operation not being taken seriously, or even thought about.

Human reactions to control systems

In various degrees, there are elements of totalitarian control implicit in this technology. There are many actions you cannot take now unless you take them electronically and in a prescribed format.

When people who are constrained can reassert some control, they do. The earliest research I was involved in was about the human implications of work study. Work study encompassed methods study and time study. It was a system of control, of trying to obtain predictable and measurable output and costs by laying down in detail the methods and movements by which operations were to be carried out, and then the time. We found that, once such a system was bedded down and familiar, operators found ways to regain some elbow-room, some elements of control. These were called "fiddles". "Fiddling" had the function not so much of maximizing an operator's earnings as of optimizing his or her total resources of time, energy, and money. And, at the same time, it allowed the operator to exercise some ingenuity and creativity for which there was no room within the formal system; some fiddles were highly ingenious and sophisticated (Klein, 1964). It is, I think, in this light that we should see some of today's hacking and planting of computer viruses, by people who may not even realize that there is potential danger or damage involved. And don't they generate in even the most sober citizens among us just a small amount of glee? Are the hackers and virus planters not doing it to just a small extent on behalf of those of us who are not in a position to, by virtue of the dignity of our role or just not knowing how?

In the work study situation, in spite of much erudite literature about time study being a scientific process, the outcome was in fact the result of a battle of wits and intelligence between the time study engineers studying a job and the operators doing the job. Around computer systems in hospitals there are similar battles of wits, and I have no doubt that there are in other situations. When the pathology system in one hospital went live, the situation of junior doctors suddenly became much easier. Most requests for laboratory tests are made by junior doctors and now, instead of constantly going back and forth to the path labs, or having to keep track of paper requests, they were able to input requests and call up results from any terminal in the hospital, an enormous improvement for them. As a result the number of tests requested soared—if you are not very experienced, it is safer to ask for more tests rather than fewer. One can tell the date on which the system went live very clearly from the sharp angle in the curve of path lab statistics. So the path lab became overloaded, and after a time began to defend itself, inserting extra screens and awkward questions. (What is the clinically appropriate pattern of tests for a particular set of symptoms is left to the lay hypochondriac to wonder about.) Equivalent battles of wits were taking place around the X-ray department and the Pharmacy.

In conclusion

There is an element of mystery about the origin of the name Ludd; Ned Ludd was most likely a mythical character. People have harnessed his name to suit their points of view—for some it symbolizes heroic resistance against oppression, for others it symbolizes blind, or at least short-sighted, opposition to progress. So I would like to harness it too, to suit my purposes.

I have said that the banner I would like to hoist is that of raising the status of operational reality. How mundane that sounds, and how important it is. It is when people cannot handle the complexity of linking vision and operation that they resort to simple solutions like executing textile workers or sacking professors of medicine. I see this as a design challenge, because it will not happen unless it is designed in, and I would like to commend it to HUSAT. Let us not avoid the complexity of it by either embracing or rejecting the technical vision wholesale; let us not avoid it either by designing user-friendly deck-chairs for the *Titanic*, when the bloody ship ought to be somewhere else. The biggest intellectual, methodological, and eventually cultural challenge to us is to find ways of connecting the macro and the micro, the visionary and the mundane, so that it becomes structurally impossible to consider the one without also at the same time considering the other. That would be a good way to honour your neighbours of two hundred years ago.

SECTION II
RESEARCH STUDIES

The two research projects described in this section are separated by forty years. The first one took place during the post-war preoccupation with productivity in industry, and was carried out in two manufacturing companies. The focus was the techniques of work study, and the research was funded to find out about their human implications; we came to see work study as part of a broader wish to control and rationalize work, and learned to differentiate between short-term and long-term consequences.

The second study took place in the late 1990s; the setting was National Health Service hospitals and the focus was Information Technology. The drive behind introducing IT was still to control and rationalize the work, this time of hospitals, and the funders still wanted to know what were the human and organizational implications, with more emphasis this time on organizational ones. The study is too recent for long-term implications to have emerged, but in view of the earlier research one could go some way towards predicting them.

So these are two studies forty years apart, both publicly funded as pieces of research. The approach in both cases was to do grounded, qualitative research to reveal the reality of the work process in its organizational context. In both cases attempts were being made to operate or introduce new "systems" into the organization—the first work study, the second computer-based record systems—and in both cases what the research reveals is the array of ramifications as the existing work system responds to these initiatives.

CHAPTER FIVE

The human implications of rationalizing work

During the 1950s and 1960s, a programme of industrial sociological research was funded in Britain as part of the Marshall Plan. It was a condition of the grants that the research should have some bearing on productivity. Work-study techniques were very popular at the time, as part of the process of rationalizing industrial production, and for five years I was involved in a research project to examine "the human implications of work study". The team consisted of Stuart Dalziel, John Snelling, and myself. Nowadays this research would be called ethnography. It took the form of detailed, intensive studies of two firms—one in which these techniques were being newly introduced and one in which they had been established for some time (Dalziel & Klein, 1960; Klein, 1964). From various outputs from the research, I have based this chapter on a paper in which the two firms are compared (Klein , 1962).

While work-study techniques may sound outdated, they have in fact much in common with—one might say recently re-emerged as—the newer-sounding "business process re-engineering". And although batch production manufacturing may not now be very common, the principle of target-setting, measurement, and payment by results, described here in a manufacturing setting, has strongly re-emerged in contemporary working life, in many other settings.

* * *

Introduction

This research was originally intended to examine the human implications of work study, and was carried out from within the Department of Scientific and Industrial Research. It took the form of detailed case studies of two firms. The first was fairly small, employing about 400 people, and work study was being newly introduced by management consultants. We called it "Pakitt Ltd". The second, "Multiproducts Ltd", was a large engineering firm, employing about 3,600 people, where a methods department and a time study department had been established for more than ten years. In both firms interviews were conducted with operators at shop-floor level, with supervisory, functional and ancillary staff, and with top management. In Pakitt Ltd we also interviewed staff from the external management consultants. Although these were different firms, and although one clearly cannot generalize from single cases, it may be useful to look at them as if they showed the rationalization of work at different points in time.

Broadly speaking, work study covers two groups of management techniques, those concerned with improving methods of work and those concerned with measuring it. In Pakitt Ltd both were being introduced by external management consultants. In Multiproducts Ltd, as seemed to be common practice in the engineering industries, these activities were carried out by two separate management departments. The methods department was responsible for reviewing existing methods and planning new processes; the time study department was responsible for determining the times required for the various operations in the factory. However, it quickly became clear that these activities could not be studied in isolation: industrial situations are complex, and their complexity is itself a relevant factor, the removal of which would distort the results of the study. Time study and methods engineering were found to be integrated parts of a wider system of rationalization, and were closely interwoven with highly developed systems of cost control, checks on labour and machine utilization, etc., the sum of which had human and social implications. Inevitably, therefore, we found ourselves looking at the whole field of rationalized management[1] and had to widen the terms of reference accordingly.

At the beginning of the project it seemed important that the research workers should know something about the actual work study techniques. We attended various training courses, among others a training course in work study organized by the Trade Union Congress for shop stewards. There was a great deal to be learned, much of it from one's fellow students. One of them, for instance, who was convenor of shop stewards in a very big company, explained how a stop-watch could be controlled. He also explained some of the factors that play a part in time study, and that are not generally mentioned in the literature. In his firm, even the distance between the time study office and the place where a rate was being decided could have an important effect. It was the established procedure that, if an operator disagreed with the rate set by a time study engineer, the convenor of shop stewards would time the job himself and then discuss the case with time study staff. So, after timing the job, he would walk to the time study office. If the walk was fairly long he had a good opportunity to work out his strategy, to decide how far he could go and what he could insist on (this, in turn would be influenced by the current state of the labour market, the balance of power, etc.). If the walk was short he had to make a quick decision, which was likely to be more cautious. So one became aware quite early that there are many subtle factors which have a bearing on the result of a time study!

Short-term consequences

In Pakitt, where management consultants were introducing work study, the initial work study assignment broke down and was terminated. Many things went wrong during the course of it and I realize that it is unusual for so many things to go wrong that, cumulatively, they lead to breakdown. Nevertheless, I also know that any one of them, taken separately, is by no means unusual. It needs to be emphasized that most of the problems arose between the firm's management and the consultants: they concerned misunderstandings about the terms of reference, the superficiality of consultative processes, different expectations about where savings were likely to come from, unexpected workloads on clerical and maintenance departments, unexpected effects on the supervisor's control over his department. The problems that occurred on the shop-floor and concerned operators were relatively less important than these, but for the purpose of comparison they are the ones I shall describe in a little more detail.

The firm manufactured printed cartons. The design of the carton was printed on to sheets of board, perhaps four or six designs on a sheet. The sheets then went through a machine that cut round the edge of the design and cut part-way through the board along lines where the finished carton would later be creased. This process was called—not unnaturally—"cutting-and-creasing". The cartons were then "stripped": an operator would collect a pile of sheets from the cutting-and-creasing machine, carry it back to his workplace, and knock away with a hammer all the pieces of waste board which were not part of the design of the finished carton.

This operation was work studied, and two changes in method were introduced. First of all a chute was designed to go under the workbench, so that waste material would simply drop away without having to be packed and carried away. It was, of course, a good idea, though it was a pity that the same suggestion had already been made some time previously by the works engineer, and that no one had taken any notice of it then.

But the more radical method change was the introduction of a "load mover", an unskilled labourer whose job was to take loads of cartons to the strippers, so that they no longer had to fetch loads for themselves. Instead of experiencing this as a relief, however, the strippers now found that they had to work more continuously. Stripping was a fairly hard physical job, and since they were now using the same set of muscles all the time, instead of occasionally using a different set of muscles, they also felt that they were working harder. (Management, incidentally, had no complaints about their previous rate of work. It was generally acknowledged that these operators worked hard.) There was much debate about the relationship between continuous work and hard work.

They lost the opportunity for an occasional change of scene and an occasional chat with others in the department. They became bored and complained of "having to look at a brick wall all day."

They also lost the opportunity, which they had previously had, of exercising some control over the flow of work. The more experienced strippers knew when good jobs were coming, and had learned to be ready at the right time, so that to some extent they chose their jobs and thus controlled their own work situation. They resented losing this measure of control.

As regards incentives, a new incentive scheme was introduced which the operators found difficult to understand because it was complicated and had an aura of science about it, slide rules and decimal calculations being much in evidence. They therefore felt unable to argue about the prices, which under their previous system they had felt able to do. They felt that its introduction implied a criticism of their rate of work, which, as has been mentioned, was acknowledged to be good. For various reasons the new scheme did not lead to an immediate increase in earnings and it seems likely that, if it had, these other difficulties would not have come to the surface. But this at least allows us to see what other effects may be present when a new scheme is introduced, even if they are masked by financial success.

In these changes one can recognize the trend of rationalization. In the second firm this trend was much further advanced.

Long-term consequences

Multiproducts Ltd was typical of the light engineering industry and manufactured a variety of products in batches of varying sizes. There were two machine shops and two assembly shops, and the work was rationalized and sub-divided so that in the machine shops, on which the study was focused, there were groups of milling machines, drilling machines, capstan lathes, etc., each of them performing one operation on a wide variety of components. This form of work organization was long-established and, unlike in Pakitt, the operators did not question or resent it. If there had ever been any opposition, it had been resolved long ago, and they probably did not think that there could be any alternative way of organizing work. They were fairly comfortable and fairly contented.

Influence on perception of the job

On the other hand, there were strong indications that the way in which the work was organized had influenced them considerably.

It influenced first of all their *perception*, especially their perception of the job.

Work study has frequently been accused of de-skilling work, and resistance to its introduction has often been on these grounds. However, the interview material did not suggest that, on the whole, the operators were worried about lack of skill, or thought their work lacked skill. For one thing, on some operations they found things to like within the immediate job, such as keeping the machine clean, handling the machine and beating a performance target, and their total situation gave them some feeling of freedom and the opportunity to vary their working pace. For another, there was an outlet for discretion and skill in getting the best out of the payment system (see later).

Mainly, the form of work organization had been too long established to be questioned. This suggests that there had been a process of adaptation, and that this may have been in the way that work was perceived. People talked about "good" and "bad" jobs. "The job" meant the immediate job cycle. When they talked about "good" jobs, as distinct from "bad" jobs, they meant jobs which had a loose price, jobs on which tools did not break easily or need sharpening too often, jobs on which production runs were long so that one could get into the swing of the job and make bonus. One woman said, "When I say it's a good job I mean they're clean, they've been well inspected, there aren't a lot of burrs to catch your hands." This is perhaps a surprising definition of a good job.

Organizationally, production was so arranged that all the planning and decision making were carried out before work reached the operators, and therefore was outside their field of vision; technically, too, there was little inherent in the job to make them aware of, or interested in, anything beyond the job-cycle. The effect of the system on the operators, therefore, seems to have been not to lessen their skills or make them feel frustrated about skill, but to adjust their perception of their jobs and with it their general perspective.

Perception of time raises a similar question. Many of the operators explained that when they had a job on which the time was tight, they became discouraged and slacked off. Only one person said that a tight price could also have the opposite effect: a tight price made him work as fast as he could, in order to get the unpleasant job out of the way. This suggests that the difference between the two reactions may be caused by a difference in the perception of time, discouragement meaning that one cannot see the end of the job, working fast suggesting that one can see beyond the end of the job to the next one, which might be better.

The operators did not appear to resent changes that were going on in the firm, perhaps because these changes did not impinge on them and they were often not even aware of them. The firm might be introducing new products or devising new processes, but for the machine operator this might simply mean that he or she was drilling a hole of different dimensions in a different grade of metal, with no indication why. The company was introducing automatic machine tools where the quantities being made warranted it (and sometimes, according to supervision, where the quantities did not warrant it). For the ordinary machine operator this meant that some good jobs with long runs were disappearing. But the nature of "the job", again, had not changed.

This narrow definition of the job was reinforced by the piece-work system. If a person was paid every time they made a half-inch cut, the implication was that this was what the firm considered the job to be, not making a good product, or being in any way concerned with the wider objectives of the firm.

Influence on attitudes

The form of work organization therefore also influenced *attitudes*. The operators were, on the whole, satisfied and regarded the firm as a good employer, but they were not very interested in it and did not feel personally involved in its affairs. A typical comment was: "They're fair enough. The money's good. As long as I can earn my living I'm not bothered. I come to work, then I go home and forget all about it". Or, a comment about the factory superintendent: "He doesn't get in my way and I don't get in his. That's how it should be". The most frequent comment about the firm, and the main reason for liking it, was that they gave one a feeling of independence, they left one alone to get on with the job, they were not breathing down the back of one's neck the whole time.

The economic and technical policies of the firm, and the market conditions within which it was operating, only affected the operators if they interfered—as they sometimes did—with the smooth running of the piece-work system. It is a necessary condition of piece-work that there must be enough work available, that tools must be in good supply and well maintained and that the planning of production must be smooth and efficient. Otherwise, piece-work is experienced as unfair. Thus it became important, and there was much pressure from supervisors as well as operators, for management to keep the operators sheltered from the problems of the firm.

In fact, these were considerable. The firm was engaged in small batch production in a difficult market and had acute problems of how to deal with urgent orders, decide batch sizes, keep down stocks, and adapt to market fluctuations.

The main reason for the complexity of production scheduling was the large variety of products, each consisting of a number of components and operations, so that, as one supervisor grumbled, "There are 3,700 jobs in the capstan shop alone."

Planning and organizing production was made difficult by the economic conditions prevailing at the time, since a credit squeeze made it necessary to keep stocks of materials, tools, and work-in-progress as low as possible. This meant that only minimum-size batches could be made, and the shorter the batch the more frequent was the need to re-set machines and the greater the call on planning ability, tools, and services. There appeared to be frequent crises, and the problem of deciding optimum batch-size preoccupied many people. In addition, the company's reputation was partly founded on quick customer service, so that it was legitimate to interrupt programmes for urgent orders. Rush and pressure were therefore the keynote, particularly for supervisors.

As well as the planning and control of everyday production, staff were concerned with the introduction of new products and processes. Innovation was continuous rather than sporadic and dramatic, and consisted of two kinds of activity: in a forward direction new products and processes were planned and introduced through a process planning department, and in a backward direction methods engineers were responsible for modifying and improving existing products and processes. Both activities were affected by a shortage of trained engineers, and a great deal of technical skill and know-how were required of production supervisors, although on paper these should now be supplied by the specialist departments. There were, in fact, signs that, at management level, the process of rationalization was not complete, showing the usual problems associated with changing skills, insecurity, and the relationship between experts and those directly responsible for production.

Taking all this together, there was certainly some truth in the comment, "The only person who isn't worried or driven nowadays is the operator on the machine". The situation I have described had, therefore, the secondary effect of establishing an enormous gulf between the operators and the rest of the people in the firm.

For the operators, life was fairly comfortable; they were preoccupied with the immediate job cycle and their bonus earnings, they were not involved with, or interested in, the affairs of the firm. Everyone else—management, functional staff, even down to hourly paid checkers and bonus clerks, was more or less rushed, harassed, and uncomfortable, but on the other hand interested in and concerned about the affairs of the firm, and considerably involved. Their problems were frequently the firm's problems, while the operators' payment system implied that their situation ought to be problem-free, or at least free from problems connected with production. There seemed to be two quite separate societies. I shall come back to this point when I have considered the incentive schemes themselves.

Influence on behaviour—the effects of incentives

The piece-work scheme in Multiproducts Ltd had been in operation for more than ten years. Familiarity with it also meant familiarity with its loopholes. For one thing, it was possible to challenge and dispute a price, and arguments generally centred on rating and on the appropriate fatigue allowances.[2] Because there was room for disagreement in these two areas, of performance and fatigue, there was scope for a certain amount of "fiddling" during a time study, as well as in the way one worked once a price had been decided, in such matters as ignoring safety regulations or running two operations together. After all, piece-work is based on the assumption that one will be able to improve one's performance, and therefore one's earnings, after a price has been set. It is a logical extension of this principle to try to increase the scope for improving performance by making the job look as slow and difficult as possible during the time study and doing it as swiftly and easily as possible afterwards.

Indeed, because the time study engineer expected this, and tended almost automatically to compensate for it, both arguing about prices and fiddling became an important part of setting the rate. It was so much a normal part of behaviour that only the more amusing or dramatic or dangerous devices involved were consciously thought of as "fiddles". One of the most revealing comments on this came from a man who made no deliberate attempt to cheat. He insisted that if one gave a fair effort during a time study the firm would give a fair time, and that he did not try to "spin the job out" a lot. The researcher asked, "Not even a little bit?" and he replied, "Oh well, you use your loaf!"

This comment gives a clue to another function of fiddling. Work in the machine shops did not give much opportunity to "use one's loaf", and there is no doubt that the battle of wits with time study gave interest and stimulus to an otherwise dull work situation. This stimulus was not confined to the operators. Some of the more sophisticated fiddles were explained by time study engineers and supervisors, with considerable humour. More seriously, this meant that the time study engineers expected fiddles and arguments about the prices, and tended almost automatically to compensate for them. This in turn meant that for the operator such behaviour became essential.

It was therefore important for the operators that time studies should be taken on those who knew the rules of the game and were strongly motivated enough to keep them—not on newcomers, those who were shy or nervous, those who were not much concerned about money or who did not intend to stay long in the firm, and so had no stake in the general level of prices. This may begin to resonate: time study engineers, because they find rating difficult, prefer to make a study on a "normal" or "average" person. (If rating were easy, the characteristics of the operator would be irrelevant.) Where the operators in the study understood this concept of the "average" person, they resented it, first because it did not correspond with experience—"no two men work alike, do they?", said one. And second, the idea was criticized because it was impossible to relate speed to moral worth—"a chap who is working slow may be working harder than a fast one", said another. Nevertheless, in spite of these criticisms, it was clear that the operators themselves had an equally well-defined concept of a "normal" person: normal, however, in this case, not in terms of dexterity and experience, but in terms of motivation and behaviour.

Because of the way that small batch production is organized, there was also a good deal of scope for manipulation and fiddling in the way one recorded one's output. In order to be able to predict and manage one's overall earnings, it was necessary to balance good jobs against bad ones, to overcome the effects of hold-ups in the flow of production, to make sure that management's attention was not drawn to loose prices and, in general, to optimize one's personal resources of time and energy. If one considers that every person is their own work study officer, it follows that they had to balance short-term interests against long-term interests, and to balance the maximizing of their cash resources against the optimizing of their total resources. The man who explained that he always worked very hard on Thursdays, hid the pieces overnight, and fed them in on Fridays so as not to be too tired at the weekend was, after all, acting quite rationally.

Altogether, by these various manipulations, the operators had regained a considerable measure of control over their working environment. (In this they inadvertently also influenced the firm's control system: time study figures and output records were not only used for bonus purposes, but also for planning production and estimating costs.) If the incentive scheme in Pakitt had been allowed to continue, one would guess that, here too, familiarity would gradually have shown up some room to manoeuvre, and the feelings of pressure and constraint would have lessened. In Multiproducts, most of the operators liked being on piece-work (although most of them also had some criticisms). The main reasons for liking it were that it meant freedom from close supervision, and freedom to vary one's working pace.

One can see from all this that the piece-work system presupposed certain personality characteristics in the operators. One can describe the person who most successfully and with least stress fitted into it. Such persons were:

- in good physical health, since the pace of work was high and, obviously, the faster they worked the more they stood to gain;
- strongly motivated in the direction of money, but not too much so. If their need for money was too urgent, operators might

book too much output and draw management's attention to loose prices;

- independent, the kind of person who did not want a close relationship with managers or a close involvement with the firm;
- confident *vis-à-vis* superiors, having the courage to challenge prices and to hold their own in the battle with time study;
- not too troubled about the quality of the product or the care of tools. They were paid, after all, for output. If tools broke or faulty pieces got through to inspection, the payment system told them that this was not their concern.

These were the characteristics one needed in order to like being on piece-work. They were also the characteristics one needed in order to behave appropriately during a time study, to challenge prices where necessary, to regulate the level of one's performance and to optimize the way one booked one's work. There was, indeed, an assumption on the part of top management that the workshop was entirely peopled by this kind of person.

But the assumption that all operators had these characteristics could be questioned. First, the operators did not always know what was in their own best interests. The idea that concealing waiting time would raise the level of bonus earnings, for instance, was a fallacy unless there was a surplus of work to be booked in. Second, there were people whose interests were different from those of the main body of operators; for instance, people who were old or in poor health and who found the pace too hard. Women and foreign workers were also mentioned in this connection. Some of the foreign workers had an urgent and overriding need for quick, high earnings, which, if it made them "over-book", went against the general, long-term interest of the majority. Women seemed to be well versed in the optimization of booking, but may have been less ready to challenge prices and more inclined to work fast during a time study because of nervousness. Nervousness of this kind may be related to attitudes to authority, which may also have been a more important factor for newcomers and, again, for foreigners, who perhaps had a greater need to be acceptable to those in authority.

Third, there were people who brought social attitudes into the factory that prevented them from responding to the system in the required way; people who wanted a greater degree of identification with the firm or who were concerned—possibly too concerned—about such things as quality or the care of tools.

Now, one way in which social scientists may describe a culture is to describe the individuals who fit into it most successfully. The fact that the people described were deviants shows what were the requirements of the situation, and many operators seemed to have adapted to these requirements. At least to some extent, therefore, the system tended to create a culture in that it encouraged people to behave in the characteristic way. Where they did so they tended to be consistent about it, and this could express itself in ways that were not necessarily intended by management. Where the wish for money became dominant, the operators responded to the financial incentive, but might also discover less desirable ways of finding money. If the incentive scheme was a major preoccupation, they also tended to demand conditions where there was no room to argue about inspection standards, or about correct methods of work. Such conditions were by no means easy to provide since, although the system has been described as one of rationalized production, few production systems are as consistently rational as all that.

It is here that we come up against a contradiction, not within the work-role but between the requirements of the work-role and other, social, requirements. Managers sometimes wished that operators would have other characteristics than those mentioned, and a wider perspective. Partly this was because they wished them to understand why things could not always run smoothly, but mostly they reflected in this social values—shared by some of the operators—rather than the production needs of the firm. Such values are frequently evidenced by policies such as joint consultation, induction training, explaining products and balance sheets to employees, all of which are intended to give people information that will widen their perspective to include more of the firm's activities than merely their own immediate jobs, and thereby to increase their involvement. But this way of doing it is essentially outside the structure of the situation. Where a wider view acquired in this way does not stem from the job itself, the stimulus has to be continually renewed to remain successful, requiring a very great deal of effort on the part of managements, and explaining why the effects of this kind of policy are so often disappointing.

At Multiproducts Ltd, a policy aimed at broadening the opera-tors' perceptions beyond the immediate experience of the task was the suggestion scheme. The mere fact that there was a sugges-tion scheme, however, reinforced the idea that there was conflict between the operator's work-role and what was thought to be socially desirable behaviour for operators: on the one hand making suggestions showed a laudable interest in the firm, on the other hand their job did not require it of them, neither did it give them the necessary perspective and knowledge to do it. Among the people in the firm who mentioned the scheme, those who had to use it because they had no means of suggesting improvements within the scope of their own jobs were least pleased.

But the suggestion scheme was almost the only interest-stimu-lating policy of this kind. On the whole there was little in the company's policy to counteract the combined effect of size, tech-nology, organization and payment system in requiring a particular kind of person as operators and in influencing their scale of vision. At the same time this form of organization sheltered them to a large extent from the firm's problems.

Two societies

Thus the work system at Multiproducts Ltd produced two distinct and separate societies, the operators and the rest. The operators tended to dissociate themselves from the firm, the rest were involved with it. The two groups had different codes of behaviour, different preoccupations, different and sometimes conflicting inter-ests; also, different values were required of them. The gulf between them was substantial, and reinforced by the tendency of the system to select particular traits in the operators. This gulf is perhaps the same phenomenon that Wilfred Brown (1960) has described as "the gap at the bottom of the executive system". He attributes it, in the case of the Glacier Metal Company, to inadequate definition of one of the work-roles in the system. But, at Multiproducts Ltd at any rate, there also seem to be simpler causes in the way work was organized and in the conflict of interests between the two groups.

One cannot compare the level of satisfaction on either side of the gulf, because there are many different kinds of satisfaction; but there is little doubt that the level of comfort was higher for the operators.

There were, of course, other conflicts of interest and other differences in attitudes and values. But the gulf described was the greatest one, because the alignments caused by differences of interest and of perspective coincided, whereas between different groups within management or within the body of operators they did not. On both sides of the gulf there were individuals whose personal characteristics or histories counteracted the pressures of the environment. But that the gulf was basically due to the environment and not, for instance, to differences in intelligence is suggested by the interviews with checkers—that is, the people who checked the quantity of output. Checkers and bonus clerks were selected on the same basis as operators; indeed, sometimes a new employee who was not thought capable of working a machine was given a job as a checker. There is, therefore, no reason to think that they were more intelligent, or that they had any different personality characteristics from machine operators. Yet the range of topics they discussed, and their interest in and understanding of production problems, was much greater and they had more frequently views on what was good and right for the firm.

Intelligence and education did play a part in hardening this situation, in that the transition from one side of the gulf to the other was becoming more difficult. As the skills required for operating a machine grew less and those required of a chargehand or foreman grew greater and different in kind, it was becoming much more difficult to promote people, and this was a cause for concern.

It is as if the tide of rationalization had reached and passed the operators. Any problems that it brought had happened at an earlier stage, and calm had been restored, but calm of a different order. They had no particular feelings about skill, or about being told how to do a job by the methods department—it was taken for granted that this should be so. Their view of work and of the firm had adjusted itself so that they only made those demands of their environment that it was able to fulfil. It was at middle management level that rationalization was still being extended and specialization spreading, and it was here, at the edge of the tide, that turbulence could be seen. It was here that there were problems due to the incompleteness of the process, the need to adapt to new demands and to changes in skill, and it was here, therefore, that problems of personal security arose.

If this hypothesis is correct, then it might be predicted that, as the process of rationalization becomes more complete in other parts of the firm—higher up in the management hierarchy or within specialist departments themselves—a similar adaptation would gradually take place: the level of comfort would rise, the view of the job would become narrower, causing new gaps to appear, and the degree of involvement with the firm would drop. The question is whether this is the development that is intended. While attention is frequently paid to problems associated with the introduction of change, it is at least as important to consider the long-term effects of changes and the kind of adaptation that is likely to take place. This may be less dramatic, but it may also be more far-reaching.

Coming back, then to looking at the two firms side-by-side: in the short term the reorganization of work and of the payment system caused problems of adaptation and adjustment. In the long term, they had the effect of creating a particular culture. For the operators the environment was consistent, requiring certain personality characteristics and tending to influence their perceptions and attitudes in certain directions. For everybody else, whose work was not yet highly rationalized, the demands of the environment were much more varied and conflicting, their perception was wider and their attitudes were less homogenous. The situation therefore also had the effect of creating two separate cultures in the firm.

A lot of attention is paid to the phenomenon of resistance to change. But after changes are introduced, and after the initial troubles, if any, are smoothed over, everybody makes some kind of adjustment to the new situation. It is an awareness of the long-term environment that is created by changes in the structure of work, and of the kind of adjustment that people are going to make to it, which ought to play perhaps the more important part in our thinking.

Notes

1. This "move away from simplification" was becoming increasingly accepted as being the most meaningful, though difficult, way to study industrial systems. For a discussion of it as applied to industrial engineering, see Eilon, 1959.

2. A time study engineer measures how long it takes an operator to do a job. He then "rates" the operator's performance, that is, he compares it with that of a notional "average" operator. Then he applies "fatigue allowances", which are negotiated according to the type of job.

CHAPTER SIX

Living and working in hospital wards. Using electronic patient records

The Bayswater Institute was established in 1990–1991, and during its early years much of its work was in National Health Service hospitals. Between 1995 and 1998, we were part of a consortium carrying out evaluation research around a programme in NHS hospitals called the Electronic Patient Record, and a broadly similar one called the Integrated Clinical Workstation. The project originally involved five hospitals (later three) and four research groups. Our part was to look at the human and organizational aspects in the three hospitals.

An Introduction explains the programme, and the main paper is a short version of the Institute's part of the consortium's final report (Manchester Centre for Healthcare Management, University of Manchester, The Bayswater Institute, London, Medical Informatics Group, University of Manchester, School of Postgraduate Studies in Medical and Health Care, Swansea, 2001). It has been slightly modified to fit into this collection. The work and writing of the Institute's paper were done jointly with Dr Lesley Mackey.

*   *   *

Introduction: the research programme

Computer systems in hospitals are in evolution. The first generation of such systems was known as HIS (Hospital Information Systems) or HISS (Hospital Information Support Systems). In 1994, the National Health Service initiated two programmes of work intended to apply information technology to patient records, known as the Electronic Patient Record (EPR) and the Integrated Clinical Workstation (ICWS) programmes, and this may be seen, broadly, as the next generation. The Electronic Patient Record depends on the pre-existence of a basic HIS, but is much more sophisticated. It is capable of being populated in real time with data at each stage of the clinical process, over an episode, or series of episodes, of a patient's care. These include: presenting problems, symptoms, signs, a working diagnosis, investigations and results, treatments, procedures, care plans, and clinical outcomes. The data collected at each stage of the patient episode are made available at subsequent stages to clinicians caring for a particular patient throughout the organization. In 1994, two hospitals were selected as demonstrator sites for the EPR programme, and three for the ICWS programme. The difference between the two lies mainly in the background and history of their funding, and for practical purposes there is no need to define it here.

The research was funded by the Department of Health Research and Development Division (RDD). Both the EPR and the ICWS programmes were overseen by Programme Boards, RDD being represented on both. They eventually decided to carry out a joint evaluation research project, with different levels of emphasis. The EPR Project Board expressed a wish for an element of action research, which should make the research useful to the sites themselves. The IT staff in the sites, however, were ambivalent about this and the research was not set up as action research. There were, nevertheless, a number of action elements, most notably the feedback discussions that took place around draft site reports.

Five hospitals were originally selected as demonstrator sites, but in the event only three were involved in the research. These were:

Burton Hospitals NHS Trust (later Queen's Hospital, Burton-on-Trent) (EPR)
Queen's Hospital, Burton, serves a wide geographical area around Burton-on-Trent and had at the time 465 beds, forty-two consultants and a total annual budget of £43 million. It provided all the services of a District Hospital and served a population of 250,000.

Wirral Hospitals NHS Trust (EPR)
The Wirral Hospitals NHS Trust was based on two sites five miles apart on the Wirral peninsula, across the river Mersey from Liverpool; the main study took place in Arrowe Park Hospital. This was an acute hospital with 1,200 beds serving a population of 350,000 and taking referrals from other parts of Northern England and Wales. It had an annual budget of £100 million and over 100 consultants.

Winchester and Eastleigh Healthcare NHS Trust (ICWS)
The Winchester and Eastleigh NHS Trust was a fully integrated organization comprising acute, community, and mental health services. It served a local catchment population of 218,000, with an annual budget at the time of the research of £64 million. There were four hospital sites within the Trust; St Paul's Hospital, Winchester, where the study took place, had forty beds comprising elderly and rehabilitation wards and a day hospital.

The research was carried out by a consortium of four groups. Briefly, they were looking at:

- clinical aspects of the systems (the School of Postgraduate Studies in Medical and Health Care, Swansea);
- organizational and sociotechnical aspects (the Bayswater Institute, which also edited the final report);
- economic and management aspects (the Health Services Management Unit, Manchester);
- information systems aspects (the University of Manchester Medical Informatics Group).

Evolution of the research proposal

The consortium's original research proposal was one of three that were short-listed and sent to referees, including representatives from the two EPR sites. The referees from the EPR sites were severely critical of all three applications, and recommended that all three should be rejected. This clearly created a problem for the funding body.

In the consortium's verbal presentation, which had been planned as the next step, I pointed to a structural problem: in a situation of competitive bidding it is not possible to engage with the field sites while designing the research, because that would be improper. In any other situation one would not dream of designing a research programme involving field sites without engaging with those field sites in the process. It was not surprising that they had rejected plans in which they had not been consulted; what was needed was an opportunity for at least one of the bidding teams to do some exploratory work together with the field sites, in order to see whether an agreed research plan could be achieved. This reasoning was accepted, and a small budget was agreed for our consortium to carry out a preliminary study, which came to be called the "scoping study".

The proposals originally made by the hospitals themselves for funding to become part of the EPR programme had also been affected by the format and assumptions of the process of making funding applications: their bids were neatly formulated in terms of sub-projects. In the course of time these sub-projects became much less salient than they had been at the beginning, and some quietly faded away. Since the only information about the field sites available to potential researchers was contained in the hospitals' Project Initiation Documents, our early methodological thinking, and no doubt that of other applicants, was also focused on the sub-projects.

The scoping study took three months. It provided explicit opportunities:

1. For familiarization and exploratory work with the field sites;
2. For the researchers to think and explore alternative configurations for the main study and to arrive at a research plan;
3. For a literature search.

As well as these explicit purposes, the scoping study also had a number of other functions:

4. It set in train a pattern of iteration between the evaluators, the site personnel, the two managers of the Programme Boards, and the Research and Development Division.

5. It started the process of the research teams getting to know each other and discussing and comparing methods.

The different member organizations of the consortium used the opportunity of the scoping study in very different ways. But, at the same time, a degree of commonality was established in that pairs or a group of researchers made up from two or more of the teams visited each of the field sites together, to carry out preliminary interviews, learn about the systems being used or developed, and collect documents. In this way the teams not only learned about the field sites but about each other's methods and approaches.

One important difference that emerged was between those researchers committed to formal and those committed to grounded approaches; that is, between whether one formulates models before going into the field, or whether one goes into the field to explore and then conceptualizes from the data (Glaser & Strauss, 1968).

At the same time as experiencing such differences, which were substantial, the teams also found that they shared and could articulate views about evaluation which they held in common:

●   evaluation, both of systems and processes, should be an intrinsic part of any systems implementation;
●   comprehensive evaluation of a complex process is inevitably time-consuming and expensive;
●   it needs to include the impact of the implementation in social, as well as in technical, operational and economic terms;
●   diffusion of the lessons learned should be embedded in future evaluation methodologies.

The evaluation research questions

In the course of the scoping study, the team's original research ideas were considerably modified. A major outcome was an agreement to concentrate on a number of research questions. As these originated from the different research teams, one function of this emphasis on research questions was to manage the dynamics of the research group. If one question could be allocated—more or less—to one research team, not only would the logistics of organizing the fieldwork become easier—four teams from different geographical locations were to work in five hospitals which were also in different geographical locations—but potential competition and conflict between the teams would be minimized.

The questions that were formulated, and the disciplines within which they were researched, were:

Q.1   What is the impact of the technology being used on clinical management, at three levels:
(a) individual patient care;
(b) by reviewing clinical practice through aggregated data;
(c) resource management (at specialty level or by types of clinical problem)?

Clinical

Q.2   (a) What is the experience of living and working at the implementation sites?
(b) What is the impact on roles, the organization of work, and work satisfaction of staff?

Social Science

Q.3   Can the costs and benefits of such developments/technologies be valued?

Economic and Managerial

Q.4   Patient record systems and technologies—how usable and useful are they? Criteria provisionally identified were:
(a) availability of data;
(b) data entry and display;
(c) confidentiality, integrity and availability;
(d) concurrency, timeliness;
(e) update consistency or anomalies;
(f) appropriateness to the task, situation and the user;
(g) training requirements.

Computer Science

Q.5   What is the relationship between electronic and paper records on these sites in respect of:
(a) availability of data;

(b) integrity, i.e., completeness/duplication;
(c) compliance with professionally required standards for record keeping;
(d) volume of paper generated;
(e) clerical activity?

Computer Science

Q.6   What is the relationship between the general management of the Trust and the information systems in use?

Managerial

Our task was to address Question 2.

A reflection on the programme

Looking back from the perspective of some years, it becomes clear that the programme of evaluation research reported here not only included multiple approaches—which we knew—but also had multiple hopes projected on to it—which we did not know so clearly. One was the hope of objective research, motivated only by curiosity and driven by scientific standards. Another was the hope that these systems would be shown to be successful, justifying the large investment. And another was that the research would help the developments under study. There were inevitably tensions between these objectives.

Moreover, as the work got under way, it gradually became clear that the research aims had been too ambitious. A complex and developing set of changes was being introduced into complex and developing institutions at five sites and was researched by four teams. The multi-method and multi-disciplinary approach was undoubtedly appropriate. But, although the research budget was reasonably large, at any rate by the standards of UK research funding, it would have required considerably more effort to do it all to the full potential of each discipline. And, on the other hand, more researchers spending more time at the sites would have been hard for the sites to cope with and would have distorted the situations being studied. It was a case of optimizing according to the dictionary definition: "to find the best compromise among several often conflicting requirements, as in engineering design".

Living and working at the implementation sites; the impact on roles, the organization of work, and work satisfaction of staff

The rest of this chapter will focus on Question 2.

Methods

While much of the evaluation was concerned with specific characteristics or specific impacts of the various technologies, this module was concerned with their combined impact and interaction in the real-life settings in which they (a) came together, and (b) affected the work being done in the hospital. The question we set out to answer was "What is the experience of living and working at the implementation sites?" The methods used were mainly observation, interviews, and tracer studies, that is, tracking an item, or a transaction, or a person through everything that happens to it/ them, and then pursuing the leads which that yielded. We did this in three of the hospitals, the Queen's Hospital, Burton, the Wirral Hospital, and St Paul's Hospital, Winchester.

The "gold standard" in health-related research is the randomized, controlled clinical trial; the received wisdom is that there is a dichotomy between quantitative methods, which are considered rigorous, and qualitative methods, which are not. In fact, qualitative methods make enormous demands on rigour; they are not the sloppy alternative for when there are not the resources or the opportunity to do quantitative work. There is indeed a dichotomy, but it is between rigorous and non-rigorous work, in both types of approach, and one may postulate a two-by-two matrix:

	Quantitative	Qualitative
Rigorous		
Non-rigorous		

In both approaches, the methodological hazard is self-deception. It is precisely because people engaged in qualitative methods realize that they are vulnerable to bias, to selective perception, and to the other various hazards of being unsystematic, that they are fairly likely to be self-conscious about what they are doing, to take steps to become aware of these hazards and to guard against them. It may even be that the scientific status of quantitative methods, the rigour that the very name implies, may make researchers feel secure, feeling that the category itself, and by itself, is enough to protect them against these hazards.

There are, in fact, considerable disputes about rigour in randomized controlled trials, where

- the condition may be one which does not produce many cases;
- starting conditions may not be the same; and
- coding/scoring is different in different centres or countries.

For example:

The choice of medication and the methods of administration are based on idiosyncratic physician experience and on reports in the literature that have different criteria of patient selection and vary in the stringency of analysis of the results of treatment. [Kohorn, 1996, p. 279]

The main problem about descriptive research is that the richer the data, the more difficult the analysis. Both the amount of data and ways of analysing them are potentially infinite, while resources are limited. Deciding on methods becomes partly a matter of cutting one's coat according to one's cloth, taking steps to guard against bias and selective perception, and coming to terms with the fact that analysis and writing up will outstrip the funded time, and will still be incomplete. We are very conscious of the fact that our accounts do not do justice to the richness of the situations observed. In the body of work around the implementation of new technologies in the NHS, a precedent for such a descriptive evaluation is the study carried out by the Bayswater Institute at Greenwich District Hospital (Scott & Buckingham, 1994).

Fieldwork was carried out as follows:

The scoping study

(i) At Burton, exploratory interviews were held with the Chief Executive, the Medical Director, the HISS/EPR Project Manager, a consultant surgeon, a consultant physician, the Director of Nursing and Quality, and the Assistant Director of Finance and Information.

Some feedback from this small exploratory study was given, partly as a demonstration of the nature of our work. It was agreed that we should carry out descriptive research at some locus where work is done and where the elements of the EPR would therefore come together operationally. At a meeting with sub-project managers it was decided that this locus should be a medical ward and an orthopaedic ward, and the two wards were identified.

(ii) At Wirral, exploratory work took the form of visits to the day case unit, the pharmacy, and a surgical ward; accompanying a consultant on her ward round, which included seven wards and the ITU; one ward drug round; and discussions with the project manager.

Again, feedback was given at a meeting with those who had been involved in the study and other key people. At this meeting it was suggested that an additional small study should be made of junior doctors as they move from EPR sites to non-EPR sites. As they move from one hospital to another, junior doctors are in a good position to compare experiences of different systems. A number of junior doctors at Wirral had already been mobilized and agreed to take part in such a study. This was later agreed and carried out (Merrifield & Mackay, 1999).

(iii) At Winchester there was little opportunity for exploration, since this site was added to our research programme after the scoping study was over. Two days were spent here in exploratory discussions.

The main study

At Burton, the initial EPR implementation was in orthopaedics and general medicine and the locus of study was an orthopaedic ward and a general medical and coronary care ward. At Winchester, also for reasons of the technology implementation, it was decided that we should study two linked wards for the care of the elderly.

The research in the two wards at Burton was repeated after eighteen months. That does not make it a "before and after" study, which, in the gradual evolution of the EPR development, would be impossible; it is more an "early and late" study, permitting some element of comparison. We also, each time, studied an orthopaedic outpatient clinic.

At Wirral, there was no such obvious locus for study, and it was decided to track two consultants on their ward rounds, which took them across several wards. This is known as tracer methodology, which then also requires studying the various departments and professionals whose work either fed into or arose from those ward rounds.

Activities during the fieldwork included: observation, planned interviews, interviews which developed spontaneously, accompanying or "shadowing" a person (for instance, a ward sister, a health care assistant (HCA), an outpatient), tracer studies of activities (for instance, an occupational therapist's home visit, a discharge as far as the patient's GP practice and district nurse), sitting in on ward meetings and outpatient consultations, observing activities (ward rounds, drug rounds, nursing shift handover), getting people to talk us through what they were doing.

As a result, we had an enormous amount of data. The individual hospital reports are quite long and are in the source document. This chapter is an attempt to synthesize some of the findings. Where relevant, it will refer to the different elements of the empirical work as:

Burton:	B-orth, or B-orth1, B-orth2; B-med, or B-med1, B-med2;
Wirral:	Wr;
Winchester:	Wn.

Feedback meetings to discuss preliminary findings were held with staff at the sites as follows:

at Burton after the scoping study and after each of the two field studies;
at Wirral after the scoping study. It was not possible to get feedback discussions on the main study or comments on a draft report;
at Winchester after the fieldwork phase.

All three hospitals cleared the report for publication.

Conceptual framework

Our conceptual framework is made up of three elements. The first is concerned with the interplay of structure and behaviour in organizational life, and is known in organizational sociology as contingency theory (Donaldson, 1996; Perrow, 1970). Structure here is taken to mean those things that cannot be changed quickly and have to be taken as given. Important structural factors affecting behaviour, attitudes, and relationships in an organization might be the legal framework within which it operates, the type of ownership, the type of market, the nature of its production system, its size, its geography, its architecture. A great deal of organizational life can be understood and explained in terms of such cause-and-effect chains. It is this frame of reference that led us to notice the clinical condition of the patient as a determinant of organization (see later).

The second element in our conceptual framework concerns the interplay between technology and people and is known as socio-technical theory. It involves a similar approach, of eliciting how "hard" and "soft" factors in the situation interact, but at a more detailed workplace level. For instance, when ordering tests becomes easy, more tests are ordered, so the path lab puts in extra screens to make ordering tests more difficult again.

The third element in our conceptual framework is generally action research, but this study was not action research; or rather, the action element in it was minimal. The research was intended to be "formative", but the action element was limited to the feedback discussions referred to above.

Findings—life and work at the implementation sites

Much of this discussion will highlight the importance of context: computer systems are developed within a policy and funding context; they are introduced into an organizational and working context; in turn, they then help to create the context for people who carry out the organization's work. It is context that makes sense of what is observed or experienced.

The context into which the computer is implemented

If the question being asked is "What is the effect of computer systems on the life and work of the hospital?", it needs to be said first that there are other influences which are stronger. The first such influence is the clinical condition of the patient. Obvious as this may sound, it may be so obvious that it is no longer noticed or its implications for organization always drawn.

The clinical condition of the patient

At Burton, an important feature of the work in the orthopaedic ward was that much of it was predictable. The patients had been booked in in advance—when they came in they were already known, because of their history as outpatients and because they would have had a pre-operative assessment. Their recovery after their operation was monitored against well-established paths. When staff introduced a patient to colleagues, during ward rounds or nursing handover, it was in terms of "This is Mr X. He is total hip replacement plus three", meaning it was three days since his operation. Everyone then had a broad idea of what to expect in relation to him. Operations too, were predictable, not only the operation itself, but the habits of the surgeon—"The computer records and updates how long I take for a hip replacement or a knee". The general atmosphere was one of calm and order. The patients were lying quietly in their beds, or being walked by physiotherapists, visitors were calm and quiet, there was little overt excitement or distress. Also, during this first period of fieldwork on this ward (B-orth 1) there were some empty beds as two consultants were on holiday.

A number of things impinged on this pattern: there might be emergency admissions because the trauma ward was short of beds; there might be operating sessions with a large number of small operations which create a lot of work; or very rarely there might be a transfer from ITU (Intensive Therapy Unit). The life of the ward around the patients itself contained a good deal of incident, but the dominant pattern for elective orthopaedic surgery was calm, order, and predictability.

Also, orthopaedics is a very optimistic specialty. Patients arrive in pain and in difficulty, have their operations, and can then be observed recovering and progressing. It is very satisfying to look after an orthopaedic patient and to see them going out in a substantially better condition than when they came in:

> Orthopaedic patients are lovely to nurse, you see them getting better. I couldn't work in a hospice. They come in in pain, you can see the pain in their face, the greyness, they're bent double, but after the operation you can see them improve.

Death is very rare on this ward. When there is a death it is very traumatic for the staff. There had been a death some two-and-a-half months before this first period of fieldwork, and staff were still dealing with it and talking about the unusual combination of circumstances that had led to it.

At the beginning of the fieldwork there was a ward audit. The outcome was positive, there was very little to criticize. One of the few critical comments was about the crash trolley: it needed updating, some things about it were out of date. Having started to learn about the climate and work patterns described, I suddenly thought, "Hang on a minute! They don't use the crash trolley. They don't have that kind of emergency." The fact that this equipment did not have equal relevance for all wards alerted me to the idea of the clinical condition of the patient being a major determinant of the life and organization of the ward.

It had already been becoming clear that there were strong differences in climate and activity between the orthopaedic and the medical wards. In the medical ward there were patients with many different conditions, non-planned admissions, medical emergencies. And there were deaths—"We are level pegging with A&E in cardiac arrests," said a nurse. Diagnosis was sometimes a complex process happening over time. Many of the patients were immobilized, either because of their condition or because of monitors and IVs (intravenous drips). A few patients were confused. Although some of the conditions were chronic, most patients did not stay long. They moved in and out of the ward quite rapidly, and were often moved from bed to bed within the ward, to free the limited number of beds with monitors for new patients. It was challenging for staff to keep up with them.

The telephone at the nursing station rang constantly during the day—patients' relatives seeking news, social workers, other hospital departments and wards. During B-med1 there was no ward clerk, and the phone was felt as a constant burden by nursing staff—"it never stops".

Visitors came and went throughout the day—not only patients' friends and relatives, but specialist staff (physiotherapists, social workers, occupational therapists, phlebotomists, and others). Consultants arrived in a flurry of activity, requiring notes, X-rays, nurses. Junior doctors came to use the computer terminals, check patient notes, examine patients, ask questions.

In this context, the ward staff were able to maintain the appearance of calm, routine, and preparedness through apparently seamless teamwork. Staff noted the high level of qualified medical staff on the ward, and many spoke of the strong degree of teamwork achieved. There was hustle and bustle, a constant coming and going; but ward staff gave the impression that they took things in their stride. Health care assistants (HCAs) and cleaners collaborated in this smoothness, referring to nurses things of which they should be aware (a patient is looking sick, needs a cuddle, is anxious). The only time the smooth routine was disrupted during fieldwork was when a patient died: the "crash" brought staff at a run, and it was clear that something untoward was happening. For the most part, staff were constantly working to create routine and calm in a situation which was often unpredictable and defies standardization; where patients' conditions were irregular, changing, serious.

In addition to experiencing this contrast between the medical and orthopaedic wards, we had by that time also experienced two wards for the care of the elderly at Winchester (Wn), which were different again:

Care of the elderly is difficult; so much so that we were told nurses used to be put on to it for their first three months because if they could handle that they could handle anything. There were occasional triumphs—for instance, a patient who turned out to be only suffering from neglect: short-term memory loss made him forget to eat and with warmth, rest, and three meals a day he flourished. There were also, of course, tragedies, not only when patients died but when they discovered that, although they knew they were going to die, death was nearer than they expected. One patient died during the week we were there, and some staff were quite distressed; four had died during the previous six weeks.

But most of the experience is not at these levels of triumph or tragedy. It is caring for people whose progress is slow, who are there for a long time, who need help with ordinary things like washing, dressing, and toileting, who may be incontinent, or demented, or both, who forcibly remind one of what is going to happen to oneself and one's parents, and whose own frustration may make them just plain difficult. We asked a nurse, "Do you ever feel like hitting them?" "Oh yes!" she answered. "What do you do then?" "I just walk away till I've got hold of myself." We don't, of course, know how often it gets like that.

The work of the ward is organized within a framework of "care planning" and "discharge planning" (a slightly misleading term for the lay person, since discharge planning in fact begins already at the point where the patient is admitted). The process of care planning, and especially of collaborative, i.e., multi-disciplinary, discharge planning is an opportunity for staff to make up for these negative feelings and experiences. An important function of collaborative discharge planning is that it helps to take care of the staff. All one's positive skills and intentions can come into play. The multi-disciplinary ward round, and especially the multi-disciplinary review meeting that takes place after it, seal the integration of the different professional contributions with doughnuts and chocolate biscuits, in a kind of celebration. This is very different from the mundane nursing shift handover meeting, concerned with the tedious realities of levels of continence and who wandered during the night.

However, multi-disciplinary assessment and planning are not the same as multi-disciplinary care, and there may be occasions when there is a difference between the quality of the strategic level of planning and the patient's immediate experience of care. Also, at the boundary of the hospital, multi-discipline becomes multi-agency, and that is a very different matter.

So it began to look as if one—or perhaps the—major determinant of the life and work of the ward is the actual clinical condition of the patient. While this may seem stunningly obvious, much of professional practice seems to be predicated on general rather than condition-specific bases.

Both hypotheses—that the clinical condition is a determinant of work organization and that this is not explicitly recognized in practice—were further fuelled in the course of the second period of fieldwork at Burton, B-orth2. The patient population had changed in the intervening eighteen months, and this provided the opportunity to observe the organizational consequences, in a kind of "natural experiment".

The same four consultants still had their elective orthopaedic patients in the ward but there was now, in addition, a rheumatology consultant with four rheumatology beds. All the beds were occupied, not only by the orthopaedic and rheumatology patients, but by some trauma patients, more than there had been before, and also by some "outlier" medical patients, one with cancer that was described as terminal.[1]

Life was not only very much busier than before, but staff were encountering situations they were not used to and having to do things that were unfamiliar. For instance, a patient needed to be weighed every day but the nurses had not known this. The doctors responsible for these outlier patients were not generally on the ward to give these new and different instructions. There was therefore also not the same opportunity to develop collaborative relationships between doctors and nurses. Responses on the phone to the worried wife of the cancer patient would have needed to be different from the usual upbeat responses to relatives of orthopaedic patients. Caring for trauma patients was also different from elective orthopaedic surgery, because one was generally not sure what was happening with them and was waiting/looking for indications. For instance, a patient cannot pass urine—does that change the picture of what has happened, is it the effect of the accident she was in? Did she black out and then drive into something, or drive into something and then black out?

Again, whatever clinical connections there may be between rheumatoid and osteoarthritis, the kind of demands they make on staff appear to be very different. The conditions subsumed under rheumatology brought with them a great deal of ambiguity. Patients were brought in for assessment; there was one patient whose diagnosis was uncertain during the whole week of fieldwork and was still uncertain at the end of the week. The patient needed to be able to tolerate ambiguity, and so did the staff. This was very different from the clarity and predictability associated with ortho-paedic surgery. Rheumatology also had other kinds of impact on staff—"She's only just older than us!"

This framework of explanation, that a major determinant of organization is the clinical condition of the patient, seems to be fairly robust. It also brings coherence to some other findings, which otherwise seem arbitrary. Some show some interaction with the computer system.

- Care of the elderly requires the collaboration of physiothera-pists and occupational therapists with doctors and nurses; multi-disciplinary working is a matter of necessity, not of dogma or lip-service. The reality of this need may then influ-ence systems design, and in Winchester there was congruency between systems design and the objectives of ward staff. Written records from the different professions were colour-coded, nursing staff writing in black, physiotherapists in blue, occupational therapists in green, social workers in red. Others (dietician, chiropodist, speech therapist) did not have a code and usually wrote in blue. The colour coding was copied on the system. Discharge planning came out multi-disciplinary, for admissions the physiotherapist and the occupational therapist had their own screens. But their notes could be transferred to the multi-disciplinary screens and accessed there by others. The screen, with its colour-coded contributions, reinforced the culture of multi-disciplinary working every time one looked at it. It could not by itself have created such a culture, but clearly was helping to sustain it.
- Consultants tend, on the whole, to be more sceptical about the hospital's computer system than junior doctors, who have to use it in the nature of their work and who are saved a lot of running around by it. Often this is because consultants have developed their own departmental systems, evolved over time to meet their needs, and dislike having to give these up for a generic hospital-wide system. Yet in Wirral we encountered a consultant who both had his own system and was enthusiastic about the hospital's. It turned out that his specialty was diabetes. A high proportion of the work with diabetics is out-patient work; they are only rarely admitted for in-patient

episodes. So it was perfectly possible for this consultant to have his own system, tweaked to his own needs, and still support the hospital's system. Patients only rarely needed to be transferred from one to the other. An orthopaedic surgeon at Burton, on the other hand, said that he did not use the system in his outpatient clinic—"Fracture clinics are very hectic."

Other findings are independent of the computer system.

- The clinical condition of the patient influences the presence of doctors on the ward. In B-med there was always at least one junior doctor present; in B-orth, junior doctors mostly spent their time in theatre or clinics. There was, therefore, also a knock-on effect on relationships—"I'm going down to the main theatre to find a surgical doctor, and I'm not coming back till I find one. Seven bleeps annoys me; I've tried three different ones."

Professional frameworks

The second major influence on the life and work of the hospital, still long before the influence of the computer system, is the way in which professional practice has been institutionalized. Much is known about this and it is not the subject of this study. We simply need to say, for the sake of maintaining perspective, that the way in which doctoring and nursing and the other professions are organized and institutionalized, sometimes in terms of their legal responsibilities, is, of course, a major determinant of what happens.

A small instance of how this interacts with computer use lies in the way terminology is used by the different professions. In Winchester it had led to some difficulties in systems design. "Reason for admission" and "Aim of hospital stay" are subtly different and come from the traditions of different professions. And when these need to be harmonized for the purpose of integrated recording, status differences come into play—"The physio is at the top of the pile, the nurses are at the grass roots . . . it comes out in the terminology . . . ."

Giving and receiving help

A hospital is not just a place of much activity; it is a place where intense and personal needs are being dealt with. Patients may be anxious about whether they are getting enough attention, resentful if they think they are not, grateful to an extreme degree, as well as feeling guilty about the pressure that staff and the NHS as a whole are under.

For staff, the best reward for efforts to help is the recovery of the patient. In B-orth, a patient who had recovered from major surgery faster than standard was a source of much pleasure and gratification for the staff. On the other hand, a patient who had been admitted labelled "Query MRSA" had created a lot of frustrating work to find out why she had been labelled in this way, and by the end of her stay—expedited as rapidly as possible—was clearly resented as a nuisance—"And we haven't even done anything for her."

In this helping relationship it can be a problem for staff if patients are financially better off than they are. How personal the relationship of help gets is also influenced by the length of contact. In the medical ward, patients tended to stay only a short time, and by the time they were leaving other things were preoccupying the staff. A patient walking out was not noticed. In the orthopaedic ward, where patients stayed longer, a nurse interrupted an interview with "Oh, there's Mr X leaving—I must just go and say goodbye." Indeed, a patient who had been there for three months had won the affection of staff to the extent that they went to visit her in her new nursing home. On the other hand, there were other phases of life in B-orth when the patient seemed to become depersonalized. On the way to theatre the patient almost tangibly ceases to be a person and becomes a collection of X-rays, test and observation findings, blood pressure readings. If this bundle of data then announces that it needs a lavatory, this can be very disconcerting and evoke displeasure, either in the porter or in theatre staff.

Continuing learning and continuing monitoring

Teaching and learning, both within and across professional boundaries, are a constant part of what goes on. At Burton, a striking thing about the work of the ward was how many people, especially nurses, seemed to be doing a lot of things at the same time. Another was the way in which the work itself, teaching, training, being taught, being trained, auditing and monitoring, being audited and monitored, seemed somehow seamlessly interwoven. Also at Wirral, in the course of a ward round: a house officer asked an associate nurse about some terms used when prescribing; two nurses used a few minutes while waiting for the consultant to discuss how one does a literature search; the pharmacist gave help to the junior doctors and advice to the consultant; a primary nurse asked a Senior House Officer what colour bag is used for a thyroid test; the HO asked the SHO how to order an EEG.

Context and culture

These elements of the life and work of a hospital combine to form a number of distinct cultures. It is a term that is much misused. When someone says, "What we need is a culture change", it often means that people are not doing what he or she wants. We take culture to mean the things that are done and not done, believed and not believed, said or not said, by a group or population; the things that are so much taken for granted that they are not voiced or questioned.

As we have seen, in a hospital ward a main determinant of culture is the clinical condition of the patient and the consequences this has for the customs, practices, and expectations of staff. A second set of influences is the particular situation of the hospital, its geography, history, architecture, economic circumstances. A third, criss-crossing with the others, is the cultures of the different professions. And a fourth is the behavioural style of senior people: where use of the computer is optional, junior doctors use it if their consultants do, and don't if they don't; the style of the consultant geriatricians at Winchester strongly influenced the culture of the wards.

The context within which the system is developed

There are contextual factors which influence the development of the computer system, such as the need to tame complexity.

In all large and complex systems, efforts are made to systematize and rationalize what is happening. It is the effort to cope with large numbers, to reduce the level of skill required (and therefore not only cost but risk), and to cope with differences in levels of skill. Quite independently of the introduction of computers, there are already traditions of routinizing and standardizing the tasks in a hospital.

The hospital-wide perspective created by the tracer studies of consultant ward rounds at the Wirral laid open a picture of enormous complexity. When one considers the multi-faceted nature of life in a large hospital, the myriad issues that crop up, both small and large, routine and unexpected, the wonder is that it functions at all. The outside observer is struck—sometimes almost overwhelmed—by the complexity of what is going on. The overall task involves a multiplicity of roles and these are interdependent: the physician needs an X-ray report, the physiotherapist needs to know the patient's medical history, the patient's relatives need information and reassurance, the junior doctor needs a consent form signed, the nurse needs to get a report up-to-date before going off shift, the ward manager is under pressure to get a bed freed . . . The unifying element is the patient: at his or her bedside (metaphorically) the history, the results of tests and X-rays, knowledge of the personal background, and the various kinds of professional knowledge and judgement, come together. And the patient struggles to make his or her individuality known to the professionals.

There are ways in which both individual professionals and the system as a whole try to tame and control this complexity. Individuals and professional groups "get to know their own pathways", and not only in the computer sense. For the system as a whole, complexity and the overpowering demands on skill and judgement are tamed by rationalizing, specifying and standardizing procedures and criteria. To give one example among hundreds: formal discharge criteria are specified for many kinds of clinical condition. But these do not necessarily coincide with the personal experience of the patient: one patient (with asthma) is anxious to be back at work before the formal discharge criteria have been met; another (with diabetes) is afraid of what may happen when she is back at home on her own.

As in other large systems, it can happen that standards and procedures come to develop a life of their own, independent of the purpose they were originally intended to serve. A good deal of discussion, and many of the day-to-day differences in perspective, were about this. In one situation nurses would sometimes move between using the computer and paper, according to the needs of the situation; for instance, using paper to draft notes for an assessment or in order to be able to look at and empathize with the patient in front of them. But this was not seen as the "right" way to do it. In another situation a student nurse had found a way to adapt the use of a hand-held computer, downloading her observations in batches. This was criticized when our local report described it, for creating a time-lag between the observation and its recording. Eighteen months later downloading observations in batches had become the norm.

The process of rationalizing brings with it managerial functions or professional routines which may come into conflict with hands-on care for the patient: "The powers that be want people out on the ward, working, *and* they want someone in here [the office]. We find it very, very hard." "Routines dominate, for instance everyone has to be washed. Last week one patient didn't want to be washed, so I didn't. Then someone said, 'that gentleman has to be washed *now!*' It's rituals. My patient with a sore bottom comes first."

The consultant ward round is a focus for this complexity. It has a number of functions:

- to remind the consultant about the patient;
- to find out what is happening with the patient;
- to arrive at decisions about what should happen next;
- to inform and/or teach patients about their situation;
- to arrive, where possible, at a safe discharge;
- to exchange experience and teaching with colleagues.

To meet the goals of the ward round there is a continuing search for information and need for communication between colleagues. The number and throughput of patients, the number of tests and investigations, the number of colleagues in one's own and other professional groups, mean that individual cases cannot be remembered at the point of action but must be painstakingly recorded. Information is what holds the system together, not so much glue as lubrication.

In effect, there is a need for everyone to leave a trail behind them, recording what they have done, what decisions they have taken, what they have requested. The systems of shifts, rotas, hours and patterns of working, mean that there can be no assumption that any one individual will be involved in the care of that patient tomorrow or the next time a case conference or ward round is held. The trail needs to be evident for anyone who might be involved, whether they are dealing with an emergency, temporarily filling in for someone else, or simply the next shift coming on duty. We came across an instance where a doctor's phone call that he was ill reached his secretary, not his ward, with multiple knock-on effects. Moreover, the information trail is not only needed for clinical purposes, but for audit, research, and legal purposes.

Efforts to tame this complexity take the form of standards, procedures, protocols. Again, some of the effects of these are not necessarily due to the computer. Doing discharge letters for a patient whom one does not know is a chore, very different from doing it for a patient whom one has admitted and cared for, irrespective of whether it is done by computer or by hand. But, clearly, a major function of the computer systems is their part in this effort to systematize.

The context of funding and development

There are many influences on the life and work of the hospital that come from policy directions outside it. In the funding and procurement of computer systems, where large amounts of public money are to be committed and outcomes are uncertain, this uncertainty creates a context where people—suppliers, IT departments, "champions"—are likely to be constrained to make over-optimistic promises. This then, in turn, creates the conditions for a culture where it is not permitted to be tentative, to try things one is not sure about, to admit mistakes; and this culture cascades downwards. Implementation becomes a matter of having to prove oneself, and wrong avenues or mistakes have to be very dramatic before they are acknowledged. Where outcomes are only defined as "success" or "failure" this can affect, for example, design processes. Pilot exercises become efforts to prove something rather than efforts to understand how something functions and explore alternatives.

Research, too, comes to be seen in a framework of judgement rather than enquiry.

The IT world is full of this kind of situation; it is not specific to the EPR project. We came across one example of this interpretation of piloting in relation to the first pharmacy module at Burton. We also found that hand-helds had fallen into disuse by B-orth2 because they were difficult to use in the real operational context. This suggests that they may not have been realistically piloted, i.e., in their operational context, although we have no knowledge of how this was done. In Winchester, the acute hospital was said to have had IT "done to them" and was still "suffering from the consequences". Of course, such problems eventually get ironed out, but at a cost.

Living with the information technology

Finally, there is the context which the computer system in turn creates.

In industry, there has been much research on the effects of introducing new systems of working. It has been found useful to distinguish between short-term effects, whatever issues and ways of dealing with them may arise, and longer-term effects once a change has bedded down, which may amount to changes in culture (see Chapter Five).

In the case of the EPR, one could think in terms of four phases: (a) procurement, design and development, (b) implementation, (c) short-term effects, and (d) long-term effects. This study was too late for the first two. A good deal of the material we have is about the third, that is, the process of integrating the system with the primary task of the hospital. And we have some tentative indications of the fourth.

The system makes many tasks easier

There are many examples of this. Finding case notes, not having to repeat getting demographic details, ordering X-rays and tests (not experienced as easier in all cases, but very often), getting test results, writing discharge letters—many of these oft-repeated tasks have become easier.

The justification for computerizing is frequently made in terms of support for clinical decisions. We did come across some instances of this; for instance, being able to plot the trend of a condition. But mostly the effect on clinical decisions and outcomes seemed to be indirect, via task support of the work of the professionals. This suggests that the function of task support needs to be looked at in the course of system design as explicitly as decision support.

The trouble is that making a department or function process its work more quickly may simply mean that it gets more work to do. With the relentless pressure of numbers of patients, we saw this in the B-orth outpatient clinic. In the longer term, some departments begin to defend themselves against somebody else's easier work, and a kind of battle of wits develops: when the system went live at Wirral, the number of tests ordered from the path lab shot up. Over time, the path lab began to defend itself by making ordering more difficult again; Radiology made ordering pre-operative chest X-rays more difficult again; the Pharmacy did the same with the ordering of some standard drugs.

It puts a value on formality of recording

The advantages of this are for consistency and for safety, that is, not being able to take step B if one has not taken step A. But there are also problems.

1. It makes you tick boxes of categories which someone else has devised, and which may not express what you want or need to say. This was voiced in all three hospitals. A radiographer explained that X-ray requests used to be in terms of "the patient fell on a broken bottle", whereas now they were in terms of "query foreign body", which was less informative and less helpful. A nurse said, "If you're with a patient and something doesn't seem quite right, on paper you might say 'keep an eye on him'. On the computer you have to give an explanation. So you don't."
    Another said, "You get the choice of constipation or diarrhoea—that's your lot for your bowels."

While we have no evidence of long-term effects of this, they may well be that professionals come to think in terms of the system's categories rather than the other way round. Certainly some are beginning to identify "professionalism" with the format of a report rather than with its content.

2. It makes demands on spelling and grammar which may be uncomfortable.

Formality in turn appears to imply precision and makes it difficult to express uncertainty, nuances, hunches, to say that one does not know what to do. What worries nursing staff is "the things you write that are not totally professional but things the patient thinks are very important". This leads to questions about whether the system may affect the way the professional nurse thinks. The amount of space available for recording comments plays a part here—it is thought that it may inhibit the hunches of nurses in preference for the tangible realities.

It has a synthesizing function

In building up the multi-disciplinary assessment on the computer at Winchester, staff had to bring together information from many different sources, and found this a valuable way of getting a complete picture. It was the same on discharge: a wide range of information had to be brought together—the nursing diagnosis, how the patient sees her own condition, whether the patient's family had been informed about the diagnosis. The Occupational Therapy assessment would indicate whether she is independent, then there was continence, Waterlow score, dressings, colostomy care. Conversely, it acted as a prompt at this point for all the different aspects out in the community that needed to be considered: alerting social services, meals on wheels, home care package, visits to the day hospital, appointments for clinics, medicines to take home, etc. We wondered how, in the absence of the computer system, such synthesizing takes place.

The computer affects where and when work is done

Making notes on the computer can only be done where the terminal is, whereas making them on paper can be done in many places.

Specifically, there were comments in all three hospitals that the computer takes the nurse away from the patient's bedside. Handhelds had not overcome this problem, although laptops may. With regard to when work is done, staff tended to collect notes about their interventions and input them towards the end of a shift, as it is obviously unpractical to keep going to the terminal for a very short spell. The comment "I can go home without doing a dressing, I can't go home without doing my computing" was accurate: doing a dressing could be delegated to someone else if one was late, while entering one's interventions could not; they were in one's head or on one's own scraps of paper. The conclusion drawn, however, that computing might be considered more important by the authorities than hands-on nursing, may not be accurate.

It affects inter-professional issues

Our impression during the Winchester study (our first) was that more was being put into the computer than was being taken out. This may have been partly because there is relatively little medical presence in care of the elderly work. We would now say that nurses put more in, while doctors take more out. It remains true, however, that the greatest value of the record in the care of the elderly ward was said to be if a patient was re-admitted.

Because different professions use different pathways, there is a tendency to ask for help from the same profession rather than from the IT professionals, which is experienced as an admission of defeat. It seems possible that this may create professional "blinkers" that are more limiting than previously.

The computer and other media

In the policy and funding context that has been described, the use of paper tends to acquire some aspects of an ideological rather than a functional debate. The dreams of a paperless hospital have not been realized. Indeed, some people feel that there is more paper now than there was. There is visible evidence on the wards of the continuing need for paper, with numerous boxes of computer paper being stacked under desks and in the corridors. The way in which printouts present information is sometimes perceived as wasteful of paper. At the same time, there are clear uses for paper.

1. In all three hospitals we have numerous examples of informal scraps of paper being used to remind one of things one has to do, to record something temporarily until it is entered into the permanent record, to save the embarrassment of having to go to the computer when relatives enquire about a patient. Much of the information that staff have is incomplete, their questions unanswered, and the answers may not be forthcoming for some time. It is these open-ended, nebulous, or tentative kinds of information for which paper seems more useful than the computer.

2. There are also situations where paper still has to be used formally, duplicating the function of the computer—"The only thing that I do mind is that you're doubling up on everything because you still have to write—I've got eight Kardex to write this morning."

3. Paper also has some specific advantages. A consultant said, "Although the case records look awful, as you flick through them you get so much information—a consultant's name which, yes, they've seen so-and-so . . . The odd words . . . That's a big problem in my mind. Though you can get things in books, it's not the same. In handwriting the downside is you can't read upside down, but you recognize the handwriting. If someone writes 'bloody fool' in the notes, you get some idea of what they were thinking . . . ." The "feel" and "look" of case-notes is lost: "A lot of useful information has been put on the system by various disciplines, but you can't get it out. It's unlike the case notes where you know what's there because it's fat."

So the technology interacts with the characteristics and dynamics of the human user. The telephone, too, is used more than is theoretically necessary. There appears to be a need to "ask nicely", i.e., in person, for some things to be done and not simply to request them anonymously on the computer. The automated computer request is reinforced by the individual and personal telephone call. There is a clinical need to report urgent test results and "panic values" back to the ward staff immediately. But there is also a human need to work on unusual events with a person, whether this is finding out why a colleague has not turned up for work; seeking clarification about the procedure to deal with a suspected case of

MRSA; or laboratory staff wishing to check manually through unusual test results. The computer also cannot summon people in the way that a ringing telephone can.

> The original paperless office concept, we're miles away from that. You'd have to have terminals everywhere. Do it there and then or write it down, that's relatively easy to solve. The harder one is how to get information out of a computer in a working environment into your brain, so that you can use it and act on it in a comfortable way . . . So that when the patient comes into Casualty the first time . . . "Yes, Mrs X, you are known to us". In assimilable form—getting it off the screen into your head—*that* will have an advantage over case notes.

Summary

In all three hospitals the general impression was that people felt the advantages of the computer system outweighed the disadvantages. One could name positive aspects: "Legibility, which is a great thing in this profession"; where there was electronic prescribing, drug administration was found to be much safer than the manual system; the computer helped with simple things like locating a patient when a visitor came into the ward. Many tasks had become easier. Advantages came to be taken for granted—"There are a lot of benefits happening that you forget about, it's become a part of life . . ."

It had sometimes been possible to influence the design, but in all three hospitals there were residual design issues. In all three hospitals junior people used it more than senior ones. In all three hospitals there was some sense that, in order to make the system function, an enormous amount had to be put in. Sometimes it seemed that more was put in than got out, but that depended on who one was talking to; on the whole, nurses put more in and doctors took more out. In all three hospitals there was some concern that the computer takes one away from the patient too much, and that information would be lost because of the formality it required.

We did not set out to do a systematic attitude survey, and it would in any case be simplistic to think in terms of "attitudes to" the computer system. But, in the course of the fieldwork, different types of engagement with the system could be seen.

The most single-minded enthusiasm for computer systems was expressed when people talked about what the system was going to be able to do in the future. Computerization opens up unlimited possibilities, both within and beyond the hospital, of research, trend analysis, comparisons, protocols, and these visions are clearest when they are not yet complicated by messy realities. At the other end of the scale, we were told that there were people who reject the system in a wholesale way, although we did not meet them. We did meet one person who said that he had a total antipathy to computers and had, indeed, taken a post at the Wirral in order to try to overcome it. Most people, however, were dealing with the integration of this tool into their work. If there is any conflict in this situation, it is not between "for" and "against", but between over-simplified vision and operational reality.

Note

1. An outlier is a patient who, when there is a shortage of beds, is placed in a ward which does not normally deal with his or her condition.

SECTION III

CONSULTING AND ACTION
RESEARCH

This group of five chapters is about getting involved in action. Of the five pieces of work described, one was consultancy, three were action research, and one was training within a framework of consultancy. The projects vary in scale from very small to very large, and so do the accounts.

Chapter Seven describes the German government's programme to "humanize life at work", in which I worked as a consultant between 1973 and 1980. This chapter is more about the programme itself, that is the context within which I was working, than the others. I have not written about it before, although there are references to it in some later papers.

At about the same time, an opportunity arose to make a contribution on work satisfaction and the design of jobs in the planning and design of a new confectionery factory (Chapter Eight), and soon after that there was a second opportunity to make a contribution on job design in a greenfield site, this time in the design of a new vegetable canning plant (Chapter Nine). The first of these had no trade unions, the second was strongly unionized. There were some links between the two projects, in that the works manager of the new confectionery plant was willing to record his experiences once the plant was up and running, and let me play them to the management of the cannery, who were at an earlier stage.

Getting into design activities was new to me, and I had to invent methods. In this I was increasingly able to draw on the methodological approaches that I was absorbing in Germany.

(continued)

Again at about the same time, a consultancy relationship with one of the UK clearing banks led to some management training for the sub-managers of bank branches. One exercise in this was about work organization, and this is described in Chapter Ten.

Chapter Eleven takes the issue of getting involved at the design stage into the processes of technology design. It describes a more recent, and more ambitious, effort to contribute to technical development at an early stage, this time the development of new information and communication technologies in the construction industry. It is also cast wider than the work experience of the individuals who would eventually be using the technology, going back into the systems of organization and associated organizational problems involved in getting there.

In the action research experiences, two features mark the difference between design and redesign: first, in design the intervention is at a stage where the real people who will be doing the real work are not available to be involved in the process; and second, even when organizations are interested in, and committed to, work design, there are many other agendas—managerial, engineering, industrial relations, political, career development of key people, etc., which make the issues around job design difficult to sustain through the whole process.

The "Humanization of Work" programme in Germany: some cultural influences in the design and re-design of work

The German government followed the work of the Commission for Economic and Social Change (see Chapter Two) by instigating a programme to "Humanize Life at Work". I worked with this programme between 1974 and 1980. I learned a great deal from the experience, and have referred to it in various ways in talks and papers, but have never put these together and written them up. Now that I am reflecting on the programme and on the experience of working in it, the aspect that strikes me most is that of cultural influences and differences. By this I do not mean a simplistic view of national cultures, but scientific and professional cultures within as well as between nations; different traditions of research funding and their consequences; different legal systems; different approaches to the relationship between science and politics. Chapter Five touched on the cultural consequences of work organization; this chapter touches on its cultural causes. In practice, of course, both are going on simultaneously, and they interact.

I do not want to mislead—it is a very big topic and this chapter will only touch on some aspects of it. But they are grounded in experience.

* * *

Introduction

I n 1974, the West German Ministry of Research and Technology and the Ministry of Labour and Social Affairs jointly launched an extensive programme of research and action to "Humanize Life at Work". In the policy paper announcing this programme, the social democratic government of the time firmly nailed its colours to the mast:

> Work plays a predominant role in human life. While at work, people are subjected to a variety of influences affecting their health and well-being and reaching far into other areas of life. For millions of workers, therefore, the demand for an improved quality of life is initially focused on the workplace.

The programme was initiated by Hans Matthöfer, the Minister of Research and Technology, who had joined the Cabinet of Chancellor Helmut Schmidt from IG Metall, the metalworkers' union. Thus it was essentially a political programme, part of the Social Democratic Party's election platform. The thinking behind it was, broadly, that Germany had gone very far down the road of economic development, but that in the process some other considerations might have come to be neglected. The values expressed in democratic political life were not matched in industrial life, in the way people spent their lives at work. A good deal of the impulse came from IG Metall, and the trades unions were strongly behind the policy (though they did not agree with everything in the eventual programme). Their main reasons were that Germany had institutions for representative democracy, but that this kind of representative form of democracy did not do the whole job: it did not do very much to change the actual quality of life experienced at work. Another reason was that Germans were apparently no longer willing to take some of the more low-level and least satisfactory jobs in industry and a very large number of migrant workers was being employed at the most junior levels. This was ethically worrying, as well as leading to social tensions.

The structure of the programme

In the programme, the Ministry of Labour and Social Affairs was responsible for research and action on those aspects of working conditions that were a continuation of existing practice, such as safety, health, and welfare. The Ministry of Research and Technology carried, in addition to this, the newer aspects concerning job design and work organization. The programme took the form of subsidies and grants to organizations that wanted to do something about changing the nature of work. If a company wanted, for instance, to dismantle an assembly line or reorganize work in some other way, it would formulate its plans, estimate their cost, and apply to the government for a grant. If the scheme was approved there was a formula that broadly reimbursed half the costs—up to three-quarters if the attempt was thought to be risky—provided that two conditions were met:

(a) the agreement of the company's works council had to be obtained, and
(b) the project had to be accompanied by research, so that knowledge for broader application was generated and public funds were not spent only for the benefit of that organization.

This meant that organizations generally came hand-in-hand with researchers to make applications for these grants, the company receiving about half its costs and the researchers the whole of theirs.

The programme spoke of "awakening and developing new potential through technologies which foster and encourage the development of skills, and work organization which fosters and encourages processes of collaboration". It covered every possible aspect of life at work, was concerned with theoretical questions about the relationship between work and other areas of life, and with the dissemination and application of scientific knowledge. The contents list of the original document gives some idea of the breadth of the areas covered:

- Safety and accidents.
- Effects of environmental influences.
- Physical demands in work.
- The effects of work organization on people (subdivided into content of work, opportunities to make decisions, manpower planning, payment and promotion, satisfaction and motivation).

- The need to do the research and development comprehensively and in an interdisciplinary way.
- The needs of special groups:
  young workers, women workers, handicapped workers, older workers.
- The relation between the world of work and other areas of life.
- The dissemination and application of findings.

The administrative structure of the programme is shown in Figure 6.

The Ministry of Research and Technology held the budget. To administer, or "carry" the programme, they appointed a group of temporary civil servants who were given offices within the aerospace research establishment of the Ministry (the letters DFVLR stand for Deutsche Forschungs- und Versuchsanstalt für Luft- und Raumfahrt e.V.) because of its location near Bonn. Obviously, the programme was not about aerospace research. This kind of arrangement for managing large projects by housing their administration within established major research centres, not necessarily in the same field, was common.

The Ministry also appointed a group of *Gutachter*. This is a role in fairly common use in Germany, which combines some aspects of expert, consultant, reviewer; the best translation I can think of is "assessor". The assessors were lay—i.e., not civil servants—and consisted of employer and trade union representatives and some academics. The academics came from the disciplines of engineering, from *Arbeitswissenschaft* (literally "the science of work", a mixture of ergonomics, work study, and occupational medicine)

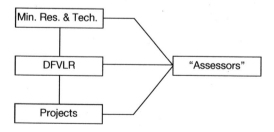

Figure 6.   Administrative structure of the "Humanization of Work" programme.

and from the social sciences. The function of the group of assessors was somewhat analogous to that of a Research Council committee in Britain: they reviewed the grant applications and advised (but did not decide) whether a grant should be given. Unlike the then Social Science Research Council (now the Economic and Social Research Council) in Britain, however, the assessment process involved discussion with the applicants. This meant that there was much clarifying of misunderstandings, and opinions sometimes changed. They also monitored the projects and reviewed progress with the people involved—the companies and researchers—which is why there is a line in Figure 6 linking them with the projects.

The first such system, in which I was invited to be one of the assessors, was set up in 1974 and was concerned with manufacturing and production. The civil servants and assessors involved were formed into a committee, which met regularly to assess applications for new grants and review progress in existing projects. Later, this method was replicated several times: there were equivalent systems concerned with white-collar work, with the special problems of coal and steel, and there was one concerned with diffusion and the dissemination of results. Within that system, for example, the DGB—the German equivalent of the TUC—received a grant to prepare a handbook of research findings for the use of shop stewards and works council representatives.

Working with the programme

As a member of that committee, I found it fascinating to take part in the discussions with the applicants, to be involved in the conflicts of ideas and priorities, and in the learning that comes from watching early ideas—and mistakes—work out in practice. Once the old notion that there is a "best way" to do a job is unfrozen, there is found to be not necessarily one best alternative. Many kinds of scientific, cultural, and ideological considerations competed for attention, and were fiercely debated. It seemed to me right that the design of jobs should be subject to controversy and cultural variation. It had been assumed for too long that, because the values of designers were not made explicit, value judgements were not involved.

The trade union side saw to it that such issues remained a matter for debate and negotiation; the employers' side complained that they kept getting involved in negotiations they had not expected. The fears of some British trade unionists, that increasing people's satisfaction in their work would lead to some kind of bland and mushy consensus, was not borne out by the German experience. There was plenty of what might euphemistically be called vigorous debate.

I am unsure about exactly how much money was spent on this programme, but a figure I saw quoted in 1980—that is, six years into the programme—was 400 million Deutschmarks, i.e., about £100 million. I found that I had to be careful about envy when I was working there.

In practice, a programme on that scale was, of course, quite difficult to set up and it ran into a number of problems, both administrative and political. It came under considerable attack from the political right on grounds of the amount of public money that was being spent; it was also criticized from the political left, or, more accurately, by the more left-wing sociologists—the social sciences, especially sociology, being rather more politicized in Germany than in the UK—on the grounds that some of the projects were alleged to be covert ways of continuing to rationalize methods of production under the cover of "humanization". There were also comments by some journalists pointing to inconsistencies in policy, i.e., between fostering a programme of this kind and some of the other, technical, developments that were sponsored under the Ministry's umbrella. Inconsistencies also showed in differences between the Ministry of Research and Technology and some other government departments, especially when it came to efforts to change the ministries' own internal work practices. The programme also ran into major administrative problems due to its size and the rapid build-up of a complicated administration. In some ways the programme was itself, and perhaps primarily, a learning process.

The first project that was proposed in the programme was in Bosch AG. It was very large and cumbersome, involving seven production plants, five research institutes, and an eventual cost of twenty-six million Deutschmark. The structural problem, however, lay not so much in the Bosch project as in the fact that it established a pattern. If that was the way to get funding, people reasoned, we must do it the same way. So the immense problems and effort and waste involved in trying to co-ordinate the work of multiple sites and many research teams became the norm. When the programme eventually ran into political difficulties, this was one of the reasons. By that time, however, it had also set the pattern for others. I do not know whether the designs of the European Commission's later research programmes such as ESPRIT, or the British government's Alvey programme,[1] were actually influenced by this German model, but they all suffered from the same problems.

When the plans for the Bosch project were first put forward, there were many criticisms from members of the committee, but eventually the head of the programme, who was chairing the committee, faced us with a difficult question: "If we don't fund this, what are we going to do?" So the project was approved, and I became the monitor for it, together with a German professor of ergonomics. This meant that twice a year we visited each of the locations, which were spread around Germany, talked with engineers, managers, operators, works council representatives, and researchers, held feedback meetings during which we might make some suggestions, and wrote a report. And, of course, we argued quite a bit among ourselves.

Once a number of projects were under way, meetings of the committee were generally held in the plants where different projects were going on, so altogether one was exposed to a great range of industrial situations and methodological approaches. Some German social scientists were, as has been said, in a strongly political framework. In one plant they had handed out leaflets at the gates about something that was happening. The company alerted the police, and next time a sociologist visited, the guard at the gate called the police and the sociologist was arrested. It happened that this was a completely non-political academic scholar, who was very shocked and distressed to find himself bundled into prison until the mistake was cleared up.

At the same time, there was great respect for the authority of science. On one of our visits to a Bosch plant, the local engineer was presenting his plans. Having detailed the proposed changes to the production system, he came to the question of where the operators would take their coffee breaks—whether coffee and refreshments should be brought to the workplace or whether a separate area should be built for this. With a little flourish he said, "And for this we look to the sociologists!"

I said, "May I make a suggestion? Don't ask the sociologists, ask the operators." He looked very disconcerted, not knowing what to make of this. Then someone said to him, "That's a sociologist telling you." And then it was all right—he thanked me for the suggestion and said he would follow it.

On the other hand, there were new forms of political correctness current at the time and they crossed national frontiers. Over the course of time, there was more than one set of administrators in the programme. One of these was a very politically orientated group of young people; some of them saw no problem in trying to insert their own ideas into the content of projects. One day one of them asked to see me. I felt immediately guilty and anxious. I found writing in German difficult, and my reports were sometimes late and, I feared, too short by German standards. But the interview was not about my late report. He had been reading my reports on the Bosch project, he said, and saw in them concern for the experiences and development of the various people in the project. Given my influential position, wasn't it time I made clear where I stood in the matter of the class struggle?

I was so nonplussed that my first response was foolish. I said that I did not think a foreigner ought to interfere in the German class struggle. Once I had collected my wits, my next response was less foolish: I said that, as a class, German workers were represented in the programme, since there was strong trade union representation. "The trade unions don't really represent them properly" was the worrying answer.

Some similarities and differences

One difference between the work in this programme and the work in the Anglo-Saxon countries and in Scandinavia, with which I was more familiar, was that in Germany social scientists were not accustomed to taking action roles. Indeed, this could extend to not getting into empirical research. I remember a debate in the committee with one young sociologist who protested that he could not be expected to interview industrial operators because they would not understand his concepts. While most German social scientists were not as distanced from practice as that, they were also not, at any rate at that time, action researchers or consultants, and most of the actual ideas for change came from the engineering professions. In the Anglo-Saxon and Scandinavian countries, the ideas for changes in the direction of "humanization" had, on the whole, come from the social science professions.

There were some exceptions to this trend: in one project social scientists ran seminars with the shop-floor workers of a particular department about job design, with engineers providing technical support; ideas about the work came from the work people themselves. However, the social scientists related to the operators of this department as to a rather privileged and self-contained entity, and any ideas could therefore only be about aspects that could be contained within the department and that had no systemic implications for what came before or after. The possibilities were therefore very limited.

Mostly, the changes introduced in the programme were engineering-led. In terms of content, engineers were using what they picked up from the literature, from visits abroad, particularly to Sweden, and from their own intuition, and applied their own methodologies to it.[2] The engineering-led nature of the changes meant, on the one hand, that in some of the projects the ideas were not very radical. For some trade unionists, and for some of the social scientists, the changes did not go far enough. On the other hand, it meant that changes were implemented. Unlike social scientists, engineers do not merely make suggestions, they take them through to implementation. For instance, in a plant making dishwashers, a dishwasher made entirely of transparent plastic was constructed and placed in a prominent position, so that operators could go and see how the different parts fitted together and how it worked. Also, engineers made suggestions and took initiatives that had not featured in the work of social scientists. For example, one idea that was seriously taken up by the engineers was the need to free workers from machine-pacing; that is, from work where an operator's physical movements are dictated by the movement of a conveyor belt or other equipment, like Charlie Chaplin's in his film *Modern Times* all those years ago. The way to release operators from being paced in this way is to introduce buffer zones between one operation and the next.

There was therefore a great deal of research and development concerning buffer stocks, and the appropriate design and size of buffers. Here, the scale of resources itself had consequences for the kind of things that could happen. Freeing the worker from being tied too closely to the pace of the machine is easy to say, but not necessarily easy to carry out, and a lot of ingenuity and engineering development (that is, money) went into designing facilities for buffer stocks. A woman said, "It's wonderful! I can go to the lavatory without having to find someone first to take my place on the line!" The remark precisely captures one of the dilemmas. If one has never had this freedom, it is indeed a wonderful improvement. (The late Professor Albert Cherns once said that, if the whole Quality of Working Life movement achieved nothing more than freeing people from machine pacing, it would have been worthwhile.) On the other hand, it is not exactly all that was meant by "an improved quality of life . . . focused at the work-place"!

Another difference arose from the fact that "humanization" is a broad and ambiguous term. For the German administrator, industrialist, and trade unionist, the concept included from the outset considerations of safety, health, and physical comfort as well as considerations of job satisfaction, autonomy, and social relations, and the former group tended to be emphasized rather more. In the work organization field in Britain, we had tended to look at these groups of topics separately and perhaps to put more emphasis on the latter.

I found that I was very ambivalent about this issue. When I was at home, I tended to think that we do not pay enough attention to sheer working conditions. When I was in Germany, I tended to think that they emphasized them too much. I remembered the operator in Pakitt Ltd, the first case study of our work study project, a paternalistic firm which took great care of its staff. With much feeling, he had said, "I'd *rather* wash my hands in a dirty bucket!" He did not want to be molly-coddled if that meant losing his autonomy and individuality (and with that he had raised all the issues about legislating about such things).

Models of science and the question of diffusion

The strategies that I was familiar with, and the theories from which they stemmed, tended to focus on small projects, which might be highly developmental for the people involved but which had, on the whole, not diffused. The strategies that I was learning in Germany were, in the first instance, not so highly developmental for the people involved, but they were aimed at diffusion and to a considerable extent they achieved it. This was partly due to a model of science that comes from engineering science and is about research in case A leading to knowledge, which is then applied in cases B, C, and D. That is also the justification for spending public money. It is very different from the culture and the model of science that I was in, which say that the experience in case A, where the research is being done, is very different from the experience in cases B, C, and D, where the research is not being done but is intended to be applied. In that model it becomes difficult, if not impossible, to obtain public money for experimentation and research.

An allied dilemma is how one may be concerned for people's personal experience at the same time as working on a large scale. On the whole, the projects one knew in the Anglo-Saxon and Scandinavian context were liked and found valuable by the people involved but did not spread, sometimes even within the firms that were famous for this work. In the German programme, partly because of different intellectual traditions and partly because public funds were being spent and had to be justified, there was a strong thrust towards large-scale application, and towards diffusion. They were looking for models that could be transferred to other situations, for design methods that could be taught to engineers and incorporated into design manuals, for findings that would feed into the law.

The rational, engineering-type model of science had some expression in legislation. There was a clause in German company law saying that "scientific findings about the work-place must be applied". So what exactly could be termed a "scientific finding" about the workplace? Legislation of this kind is likely to influence research in the direction of looking for standards and norms, and this can, of course, be done more easily in relation to such things as noise levels, lighting levels, etc. It is much more difficult in the area of work organization. There were, however, some attempts at this; for instance, to agree a minimum length of job cycle. There was a collective agreement with the trade unions in one of the *Länder* (regions) that there should be no work cycle of less than ninety seconds. This, in fact, could lead to some nonsenses in practice; but it indicates the way people were thinking.

Questions of standards and legislation

So, while the Germans were new to the topic of work organization, they brought to it approaches that were, in turn, new to me. These approaches were not alien, they "spoke to" something in me. I formulated this in a lecture at the Tavistock Institute, where I was then based, in terms of a marker buoy somewhere in the Channel: every time I passed it, in either direction, my attitudes about a whole range of things changed.

For one thing, there was the whole question of doing this by law and regulation. If one told a British audience about the clause requiring "scientific findings" to be applied, they laughed: most of the things we were talking about were not "scientifically proven". You cannot "prove" in that sense that people need opportunities for learning and decision making in order to develop. And yet, there were many things contributing to the working environment to which such a law could apply, and because of it working conditions in Germany were likely to become progressively better than in Britain.

And the range of topics to which people who were used to this legalistic approach paid attention could grow. My professor colleague was open to new ideas: "All right," he said, "you've convinced me that it is good for people to be able to communicate. So we must make it possible for them. We must have a standard specifying that components must not be piled more than thirty centimetres high on a work bench, so that people can make eye-contact." Ridiculous? Perhaps. On the other hand, the principle of creating the preconditions in this way is not a bad one and did not enter into Anglo-Saxon thinking.

A noted German work scientist, Professor W. Rohmert, tried to tackle this issue by establishing categories that divided the field into four levels:

● whether the work was possible to do;
● whether it was tolerable;

- whether people should be expected to do it (*zumutbar*);
- whether it led to job satisfaction.

The first two, he considered, were amenable to scientific research and assessment; the second two needed to be tackled in a sociological and cultural framework.

There were efforts to articulate links between the two kinds of category: people cannot behave autonomously if they are technically constrained. There was (and still is) a great deal of machine pacing, so the question arose as to how much freedom from being paced is "good" or "desirable", i.e., could have the law applied to it. One of the humanization projects tried to address this—given the legal framework there was much prestige for researchers in doing the kind of work that might produce a "proven scientific finding" to which the law might apply.

The researchers did a major attitude survey in a large company. From a range of questions in a very long questionnaire, they compiled a "job satisfaction index" for each operator. At the same time they described the jobs being done by those operators, in very great detail. The descriptions were "objective", in the sense that the categories were completed by an observer, not by the operator. The categories included the amount of buffer stock available to the operator, measured in terms of time. They then crunched the data through the computer, relating the subjective findings about job satisfaction to the various objective descriptors of the jobs. And they came up with a very interesting finding.

When they plotted an operator's job satisfaction against the amount of buffer stock available to the operator (measured in terms of time, from one minute's worth to 180 minutes' worth), there was a straight positive correlation: the bigger the buffer, the greater the job satisfaction. There was more: in their attitude survey, whenever a complaint was expressed about anything, there had been a follow-up question: "Can you do anything about that?" In so far as people felt that little or nothing could be done about a problem, the researchers compiled a "helplessness index". And when the size of buffer was plotted against helplessness, they found a straight negative correlation. In other words, the greater the buffer zone, the fewer complaints people had in the first place, and the less helpless they felt about those things that did give cause for complaint. The reasons were not investigated; it may simply have been that there was then time to complain or otherwise take some steps about a problem (Bullinger, Rieth & Euler, 1993, pp. 103–140; Euler, 1987, pp. 32–42).

The Committee found these results quite uncomfortable. They had been expecting something that would indicate a "good" level of buffer zone, say fifteen or twenty minutes' worth. So, to be honest, had I: fifteen or twenty minutes is time to have a cup of coffee, to leave the workshop to smoke a cigarette. Such a result could have been turned into a standard. But what these results were saying was the more the better, and this took implementation out of the realm of the law and straight back into that of negotiation, the Anglo-Saxon model. The Germans were discovering the limits of their approach, as I was discovering the limits of ours.

For that particular researcher, the empirical scientific approach, combined with a clear-cut boundary drawn between research and action, inevitably led to a critique of the autonomous work group concept. He found it inadequately—or not at all—tested: there were no findings about the actual nature of the co-operative work relationships which resulted for the members of such a group, and which are so decisive for the real social attractiveness of work. He conceded that co-operative work relations are only problematic in so far as interactions such as discussions, agreements, mutual help are the result of compulsion; but a group can dictate and enforce behaviour as much as any other circumstance (Euler, 1977).

Some cultural aspects

Nevertheless, having heard and read so much about the Scandinavian approach and work, the head of the Humanization Programme wanted some involvement from them. Some years into the programme he invited Einar Thorsrud, the Director of the Norwegian Work Research Institutes, who had been involved with the early Tavistock work, to act as assessor for a large project that was being launched in Volkswagen AG. He, in turn, brought in a Swiss research group. Einar did not look at things in terms of understanding legal or cultural differences, he had a mission. The first thing he did, before taking up the role, was to publish an article in the European edition of the *New York Herald Tribune*, saying that the Germans were doing it all wrong and now we would show them how. He also saw the role of *Gutachter* differently from the way I did, and set out to shape the project; he and his colleague set about implementing autonomous work groups in Volkswagen. They did not realize, or did not accept, that there was a need to accommodate to the legally established and deeply institutionalized arrangements for works council and trade union representation. When a works council representative came to sit in on the discussions of one of the groups, the (foreign) consultant asked the group "Do we really need him?" It was the representative's legal right to be there, and there was uproar in the trade unions. The rights and positions of these elected representatives had been hard-won and the legal position was very important to them. The German trade union movement set its face against autonomous work groups, and for about two years it was not possible to introduce ideas of worker autonomy—either individual or group—into the discussions of the Programme committee. When I needed to, I would preface what I was going to say with "If I may use a dirty word . . ."

But I, too, made cultural mistakes. It is dangerous to make jokes if you are not completely at home in a culture. One day the committee had before it the project application of a large industrial group. We had read the documents (always very heavy) and were now to discuss the proposal with the applicants. The atmosphere was tense, about thirty people were standing around in the committee room, dressed rather formally for the occasion and speaking in hushed voices. One could not be sure who was an industrialist, who was a researcher, who was a civil servant, who a trade unionist. As we took our seats, in an effort to break the tension, I announced, "Well, I'm open to bribes!" There was total silence, which seemed to me to last for about three weeks. Not a murmur, not a smile. Then the chairman said, "Now, item one on the agenda . . ."

And in the end I, too, succumbed to cultural differences. In the autumn of 1980, the committee was reviewing one of the projects. As usual, we were meeting in the plant of the project that was being considered. This time it was in south Germany, near Ulm. The management representatives gave their report, then the trade union, then the researchers. Then the assessor who was monitoring that project pulled out his notes and prepared to speak. But the chairman (a new one) stopped him. "No, wait a moment," he said, "we will take your report in closed session."

I protested. This was inconsistent with the values of the programme itself, one of the main thrusts of which was about openness. In any case, if the assessor monitoring the project had something to say, the people working on the project needed to hear it. This became a big argument within the committee, though I do not remember which side won. At the end of the year my contract was not renewed. At the time I thought it was because after seven years they had probably got all the contribution they could from me, and wanted a change. It was not until much later that I learned the reason had been the chairman's objection to my subversive argument about monitoring as an open process.

It was a pity. This particular committee chairman from the Ministry of Research and Technology was not typical of the senior civil servants I had encountered. And I also learned that he was not in that role for very long. A very different kind of civil servant was Günter Keil, who represented the Ministry of Research and Technology for some years. We are still in touch, and he recently quoted to me a limerick I had doodled during a committee meeting, and which I had forgotten:

> A semi-autonomous Turk
> Said, "This change agent chap is a jerk.
> I would much rather sit,
> Chew tobacco, and spit.
> Make my other half happy at work!"

Then I, in turn, remembered the complicated discussion we had had about political correctness and whether one should use the more usual English formulation of "my better half", given that this was about Germany, and its Turkish guest workers.

A personal note

Working in Germany was both important and complicated for me on personal grounds. Having lost most of my family during the war in concentration camps, I regarded it as an opportunity to see whether it was possible to work through my own history and relationship with things German, and also to make a contribution in areas that had been part of the problem. To do this, I had to be very careful about my own behaviour, demonstrating values rather than preaching about them, and not making emotional capital out of my own history. I think that on the whole I succeeded in this.

I did, however, find myself quite instinctively calculating the ages of people I met. If someone was younger than about fifty, there was no problem. If they were older, I could not help wondering "and where were you?" In the humanization programme, almost all the people I met were too young to have been involved in the war. The only exception was the professor with whom I was monitoring the Bosch project and who was considerably older than I. He did his best to find nice things to say about the English, but the greatest compliment he could come up with was that they write very good detective stories. He had been in the German Air Force during the war, in fact had learned his ergonomics and work science there. And he loved to reminisce. Quite unselfconsciously he told about having been billeted in Russian homes, and how bug-infested they had been; at times he had been so disgusted by the bugs that he slept outside the house, in his car. The thought that he had no business to be in a Russian home at all had not occurred to him then, and did not occur to him as he told the story.

Postscript

During the 1980s, the economic climate changed (I referred in the Introduction to the effect of the Arab oil embargo of the 1970s on these activities). In 1989, the programme was discontinued, or rather was replaced by a narrower programme called "Work and Technology". In 2002, under vastly different political and economic circumstances, a new programme was launched, with much less funding and with emphasis on spreading known best practice. It is called "Initiative Neue Qualität der Arbeit" (Initiative New Quality of Work).

This has been a snapshot of a major programme, written from the point of view of an outsider who was lucky and privileged to be involved in it. There is another snapshot in English, written by one of the participants in the programme (Fricke, 2003). Information about current programmes and initiatives can be found on the website of the "project carrier", now called DLR, at www.dlr.de/pt-dlr.

And Dr Keil has summarized the broader systemic implications of the programme very succinctly: "You design jobs so that the workers get to use more skill and initiative. Then they want more money. Then you build a branch factory in China."

Notes

1. The Alvey programme for advanced information technology was a government initiative that ran between 1983 and 1987. It was a programme of pre-competitive collaborative research in the enabling technologies of information technology: collaboration between companies, between companies and academic institutions, and between government departments and industry. Its aim was to double the level of IT research in the UK as well as to meet some specific technical goals.
2. Chapters Nine and Ten show how my own work was influenced by a design method that was arrived at in this way, and that I adapted. The original method is described in Chapter Eleven.

CHAPTER EIGHT

A contribution to the design of a new confectionery factory

This was a project about contributing to the design of a new factory from the point of view of job satisfaction and work design. It is an edited, fuller version of a project account that was first published in Klein and Eason (1991).

I am sometimes credited with introducing autonomous work groups into the Colchester factory of Trebor Sharp Ltd. Reader, I didn't.

* * *

Background to the project

Trebor Sharp was a family firm, manufacturing sweets and confectionery. The company had a history of solid growth, and employed some 3,000 people. At the time the project began, it had four factories. In 1977, it was decided that one of these, in London, could not be adequately refurbished within the existing building and site and should be replaced by an entirely new factory elsewhere.

Trebor was a company whose management had a strong philosophy and drive, both to "do the right thing" as far as the social aspects of industry were concerned, and to be innovative in these matters. It may have had to do with the fact that it was a family firm, which led the top levels of management to have a more than temporary and career-level involvement with the company; and with the fact that the products themselves were relatively traditional and stable, and not subject to major innovation.

When the company decided that a new factory was needed, they wanted to achieve two things: a building that would not be just another factory, but something rather special that would stand the test of time and make a distinctive contribution to the built environment; and jobs and working conditions that would be positively satisfying for the people who worked there. As the project developed, it was interesting to discover how these two aims could, in some ways, come into conflict.

I was working in the Tavistock Institute at the time and the company's brief, put to me by the personnel director, was, "We would like, for once, to get the social and psychological aspects taken care of at the design stage." The personnel director had been in Esso at the time that I was there, and knew of my interest in work organization. His own interest was in the area of Organization Development and he had already, some years earlier, introduced a form of OD in Trebor, based on managers exploring their personal relationships with each other. I had misgivings about that kind of orientation, because of the fascination it can engender in people to the exclusion of other things; but the opportunity was unique. While I had experience of working on job design problems, I had never before done this at the factory design stage where the operators concerned do not exist yet and their experience and contribution are not available.

Here was an opportunity, for the first time in my experience, to get involved early enough. Usually questions about job design are asked too late; job design work that I had experienced myself, and of which I had read, was almost entirely redesign, with limited options and within fairly narrow constraints. Therefore, at the same time as finding the assignment extremely interesting, I had to make it clear that methodologically it was to me unknown territory. It would involve designing jobs to be done by people who would not appear on the scene until much later, and so was very different from improving existing jobs with the benefit of the experience and contribution of those who were doing them.

Some early design activities

A project group at Board level had been formed and when I first met this group, in June 1977, a site had been acquired outside London and planning permission for the new factory obtained. Within ten minutes of joining this project group for the first time I discovered a big dilemma: the basic concept I worked with was that of the production process as a sociotechnical system, that is, one where the human and technical aspects are interdependent and need to be considered simultaneously, with the human needs and aspects playing a strong role. To translate this concept into practical reality and have anything useful to say about improvements, you need to learn about the product and process in some detail.

At this meeting the group was beginning to discuss the choice of architects and the general shape of the building. Two concepts for the new factory were being debated: on the one hand, the concept of a large, hangar-like structure within which there would be freedom and flexibility to arrange and rearrange things; on the other hand, the concept of a "village street", along which would be ranged small, human-scale production units, as well as social facilities such as shops, a post office, a tea bar. Within a few minutes of joining the group, I was confronted with the question, "What do you think—large hangar or village street?"

I had, of course, no basis for an opinion. The company felt that they could not even begin to talk to architects until they had some idea of the basic shape of the building they wanted (the architects later disputed this view); one could not sensibly discuss the shape of the building without some idea of the production layout; and I could not contribute to discussion about the layout from the job design point of view without some sociotechnical analysis of the production process. At that stage I had not even seen the manufacturing process. So, within ten minutes of joining one of their meetings for the first time, I had met a major methodological difficulty in design—that of phasing.

At a second meeting I worked with the project group to list job design criteria, discussing priorities among them and relating them to production criteria (a methodological approach I had picked up in Germany. The production director kept saying, "It's got to be *possible!*"). I had the opportunity to spend a day in the old factory looking at the production process, but when I attended the third meeting of the project group I was still far from really understanding the details of the production system.

I had learned that the first of the products to be manufactured on the new site, a mint, consisted almost entirely of crushed sugar with some additives, which was then compressed into tablets and packaged. Instinctively, I went back to basics. Groping for a more detailed understanding, I said: "Look, I still haven't understood the process properly—suppose I'm a piece of sugar, I've just been delivered. What happens to me?" Somebody said, "Well, the first thing that happens to you is that you get blown along a tube. But there is a physical limit to how far you can be blown." I said, "OK, what happens next?" And somebody said, "Next you get crushed into a powder." In this way I talked my way through the process in very great detail, role-playing the product. For example, I heard myself saying, "All right, so now I'm a granule—what happens next?"

"Next, we drop mint oil on your head."

"Might you miss?"

"Yes, we might."

"How would that be discovered?" And so on.

I checked back a number of times to ask whether this was just a game or whether it was useful, but they assured me that they were finding it very useful. The product was a fairly simple one, which they had been making for a long time, and their ways of thinking about it had become rather set. Now, these ways of thinking began to unfreeze, and they began to discover alternatives and to say to each other, "It doesn't have to be like that, it could be like this, if such-and-such conditions are met."

In particular, some things that they were used to thinking of in sequence could, it was found, be done in parallel. This meant that the logic of the production process was not necessarily a straight line and this, in turn, meant that one could think in terms of a short, squat building. That was the eventual shape of the "product house" that emerged out of this process.

I realized afterwards that my strategy had instinctively been about leaving options open. Once the factory was staffed and experience of the work system beginning to accumulate, there was more chance of reviewing and revising it in a short, squat building than in one where the logic of the layout led to long, straight lines. The other function of this shape, from the point of view of the people working there, was that it should facilitate people relating to each other.

Unfortunately, in the welter of things that had to be decided and done between that time and the completion of the building, the aim of leaving options open was lost sight of (phasing again). By the time operators appeared on the scene, there were not really any operating alternatives available. The main area for choice was in how the work groups organized themselves around the technology; since autonomous group working was a strong part of Trebor's philosophy, people had been recruited with this in mind.

During the early design activities and partly through the work that had been done on design criteria, it had emerged that there was a very strong value—not to say ideology—in the company, concerning autonomous work groups and team working. This emphasis was strong and, in my view, somewhat romantic, in that group working was expected to solve a wide and diffuse range of problems. I found myself putting emphasis on unaccustomed ergonomic considerations and other "mundane" aspects of work to try to maintain some balance.

Relations with the architects

Consistent with the above, when selecting architects the company was attracted by the fact that the particular practice they chose was organized in teams. In the event, it was this very team structure of the architects, and the internal cohesiveness that went with it, that made interaction between the company and the architects difficult and collaboration slow to develop. The client's staff, after all, had relevant expertise. They knew that pumps specified as delivering exactly the same litres per minute were not to be had off the shelf, they wondered whether "copper pipes will be chromium plated" literally meant all pipes, they worried when they found items in the specification which they did not remember discussing. The development engineer lost an argument about the design and siting of the silo, and thought that it would have to be changed when the third and fourth production houses came on stream. There was much argument about cost control systems and whose right it was to reallocate savings.

Paradoxically, one of the more satisfying design experiences was on the question of flooring—sugar dust causes special problems—where neither side felt particularly expert and they joined up to look for a solution together. They had formed a team that was more appropriate to the task.

A study of the old factory

Although the factory itself was to be new, the basic production technology would not be radically different from that in the old one. I suggested that it would be relevant to make a study of the work system in the old factory, once the pressure of deciding on the shape of the building was gone. Although jobs in the new factory had been offered to all staff in the old one, many knew that they would not be able to move to the new site for domestic reasons and would therefore in time be made redundant. It was very touching, therefore, to discover how ready staff were to think and work on possible improvements "to make it better for the other girls".

The study yielded thirty-five pages of comments and suggestions. For example, at one point in the process, when the mints were finished, they came sliding down a chute at the left of an operator, and were carried from left to right along a belt, on which they were shuffled into rows, before being moved into a wrapping machine which wrapped them in rolls. An operator monitored this process, picked out any that were broken or jammed, made sure that the wrapping machine was supplied with paper and glue, and so on. There were eight of these arrangements spaced along the room, each one involving a chute, a moving belt, a wrapping machine, and an operator.

In the course of the study, one of the operators developed the idea that it would be much better if the equipment was grouped together in pairs, four pairs of belts running parallel and attended by four pairs of operators, instead of eight single ones. "I'd have a mate, opposite me," she said. "We could talk. And we could help each other out. When I go to the toilet, I wouldn't have to switch off, because she could watch mine for a bit." What actually happened was that, when the supervisor was not looking, operators switched the equipment off in order to visit each other, since the work was isolated, with each operator looking at the back of another operator, several yards away.

Management liked the idea, but came back some weeks later to say that it had been impossible to persuade the equipment manufacturers to make the equipment so that some ran from left to right and some from right to left, with the controls in the mirror position, as they would have to if operators were to face each other instead of looking at each other's backs. The reason had been the cost of redesign and the special development and retooling required.

It was, of course, no kind of technical challenge, but it was a challenge to seeing the operator and her work-role as part of the system, rather than something to be added on afterwards, and this was the difficult boundary. It was a boundary that management itself had not, at that stage, really crossed. I do not know with how much conviction, as an important purchaser of equipment, the request was made. I did discover, more than a year later and by accident, that the engineer who had been sent to negotiate with the manufacturers on this issue thought that he was doing so because, if the lines were grouped in pairs, it might be possible to have one operator monitoring two lines.

Three points are worth noting about this: first, that engineering training, with economic criteria as the dominant ones, is very deeply ingrained. Second, that even in this company, which was making a heroic effort to give greater priority to human criteria, the message had not got through to all the staff. This, I felt when I discovered it, had been to some extent my fault. My early work on values and design criteria had been with the Board-level group. When I later met the site team I missed the significance of the break in continuity. It was the same company, but it was mainly not the same set of people, and there was a need, which I had not fully appreciated, to start again at the beginning. The third point to note is that the break in continuity of thinking would not even have come to light if we had not, at a later stage, done some research about the building process, unconnected with the main project.

More design activities

During the phase of designing and building the factory, I was not much involved. Payment for my work was by the day, which meant that I waited to be asked to visit and felt inhibited about proposing visits and activities. The next phase of involvement was with the management team that the company had recruited to develop, and later run, the new factory. A residential workshop with them included consideration of a rough model for the proposed product house. The team had invested £200 in Lego bricks and had worked very hard over a weekend to produce a first tentative layout. This they presented, with the question, "What do you think of it?"

In a way that was similar to the earlier experience, it seemed unreliable to translate the arrangements of the layout by a sheer act of imagination into the work experiences that might be going on around it. I said, "I'm not very good at reading drawings, I can't really think my way into this. What is actually happening down there? Suppose it's seven-thirty in the morning, what is going on?" One of them said, "All right, I'll be a press operator." Another said, "We don't know if we're going to have press operators." Gradually, they took on roles according to the tasks that needed to be done, and then someone said, "OK, it's seven-thirty in the morning, the bell's gone and the doors are open . . ." He was interrupted—"What do you mean, bell? Are we going to have bells?" And there followed a long discussion on clocking-in. Their optimism and enthusiasm about the consequences of autonomy was unbounded, and it was I who found myself playing devil's advocate—"Suppose a work group has a member who is persistently late? What will they do? How will they demonstrate it if there is no clock to give them the information?" The outcome of this discussion was that there should be space on a wall to install a time-clock if it turned out that the work groups themselves wanted one. By midday we had, in this way, worked our way through the start-up and first hour or so of production. In the process, a number of things in the layout were changed and it was interesting to see how difficult it was to undo even as ephemeral a decision as the arrangement of a few Lego bricks, given the hard work that had gone into their original arrangement.

Outcomes

The process of designing, planning, and building the factory took much longer than anyone had expected. Much of the delay was due to industrial relations problems in the building industry combined with, in the company's view, the nature of the management contract with the architects and, in the architects' view, the company's insistence on choosing the builder. The consequences were bad for industrial relations since, for two-and-a-half years, the people in the old factory who were to be made redundant did not know when this would happen.

Much of the activity during this time was not connected with work design, and the consultancy relationship became sporadic. Because of the nature of my contract, I was not present during many phases which had no overt and explicit "human" aspects but during which decisions affecting work organization were in fact implicitly made. During this long period the framework that regards the work system only as a social system was reinforced, and social systems aspects of work design highly developed, while sociotechnical aspects became eroded. This was because "Organization Development", in the sense of concern with social systems and group relations, introduced by the personnel department, was already institutionalized in the company before the project began, while thinking about the interdependence between social systems and technology depended on input from me.

Thus, there was general agreement among the participants that, when the factory started production, the group-working aspects worked out very well. This was also the finding of independent research (Wall, Kemp, Jackson, & Clegg, 1986) and is not surprising, since operators were explicitly recruited on the criterion that they should like working in groups. The considerable problems that were experienced were all in technical and production areas. The management team later said that, in their great enthusiasm and commitment for developing the work-group concept, they probably did not give enough attention to these other aspects.[1] On the work design side, packers in the new factory were still sitting looking at each other's backs, as they had in the old one. The noise level was high and the principle of feedback and overlap of roles between different operations was lost in the course of the design of the building. As has been said, another idea which had been lost sight of by the time the factory opened was that of leaving options open: in the designing, planning and building of the plant, there was such a welter of things to take care of that an abstract concept like keeping options open would have had to be very strongly internalized to remain alive and be remembered, as many hundreds of decisions were taken.

It is also perhaps a question of the formality with which a point is made: when a colleague and I later ran a seminar on sociotechnical design in the company (see below), he spoke of "minimum critical specification" where I had talked of "keeping options open". Although the audience preferred "common-sense" terms, I can see how such terms are easy to accept without translating them into practice, whereas my colleague's phrase provided a hard principle against which practice could be measured and evaluated.

Later developments

Relationships with the company remained friendly, and there was occasional contact. At one stage the works manager developed a pattern of sending me tapes on which he reflected about what had been happening, particularly during the start-up phase, and what his own experiences were. It was a kind of compromise between having a consultant and not having one. He later allowed these tapes to be used for the benefit of managers in another company (see Chapter Nine) undertaking a similar green-field development.

Two years after the start-up, I was invited to do training in the company "in the sociotechnical methods you used with us". It was a surprising request, and to test whether it was serious, a half-day presentation at Board level was made first, followed by a two-day appreciation course. This included a simulation exercise, manufacturing paper aeroplanes by different methods and comparing the experience. For the production director, the experience was one that he later said made an "indelible impression". It came from realizing how stressful a short time-cycle, with tight controls, could turn out to be. At one point one of his aeroplanes was rejected by "quality control"; without comment he slipped it in again and this time it passed. The idea that quality standards might not be absolute horrified and infuriated him. He threw his aeroplane at the "inspector" and shouted, "Now I know why we have problems between production and quality control!"

The production people in the company decided that they wanted training in sociotechnical analysis and design to become part of the training for all managers, and for these methods to be applied in the other factories. It was left to the personnel department to follow through on this decision. However, they did not. It was felt as a threat to their own approach, and management did not want to upset their own personnel department.

One reflection about this project is, therefore, that an organization's enthusiasm for innovation may make them bring in a range of innovations which are not necessarily congruent with each other. The innovations then become part of the political dynamics of the organization.

The project also shows some of the ambivalence that clients experience towards help, both wanting it and being afraid of such powerful needs. Third, the method of payment for consultancy, and its institutional consequences, had important implications for the outcome.

Notes

1. I was reminded of the introduction of integrated crewing in Esso's Marine Department (Klein, 1976b). In the company's enthusiasm to remove the barriers between deck and engine room operations, much attention and effort was given to the group relations aspects involved, and not enough to the necessary retraining.

CHAPTER NINE

Work organization in the design of a new canning plant: plant design, job design, and industrial relations

This project concerns a social science contribution to the design of a new high-speed canning plant. The project as it developed had two strands: one concerned plant and job design, and the other concerned industrial relations. At first these were quite distinct. Later they came, for a time, closer together—the project can, in a sense, be seen as a history of trying to bring plant and job design and industrial relations into relationship with each other.

Some effects of the social science intervention were inconclusive and hard to pin down, leading to some uncertainty about whether the glass was eventually half full or half empty. However, one breakthrough that it achieved was clear and important: it demonstrated to a group of managers and trade union representatives who would not have believed it, and who were in any case locked in combat, that they could design a job and could do it according to criteria on which they could achieve reasonable agreement.

Only an abbreviated version of this account has been published before (Klein & Eason, 1991).

* * *

Introduction

"Foods Ltd" was a subsidiary of a large multi-national organization engaged in processing and packaging food products. It had three factory sites. One of these (site X), in the north of England, was becoming uneconomic to run and had begun to make a loss. This was thought to be largely because of technically outdated and labour-intensive methods. It was decided to build a new high-speed canning plant at one of the other two sites (site Y) thirty miles away.

Industrial relations in the company were very tough and adversarial. In the summer of 1979 a steering committee of directors of Foods Ltd was beginning to discuss plans for the new cannery with parts of its network within the parent company, which would be funding the new investment. On the personnel side, the parent company's employee relations adviser suggested to the personnel director of Foods that the new cannery would be an opportunity to pay attention to the quality and design of jobs as part of a strategy to improve industrial relations, and suggested that they should consider me as a consultant.

The preliminaries

At a first meeting, the technical director of Foods expressed a strong wish and value that jobs in the new cannery should be rewarding and satisfying, so that the people there should be happy and that industrial relations, in turn, should become more positive. However, it soon became clear that the engineering background of the Foods staff made them hope for specifications and standards for making jobs "good" that could be taken off the shelf. They were disappointed when I said that there were no ready specifications, and that the main route towards arriving at "better" jobs would lie in the design methodology.

At one level the Foods people quickly came to accept this reasoning. But when the project was being reviewed three years later, the technical director said wryly, "I was looking for someone to tell me what colour to paint the walls."

The industrial relations strand of the project was dominated at the beginning by the fact that a plant was to be closed, involving the loss of several hundred jobs in an area where there was already high unemployment; and that, although a new plant was to be built, it would employ fewer people than the old one and would be in a different location, so that few of the people at site X would benefit from the creation of the new jobs at Y.

The announcement of these plans was scheduled for November 1979. In the meantime, there was a phase of mutual education with the management. For example, in a seminar I described simulation and the testing of alternatives as a way of arriving at design decisions in a new situation where there was no operating experience to draw on. There was some discussion about whether models or larger physical simulations might be practicable as transitional systems, a means for trying out ideas. Although it would involve costs, the costs it might eventually save were likely to be greater. But later, as time went on and people became busier, the sheer time and trouble required to build a model came to appear increasingly burdensome, and it did not happen.

The Foods project engineer internalized very rapidly the job design concepts and methodologies. He and I visited another canning company where considerable efforts in the direction of job enrichment and autonomous work groups had been made. The purpose of the visit was for him to learn about these developments and for me to begin to learn about canning technology. I could not, at that stage, be introduced to canning within Foods itself, because "the Plan" had not yet been made public.

In advance of the public announcement about the closure of X and the proposal to build at Y, company staff had prepared a strategy that, consistent with the company's culture of tough and adversarial industrial relations, consisted of anticipating every possible response and move that might be made by the trade union side and preparing clear-cut moves and steps and statements for every eventuality, at the same time linking these to a timetable.

I had not been involved in developing this strategy and, when I saw the strategy document, discovered that there was no mention of the nature and quality of jobs in the Plan, its announcement or in the strategy itself. This surprised me greatly in view of the importance for industrial relations that the technical director, as well as his colleagues, had seemed to be attaching to these ideas. It seems likely, with hindsight, that it is here that the seeds of eventual limitations lay: after this, job design considerations always had to be inserted against the combined weight of timetable, cost estimates, trade union preoccupations and suspicions, and company culture and politics. Seen in this light, it is perhaps some achievement that anything happened at all.

The waiting period

The initial trade union response to the announcement was not as strong as had been feared—there was no strike—but it was, predictably, preoccupied with the fate and the terms and conditions affecting the people working at X. Thus, once the Plan was announced, there was for a long time no opportunity to raise another new topic, that of job design.

Three trade unions were involved in the company: a general union to represent the process operators, an engineering union, and one for the supervisors and junior managers. As it developed after the announcement, the trade unions' position showed some differences between the approaches of the three: broadly speaking the engineers, whose members would be in the least unfavourable position in the X labour-market, were mainly concerned with obtaining the best possible terms for their members who might become redundant; the supervisors' union concentrated on the number of jobs that might become available for their members at Y; and the general union concentrated on trying to prevent the closure from happening.

This meant that, for several months, they refused to negotiate with the company about anything at all, and it therefore also meant that it was not possible to do any exploratory work in the X cannery, or to talk with them about the design of jobs in the new plant. Discussing jobs in the new plant would have implied accepting that the old plant was going to close.

So there then began a protracted waiting period during which the main activity was discussing strategy. The choice seemed to be between having me as a consultant work secretly in a back-room capacity with the engineers, or waiting until the problem with the general union should be resolved so that I could work openly with the trade unions.

I was not prepared to work in secret, and the steering committee's sub-group on personnel matters, of which I became a member, unanimously agreed that we should wait until I could work openly. Three years later, some members of that sub-group thought that this had been a mistake—"If you had been prepared to swallow that principle and work as a management toady, (a) you would have had more influence, and (b) we would have ended up with a management group that understood the concepts better." In the light of what happened later I can understand that conclusion. However, faced with the same dilemma and without knowledge of what was to happen later, I do not see how one could avoid making the same choice again.

Discussing strategy was, of course, not the only activity during the waiting period. Some other developments are listed below.

1. The project team was getting on with making decisions about suppliers of equipment and with developing a layout for the cannery. I was not involved, but the project engineer, who had taken on board sociotechnical principles such as the value of roles overlapping and people collaborating for a perceptible end product, was a member of the project team as well as the steering committee sub-group and this influenced the layout. He also produced a list of technical constraints in preparation for job design activities and began to experiment with role descriptions, writing a job description for one key operator in terms of the experiences involved as well as the tasks to be performed.

2. The steering committee was getting on with its work. Sometimes they asked themselves, "What would Lisl think?" and generally made accurate guesses. The use of a ghost seemed a useful device in the process of internalization.

3. In May the project engineer was transferred to another company in the group, in a career development move. In the logic of the cannery project, this signified the transition from basic design to more operational concerns. In the logic of the job design project, however, it was a great loss of continuity. He had become the in-house "holder" of the concepts. In spite of later efforts, there was never again anyone in-house who was identified with holding the know-how and concern for job

design. The works manager of the Y site now moved into the project in an active role, heading the future operational team.

4. The parent company's management services subsidiary began to be involved. The engineering project team resisted for a time, but the works manager at Y came to use their consultancy input on a wide range of personnel matters. The frame of reference of this consultancy was about minimum cost running. The language, however, turned out to be about behavioural science concepts, organization development, managerial style, etc. When the opportunity arose, much later, to discuss this, it was claimed that the aim was to harmonize the two sets of values. But it seemed to me that using the language of one set of values for the tools and concepts of another was very far from the same as harmonizing them.

5   Some of these strands came together and surfaced in a rather bizarre episode. The parent company's consultants had developed a layout proposal that was different from that of the in-house project team, and there developed a hard-fought debate about the relative merits of the two layouts. The conflict clearly had both realistic components about the characteristics of the two layouts, and political components about the source from which they came; there was a serious question about which of the teams would survive. Much of the language in which the debate was conducted was in terms of job satisfaction (which was known to be an explicit company goal), but that was, of course, hypothetical.

I was invited to a meeting, to find myself confronted by drawings of the competing layouts set out on a table, and the managing director asking me to decide between them. When I think about it, this episode still contains for me an element of craziness. My experience of canning at that stage consisted of one half-day visit to a cannery and a total of perhaps five or six hours looking at drawings. I have sometimes wondered since then what would have happened if I had met the MD's expectations and confidently selected a layout. I would dearly like to know if it would have been implemented.

I could, however, offer a method for deciding between the layouts, if job design considerations were to be the deciding factor. This involved giving priority ratings to a number of job design criteria, and then scoring each of the layouts on each criterion. The method turned out, however, to be vulnerable to partisanship since the sample was small—people scored according to the outcome they wanted. In any case, it did not reveal a clear advantage either way. What it did reveal was that both layouts gave cause for concern, and I suggested that one criterion for selecting between them should be which one had more potential for upgrading.

Management began to form the view that their consultant was not decisive enough.

In May there appeared to be an opportunity to break the deadlock. There was a small production line in the existing factory at Y, making a product for which the market appeared to be growing. A second line was to be built and the personnel director proposed that it should serve as a training exercise in job design. This would give the company practical experience of this approach on a small scale, and also did not have any redundancy implications. However, the market situation changed and the second line was not built.

The full-frontal phase

By July, the tension surrounding the timing of the project was great. In some ways, for instance as regards basic design and equipment purchasing, it was rapidly becoming too late; in other ways, i.e., as regards collaboration with the union, it was still too early. The personnel director decided to cut the Gordian knot and proposed "going full frontal". A timetable for an announcement about work organization and my involvement was worked out, involving letters to the full-time trade union officials, meetings with the X and Y department heads, meetings with middle management in both factories, and three meetings with trade unions (one with each of the unions but jointly between the two factories). The general union did not accept the invitation but all the other meetings took place at the beginning of September.

It is relevant to make a digression here.

The trade union movement as a whole was finding it difficult to know how to relate to the wave of job design activities that was causing a considerable stir in Europe during the 1970s. While in Germany, for example, the Metal Workers' Union (IG Metall) had itself been a driving force behind the government's programme to "Humanize Life at Work", in Britain the unions were highly ambivalent about these developments. For example, they agreed to take part in a steering group which was set up to oversee the Work Research Unit that was being created in the Department of Employment, but they were clearly unenthusiastic about its mission.

Some of the anxiety was about issues of demarcation: if the content of jobs was to change, so might the trade union allegiance of the job-holders. I mentioned in Chapter One that the General Secretary of the Trades Union Congress, Len Murray, had dealt with this by writing a letter to all trade union general secretaries, saying that the TUC was not in support of job *redesign* activities, but would support job *design* activities in situations where new plants were being created. I was involved with the working party that the TUC had set up to consider these issues, so I knew about this letter. I do not think that many people did, and I do not think that it had much effect. But it was very useful now in helping me reassure the trade unionists with whom I was beginning to engage.

With the agreement of those who had taken part, I prepared a "First Progress Report on a Job Design Activity at Foods Ltd". This was circulated to all who had been invited to the meetings, including those who had not come. It began by reiterating why such an activity was felt to be necessary.

Traditional ways of designing plant involve two processes:

(a)   engineers concentrate on obtaining the most reliable equipment and production methods, which to many engineers means those methods which leave least to human intervention. They work to criteria about output, quality, costs, etc., and they want variances to be controlled automatically where possible. The only area where they are required to pay explicit attention to human criteria is that of safety;

(b)   at the same time, trade unions attempt to protect the interests of their members in terms of the numbers to be employed, their grades, pay, conditions, etc.

In these processes, neither party has traditionally paid much attention to the content and meaning of the jobs that are being created and yet both know that work is a very important part of people's lives.

The report went on to summarize what had happened at the meetings, including doubts that had been expressed about the genuineness of management's intention. It ended by saying that I would be available for a week in each of the two factories to see anyone willing to discuss these matters further.

The second week was spent at Y. During the first part of my stay there I heard nothing from the general union's convenor. But on the last day (Friday) I received messages, indirectly, to say that she intended to talk to me. Since she was working on the afternoon shift and would not be on site until 2.00 p.m., I arranged to take a later train back to London than I had planned. Nothing happened, and when I realized that she was not coming I, in turn, sent her a message: it was that I had interests too, and that if I had known she did not intend to come I would have caught the earlier train, as I was going out that evening. On getting this message she came, and we had a long conversation.

That conversation contained two threads: one was that this was a management whom one could not trust, any co-operation was likely to be abused. The other was that impoverished jobs were indeed a problem. Some short-cycle repetitive packing jobs in the existing plant were so dreadful that some of her members were clinically depressed: it would be wonderful if something could be done about this.

In a second progress report I proposed that a "Y cannery job design committee" should be set up. The works manager announced that the company accepted the recommendation and invited the three trade union groups to do the same, and to nominate two representatives each. They accepted.

The Job Design Committee and the Job Design Steering Group

The Y Job Design Committee functioned for about eight months. (It may be a statement of the obvious, but one could not involve the operators who would be working in the plant themselves, because they did not exist yet. At least there was a representative system in existence.)

At the same time, there was set up a superordinate monitoring and holding institution, the Job Design Steering Group. This included the parent company's employee relations adviser, the Foods Ltd technical and personnel directors, and the works managers from site Y and the company's third factory in the south of England. I proposed some overlap, such as observers from the Job Design Committee to the Steering Group. There was no objection to this, although later events prevented it from being implemented. Although its life was short, the Job Design Steering Group was possibly the most strategically important of the institutions that were created in the course of the project. For a time there was an institutionalized, systematic and policy-level means for planning, deciding, and reviewing the activities connected with job design.

At the first meeting of the Job Design Committee the general union representatives spoke openly about the difficulty of making a contribution, since they were new to canning and were not engineers. The other two union groups, representing engineers and supervisors, wanted to talk about the number of jobs that would be created in the cannery rather than the quality of the jobs, and there was much argument with the management side on the lines of "We can't talk about job content until we know numbers and structure"; "We can't talk about numbers and structure until we know job content." A pattern emerged in which meetings dominated by "numbers and structure" alternated with meetings in which work was done on job content issues.

Five activities can be picked out from the work of the Job Design Committee.

1. We did an exercise, adapted from a method I had seen developed in Germany, first putting job design criteria in order of priority. I presented a list of characteristics that a job might have, derived from experience and the general literature, as well as from local interviews to gain some specific knowledge of jobs in canning. (For instance, "height above floor level" is a real issue in a canning plant, which would not have occurred to me otherwise and which is not in the literature.) I asked the members of the group to put these characteristics in order of priority, by selecting the one they considered the most impor-

tant; then crossing it out and selecting the most important from what was left; and so on. The results showed big differences, not only between management and the unions, but between the union groups and between individuals.

I had to decide quickly about what direction to take next. We could have done work on working through some of these differences. But it seemed more important that the group should have some early experience of success, of actually being able to influence design. So we picked a criterion which had fairly high priority and fairly high consensus—"being able to influence one's own pace of work"—to explore with the project engineers.

We asked the project engineers to take us through the proposed layout of the new cannery, only from the point of view of control over the pace of work. In this way we discovered that there was one job, at the point where lids were put on the cans, where an operator would be locked into a twenty-second job cycle.

The lids came packed in one-metre "sleeves", which had to be unwrapped and placed by hand on to a machine from which the individual lids then slid onto the cans as they passed. At the rate of 600 cans per minute, which was one of the main achievements of this new technology, one sleeve would be used up in twenty seconds.

We asked the engineers to do some thinking and research about possible alternative methods, and they came up with two: for one thing, the sleeves holding the lids could be longer, say up to three metres. More radically, one could think in terms of a carousel to be filled up with a larger number of sleeves, which would click round automatically and drop a sleeve into the machine every twenty seconds.

We then compared the three methods on capital costs, labour costs, and consequences for job design, shown in Table 1. As a result of this exercise, the carousel was installed.

Two points need to be made about this exercise:

● It was fortunate for what I was trying to demonstrate that labour costs were the same in all three methods. The main priority for the unions was employment; if the labour costs

Table 1.   Comparative analysis of work methods.

	Method	Capital cost	Labour cost	Job design aspects
1	1-m sleeve on machine	Nil (the present system)	1 person	20-second cycle
2	3-m sleeve on machine	Low (minor modification)	1 person	60-second cycle
3	Carousel	High (purchase)	1 person	12-minute cycle

had varied between the methods, the method involving the most jobs would have had priority, no matter what. As it was, when management indicated that they were prepared to install the expensive carousel, one of the representatives made the unanswerable point, "If they're willing to spent £30,000, I'd rather they created an extra job."

• Although machine pacing is extremely important, we had after all only dealt with one aspect of one job. Uncoupling the operator from the pace of the machine did not create a wonderful job, it merely relieved him from a major constraint.

Nevertheless, a major break-through had been achieved: jobs did not come from heaven, they could be designed in as systematic a way as anything else, incorporating whatever criteria one valued.

2.   Two control systems engineers were involved in the planning of the cannery. They became interested in the idea of job design, and one of them made a presentation to the committee. This showed up a problem that dogs this subject and that is not sufficiently highlighted in the literature. He said that, at that stage, the control systems could still be designed in almost any way the committee wanted; he liked the idea of working as a service to the operators who would later be doing the jobs. But once the floors were laid, with channels for the cables, it would

be very difficult to change. The representatives, at that stage, did not have enough knowledge of the process to be very specific about what they needed.

However, some useful meetings took place between the representatives and the control systems engineers about the design of visual display terminals, the placing of mimic panels, etc.

3. To help the learning process, the representatives asked for some job design work in the existing plant. Preliminary work was done, but by the next meeting the committee was in its other, negative mode: there was no point, nothing could be improved without big investment, which would never be sanctioned, and so on. Later, whenever the suggestion for a trial run or work on other jobs in the plant came up again, senior management always pointed to this experience as grounds for not agreeing. They also did not agree to the construction of a model of the cannery as an aid in developing work roles.

4. A series of visits to other organizations was planned, and one took place.

5. A residential training course was planned for the committee. Before it took place, members of the committee filled in a job satisfaction questionnaire, about their own work experiences. It was planned to analyse and feed this material back as part of continuation and follow-up afterwards.

The course appeared to go very well. However, on the last day, as the application of the learning to the plans for the cannery became more and more specific, difficulties began to emerge. At the end, the general union's representatives said that they were withdrawing from the project. I felt at the time that they may have been troubled by the fact that they had enjoyed the experience and were afraid of being seduced by it.

The final phase

There was a good deal of ongoing business to keep the committee going, even in the temporary (it was hoped) absence of one of the unions. I was going to be away for a month, and the works manager wanted to keep the committee and a number of planned activities going. The personnel director thought that the union might be willing to accept help, in confidence, with whatever problems it was experiencing with the job design activity, and I wrote to the convenor offering such help and saying that I would be in touch on my return from abroad.

When I got back, none of the planned activities had taken place. The personnel director had not conveyed his idea of separate consultancy for the union to the works manager who, when he heard about it, refused his consent. I could have insisted on keeping my promise to the convenor, but what would have been the consequences if I had deliberately undermined the works manager's authority in this way? It was hard to understand why none of the things we had arranged had taken place. It may be that I was being punished for going away.

(I did not see the convenor again until the official opening of the cannery, a year later. As a result of that conversation, the convenor said, "All right—have another go and we'll co-operate." But that time it was the management that did not agree.)

I thought that the project was dead, and was surprised when at the end of the year the personnel director contacted me about continuing work. I said that, if work was to start again, there should first be a formal review. This was done and considerable agreement reached about the nature of the issues. The review revealed that changes in the external economic climate had led to some shifts in priorities. Nevertheless, a plan of action was agreed consisting of eight items, including, for example, dealing with "unfinished business" at Y, reviewing what institutions I should routinely take part in, planning training and development for in-house people, planning a continuous audit of the jobs as they developed when commissioning got under way, and so on.

None of these things happened. The main obstacle in this phase appears to have been the time pressures of the stage that the cannery development had reached (it was due to be commissioned within months) and the associated negotiations.

In reflecting about the whole experience, it seemed to me that there was an almost aesthetic quality about the industrial relations symmetry. Each side was able, always with good reason, to point to the intransigence of the other as a reason for not making any changes itself. What is particularly striking about this symmetry is the timing: those moments when one side was temporarily locked into the most negative aspects of its stance freed the other to express the most positive aspects of its own, without any real risk of change.

Both sides did have a genuine wish for change but, when one considers the system as a whole, the need for equilibrium was clearly greater.

I wrote this in a report to them. As an Appendix, I wrote a little fable about industrial relations as Cinderella, caught between the two ugly sisters, Mangie Mingie Annie and Terrible Trudy, who are building themselves a new castle in a country called Northof-watfordgap.

I said in my report that I thought the project had had very little effect, and that was the only part of it that made them angry. They said that the organization of work in the cannery was very different from what it would have been without the project.

Oh, and they said that access for maintenance would have been designed better if they had had a model.

There is a postscript. When I approached the company for agreement to publish an account, I found that every one of the members of management who had been involved had moved on, to other posts in the parent organization. That could help to explain some of the things that had been so puzzling: if a post of this kind is transitory, that would affect the amount of engagement one invests in the problems of a particular site.

CHAPTER TEN

Work organization in branch banking

It was not all manufacturing. For seven years during the 1970s I had a consultancy contract with one of the four clearing banks in the UK, and Ken Eason has reminded me that this included some work on the organization of the work of a branch. While the overall consultancy has been briefly written up before (Klein & Eason, 1991; Chapter Six), this piece of work did not feature in that account and is described here for the first time. Ken and I did the work together, and have written this account together.

* * *

Introduction: a study of branch banking

After a merger and a strong wave of computerization, the Domestic Banking Division of one of the UK clearing banks thought that customer service might have suffered, and set up a Customer Service Working Party. I was invited to be a member of this working party, but, in order to be of help, thought it necessary to understand more about domestic banking first. A study of branch banking was commissioned, and a team of five researchers spent a week in each of four branches—one in central London, one in a London suburb, one in a provincial city, and one in a small country town. One of the things we learned concerned the division of labour between the manager and the sub-manager of a branch: the main job of the manager was to make lending decisions; the hallmark of a good banker is to be a good lender, and that was where training was focused. The sub-manager ran the office. This included organizing the work of the office and allocating tasks among staff. However, that was not seen as "real" banking. Sub-managers tended to be marking time until they could get back to "real" banking, they hoped, through being promoted to manager. Training played a big role in branch life, but it was training in banking. It seemed that sub-managers were not trained in management and did not think of themselves as responsible for effective work organization.

One of our recommendations following the study—really a side-effect of learning about customer service—was for some management training for sub-managers. (But we did *not* make glib assertions about happy workers giving better service!) This was agreed, and we ran two three-day workshops for sub-managers in the London region, aimed at developing their problem-solving and management skills. Sixteen sub-managers attended each time, and a member of the Organization and Methods Department was on hand to help with technical questions.

Work organization in a branch

Spending time in four branches of the bank, of different sizes and in different parts of the country, had given us a rich view of the daily life of domestic banking and of the great variety of tasks that the staff undertook. In addition to the work of the cashiers that one saw as a customer, there were many "back of the office" tasks: opening and closing accounts, setting up direct debits and standing orders, looking after safe boxes, processing loan requests, organizing foreign money transfers and so on. Somehow, and in some combination, all these tasks got allocated to members of staff. Part of what we were looking at in the branches was the kind of jobs that resulted and the process by which this happened.

Some conclusions stood out:

- There were detailed procedures for undertaking each task. Banking is highly regulated and every branch had rows of manuals with standard procedures for every imaginable situation. This meant that staff had little discretion about the rules they followed in completing a task. On the other hand, there was considerable discretion about who performed each task.

- There were commonalities in the work organization of the branches. In every branch there were workstations where cashiers managed tills and were the first point of contact for customers. Also in every branch, at the "back of the office", was the "machine room". At this stage in the application of computing to branch banking, customer accounts were held in large computer centres, but only a few online terminals, located in the machine room, provided continuous access to these accounts. The machine room was staffed by operators whose job it was to enter into the computer every change in the customer account made in the branch. These were in junior grades and it was a great source of satisfaction that, for the first time, there was a subject—computing—about which the juniors knew more than their managers.

- There was variety in the middle of the office. All the other paperwork tasks were done in the middle of the office and different branches organized them in different ways. Some of the jobs were organized by service, e.g., the foreign clerk dealt with all foreign transactions. But some of the other jobs were made up of a collection of tasks that had little overall coherence.

- There was a grading structure for the jobs in the office that created some career progression for the staff. Beginners did the tasks that required little knowledge of banking and then graduated to become machine room operators. As they developed banking knowledge they moved to cashier roles, and then to the more complex accounting and document handling tasks in the middle of the office. However, within this broad structure, most staff contributed to a range of the tasks of the office.

- While there were some fulfilling jobs in the office, there were also unsatisfactory ones, and stresses and problems in the work organization. Some junior jobs were perceived as mixtures of routine tasks that lacked integration and were "going nowhere"; one girl said she prayed for someone new to be recruited so that she would no longer be the newest, with all that went with that. In some places juniors were given the task of answering the telephone, which was stressful because they did not know enough to respond to the customers (not to mention its implications for customer service).

- Many tasks required the co-operation of several staff, and one common feature was that the work of one person was checked by another. This led to a very noticeable feature of branch life: staff were continually interrupting one another. As one of the senior staff commented, "Branch work is constant checking with constant interruptions." Senior staff found this feature of the middle of the office quite difficult because many of their tasks were long and involved and needed attention. Keeping your place and your concentration amid all the interruptions was a widely perceived problem.

The exercise—staffing a branch

The workshop consisted of a number of talks and exercises, one of which was about the organization of work. It was intended to explore their approaches to staffing and to introduce them to some social science findings about job design.

The study had shown that there were significant work organi- zation issues to be addressed. It also showed that, although there were outside forces shaping the tasks to be undertaken, there was also considerable discretion that could be used to identify the best form of work organization for each branch. The shaping forces included the detailed banking procedures, the computer system used in the machine room, and the grading structure in the branch. Within the framework these factors created and the mixture of work the branch had to do, it was up to the sub-manager to use the flex- ibility that remained to organize the staff to get the work done.

As a vehicle for working on this we created a paper-based simu- lation of an average branch, describing the locality and the type of population the branch was to serve. It was a branch with thirteen positions for staff, eleven if we took for granted the work done by the manager and the sub-manger. They included individuals of different grades, some of them part-time. On the basis of our study, and with help from the Organization and Methods Department, we specified a long list of tasks that the eleven members of staff would have to undertake and the average amount of time that each of these tasks would take each week. At the workshop we gave each sub-manager a sheet of paper on which were listed positions one to eleven, and asked them to allocate all the tasks to these eleven positions. As they did their allocation, we asked them to write down the criteria they were using, but although they allocated the tasks and organized the work, they did not articulate criteria. We then made an exhibition of all the allocations and allowed the sub-managers to see how their colleagues had approached the exercise.

It was a revelation to the sub-managers to discover that they had not all done it the same way. There was a common core in the way they had allocated tasks to the cashiers and the machine room, but beyond that there was in fact a lot of variety in the ways they had all done it. A common practice was to take the next big jobs, such as dealing with foreign business, and make these the responsibility of one of the more experienced staff. This process tended to leave a collection of relatively small tasks, mostly routine, that were put together into "rag bag" jobs for juniors.

The criteria they had used had been tacit, but once the sub-managers were aware that different allocations were possible one could get them to think in terms of their criteria and articulate them. Some of them had tried to group tasks together so that the overall job had meaning, some had had learning and training in mind, but most simply thought of their allocations as "following tradition". Having brought the idea of criteria to the surface, it was then also possible to discuss criteria in terms of alternatives and their possible consequences. To do this, they were given a list of job design criteria that included having variety but also performing an overall task, having opportunities for learning, getting feedback, etc.

We had also prepared two "example" allocations. One was based on what they called the traditional approach, in which emphasis was given to allocating large service tasks to senior staff, and which was very similar to the allocations that many of them had made. The other was based on a different rationale: it accepted that there were two relatively autonomous sub-groups within the office (the cashiers and the machine room) and noted that there was a leader (a chief cashier and an accounts clerk respectively) who took responsibility for each group. In technical terms, a lot of "variance" was contained within each of these groups. This example allocation then examined whether this structure could be replicated in the rest of the office. There was a natural group of relatively senior staff doing the more complex tasks in the middle of the office. They were the ones who needed "do not disturb" notices. There was then a range of relatively routine tasks and also the task of dealing with all customer enquiries that did not come to the cashiers. In this allocation a senior role was created called "Enquiry Clerk", whose function was to deal with all these customer queries and to supervise the undertaking of the routine tasks around the office (including much of the checking of work). This person then became responsible for some of the junior staff and for ensuring they got learning opportunities. This approach to work organization was an attempt to handle two of the other issues that had troubled staff in the branch study: first, it was an attempt to contain the interruptions within each sub-group, so that interrupting everybody became less necessary. And second, it meant that a lot of very routine but not very time-consuming tasks got shared out across all the positions, even the quite senior ones, so that they were not bundled together into one unattractive job.

These examples were not offered as "good" or "bad", but in the sense that there were alternatives that had a logic behind them and were very different from one another. The sub-managers explored the possibilities and implications of these different approaches for different kinds of branches; for example, large ones in city centres as opposed to small ones in market towns. They concluded that there was not a single best solution but that, as sub-managers, they had a responsibility to work out what would be best for each branch they worked in.

As often happens in our work, we did not have the opportunity to follow this up and see what kinds of work organization they went on to create, but one outcome was that the sub-managers who attended these workshops decided to meet regularly. Once a month they met for lunch and hired a room for the afternoon to work together. It was significant that they managed to persuade their managers to agree to this. The process of attending the workshop had caused them to recognize that they had shared experience of a management responsibility that was not reflected on and discussed in any other forum in the bank. We had initiated a process that filled this gap and they took it over for their own purposes.

CHAPTER ELEVEN

Putting information and communications technology to work in the construction industry: testing a model

ProCure was the acronym of a project funded by the European Commission, called "ICT (Information and Communications Technology) at work for the LSE (Large-Scale Engineering) Procurement chain".[1] It was carried out by a consortium of partner organizations in three countries: Finland, the UK, and Germany. The Bayswater Institute's role was to accompany the project from the point of view of human and organizational aspects.

The project represents the only opportunity I have had of accompanying a technical design and development programme from its inception. Changes in the work content of individuals play a smaller part than in the other action research cases. On the other hand, it shows how closely linked the characteristics of work roles are to the systems that give rise to them: chains of cause-and-effect can be traced back on the one hand to the economic context of the participating construction companies, and on the other to the vendors of software and their problems of timing. The social science aims of the project were therefore very ambitious. Since the technical aims were also very ambitious (ambitiousness squared?) the account is untidy and the outcomes inconclusive—it would have been simplest to leave this project out! However, there is an itch that tells me it was worth trying to make a contribution on human and organizational aspects to technical development in a way that is more systemic than concern for the eventual nature of the jobs involved alone, even where the circumstances turn out not to be particularly favourable, and that it is worth trying to write this effort up. It would have been better to try the model first in a simpler situation, but one has to make use of opportunities where they arise.

From the point of view of content we (the social scientists) decided, in this project, not to draw any artificial discipline boundaries around topics or to put limits on the human and organizational features considered relevant. That is what makes it ambitious. However, the amount of effort expended on different aspects varied, as it was determined by the limits of staffing, budgets, geography, and receptiveness to the ideas on the one hand, and changes in the circumstances of the client systems on the other. (Among other things, the story of this project shows how arbitrary it can be to allocate project work into topics: this paper could equally have featured in the volume about the use of the social sciences, Working across the Gap.) The impossibility of drawing time boundaries beyond the artificial one of project funding is what makes it inconclusive; we do not know how things worked out in the long run in the organizations taking part. Several years later, the project manager says that he and his organization have found it, and are still finding it, useful. As an exploration of the usefulness of the social sciences I very much believe it was worth trying—and would greatly like to try again.

The main part of the chapter is largely drawn from the Bayswater Institute's part of the final project report. Alan Dale and Emily Hutchinson took part in the project; their contributions will be acknowledged along the way. The material has not been published before.

*   *   *

Introduction: the model and the project

The model

In 1981, after giving a talk at the annual meeting of the Collège International pour la Recherche en Production, I was confronted with this question: "What research should we—the CIRP—sponsor, to increase understanding of why people resist new technologies, so that it becomes easier to introduce them?"

The assumptions underlying the question were familiar: there must be something wrong with "them"—the users—if they do not see the advantages of these developments which "we"—the technologists—are introducing, and do not want to embrace them. If only "we" understood more about how "they" function, "we" would be able to deal with "their" resistance.

Because this question is asked every time there is some new technical development, there has in fact been massive research during the past decades, going back as far as the 1920s (for example, Harding 1931; Wyatt & Fraser, 1928). The answer to the CIRP questioner was, therefore, that there was no need for yet more research, but a need to insert findings and methods gained from already existing research into the processes of developing and implementing technology, and to research *that* activity. A model for doing this could be for social scientists to accompany such developments in a longitudinal way, making contributions on methods, findings, and processes as need and opportunity arose along the way.

CIRP liked this idea, and it became the subject of a CIRP-sponsored application to the European Commission's research programme ESPRIT 2. We proposed a programme of "accompanying research", which would take the form of tracer studies in an action research framework.

The use of tracer studies in industrial sociology originally derived from medical research, where a "tracer" is sometimes introduced into an organism and studied, at intervals or continuously, on its way through. In organizational research, it consists of taking a key item, usually a product but in this case a process, and tracking it through everything that happens to it, as well as examining the roles and institutions involved.

However, the framework would not be that of research but of action research, for three reasons: first, and most obviously, feedback from the work should provide a contribution and not mere *post hoc* analysis and critique. Second, much relevant knowledge, experience, and research do not generally find their way into practice. And third, the range of issues is great and changes over time.

Action research can and should be totally rigorous. It is not a matter of intervening in an *ad hoc* and uncontrolled way, but of selecting and agreeing strategies with the participants in know-ledge of their consequences, documenting them, and staying in role. An action researcher attached to a design or development activity might:

- make predictions: "If you set it up in this way, there are likely to be consequences of that kind. Is that what you intend?";
- help work through dynamics: the dynamics at the input end of design have direct consequences for the output end; in fact, that is often where the origins of poor design decisions are to be found. If design decisions are made for reasons other than design needs, the outcome is bound to be problematic;
- give feedback about patterns that are observed, such as how outcomes differ when some parties are not able to come to meetings;
- offer research findings or experience from other situations;
- offer methodological help; for example, with prototyping or other forms of transitional system, or with methods of evalua-tion;
- ask questions that stimulate people to consider a wider range of alternatives than might have been considered.

None of the interventions mentioned are "consultancy" in the sense of telling people what to do. It is axiomatic in action research that ownership remains with the client system. The point, in any case, is to find a methodology that does justice to the complexity and dynamic nature of design.

The project

The proposal was turned down, with a strong recommendation to re-submit, and was then turned down again. This process took several years, and in the course of it one of the Commission's project officers came to like the idea and to respect its proposers. In 1998, when he was in preliminary discussions with engineers from Taylor Woodrow Construction Ltd about a project they were considering, he suggested it to them and also suggested that they explore involving the Bayswater Institute. They did, and this time the application was successful.

The project was carried out by a consortium of partner organizations in three countries—the UK, Germany, and Finland. In each country there were industrial partners, engaged in large-scale engineering construction, and research/consulting partners.

The industrial partners were:

in the UK:	Taylor Woodrow Construction Ltd (the project leaders)
	British Steel [later Corus] plc;
in Germany:	Daimler Benz [later Daimler Chrysler] AG
	Ed. Züblin AG;[2]
in Finland:	Fortum Engineering Ltd.

The research/consulting organizations were:

in the UK:	The Bayswater Institute;
	University of Leeds School of Civil Engineering;
in Germany:	Haas + Partner Ingenieurgesellschaft mbH (an IT consultant);
in Finland:	VTT Building Technology (Technical Research Centre of Finland).

The technologies and concepts

In essence, the project was about advanced technologies that the partners wanted to test and apply, rather than a task for which they wanted to design a system. When they started, the industrial partners were thinking in terms of finding better ways for construction projects to operate, facilitating trading messages between partners, but ". . . we didn't really get on to that." There were many changes along the way, mainly in response to changes in the environment. The project was technically very ambitious, and the summary that follows is greatly over-simplified. It is also the product of hindsight; the situation was not nearly so clear to us at the beginning. In a very over-simplified way, and with some overlap, the eventual technologies were of three kinds, listed below.

1. *A simulation tool.* This was the technology that the Finnish partners planned to test. It consisted of a business model, specifying

resources and prices; a product model, modelling parts; project modelling (contracts, equipment buying, etc.); scheduling of operations. The original plan was to test the technology on a coal and biomass (waste) power station in Poland, looking at the delivery process of the whole plant—building, design, equipment. But the client withdrew during the course of the project, and different plans had to be made (see later).

2. *Three-dimensional working.* The computer-based three-dimensional presentation of buildings had been in practice for some time, mainly for marketing purposes, allowing potential clients and others to "walk through" a building, to experience the building to some extent, and to suggest and try out changes. Now, however, the partners wanted to develop 3D working in a sophisticated and detailed way for operational purposes, so that it would wholly replace two-dimensional drawings. They had recognized the limitations of drawings, realizing that an object is not just a series of lines that describe it, and were beginning to look at the properties of objects.

3. *Project website.* The aim here was to create a website for the construction site of a large-scale facility, for contractors, subcontractors, professionals, and suppliers to communicate with each other and with client staff, exchange data, etc., with different levels of security and degrees of access, and so on. It would provide detailed audit trails, that is, information about who had done what to what, when information was created, when it was published, who it was sent to, etc.

Both the UK and the German partners were intending to test the last two technologies, in the case of the UK on an office building and in the German case on a production facility and a remountable car park. But the UK office building ran into organizational difficulties within the host company (see later); the German buildings ran into difficulties with the Commission's reviewers when it was discovered that they existed already, so that the work had less innovative content.

All these technologies would, of course, have major effects on the various roles in the system—for instance, the roles of professionals such as architects and structural engineers. (Existing information technology was already doing that. A consultant structural engineer, not part of this project, discussed the anxiety created by the great increase in speed in processing information: "By the time I realize I've made a mistake, they've built the bloody thing!" He was not entirely joking.) The technologies would also make demands on the equipment and skills needed by building contractors, who are often small firms.

From the social science point of view, I had developed a model about the interaction between technology and its contexts, which is shown in Figure 7. The model shows two things: first, that interdependencies between technology and human and organizational aspects exist at many levels; and second, that these interdependencies are as relevant at the input end as at the output end.

The project proposal

As the Commission's project officer had suggested, engineers from Taylor Woodrow (TW), the lead partner, first tested out the

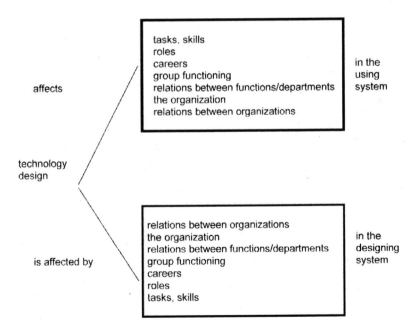

Figure 7. Factors affected by and affecting technology design.

Bayswater Institute and its staff in terms of experience, practicality of approach, and ability to use straightforward, non-jargon language. When they were satisfied on these grounds, they decided to incorporate a social science component in their plans for Pro-Cure. It is significant for what happened later that the other partners did not have the opportunity to do this exploring and testing out to anything like the same extent. The process of developing a project application exerts pressures and constraints of its own. It is dominated by deadlines and the need to meet administrative requirements, and the "working through" that had happened between TW and the social scientists before the project did not happen with the other partners until the project was under way. By that time it was under a certain amount of constraint, at first from the way the proposal had been formulated and later from the Commission's reviewers, who were very enthusiastic about the social science component; the partners were obliged to include this component rather than choosing to.

Then there was the question of scale. As Figure 7 shows, the "human and organizational issues" potentially relevant in such a project are virtually unlimited. The issues are many and varied and they can arise at any point, as much in the designing/developing system as in the user system. They will arise at different times and they will have different degrees of importance or seriousness.

This has consequences for budgeting: it is impossible to make a rational decision about what is an appropriate budget for the work, and the decision becomes rather arbitrary—it is easier to cut one's coat according to one's cloth than to decide at the beginning what will constitute a good coat. The proposal was mainly prepared by Taylor Woodrow, the lead partner, who recognized the need for this contribution. At first they proposed a much larger budget than the one that eventually featured in the proposal. One of the other partners had protested that it was out of proportion in relation to the whole project, and we (the social scientists) had tended to agree. It is partly a matter of what one is used to—we were not used to so much confidence being placed in our ability to be useful—but it is also a matter of what was going to be acceptable to the other partners. The fact was, in any case, that the eventual budget was too small for the comprehensive nature of the proposed work. There should have been an experienced social scientist attached full-time to each of the three pilot projects that developed. Although this was suggested, we "went along with" the situation when it proved impossible to carry out.

Towards the end of the project, when the final report was being written, there was general agreement among the project partners that it is important to integrate activity around human and organizational issues of the technical implementations in the mainstream reporting of the industrial partners, rather than to label such activity as "social science" and report on it separately. This sense of the importance of an integrated approach can, in fact, be seen as one of the outcomes of the project. All the industrial partners included this activity in their reports; indeed, some of their reports appear to be dominated by human and organizational issues.

The first phase—preparation

Familiarization

The plan was that, during the first year, the engineers would be working on the technology and developing their plans, while the social scientists would be familiarizing themselves with the construction industry and with the partner firms.

For familiarization we first conducted interviews with a range of professionals in the construction industry, both within and outside the project, read documents, and attended industry events. We then looked at the partner firms at the level of the organization and prepared reports on their corporate strategies: interviews were conducted in the industrial partner firms and led to individual firm reports. These were fed back to key professionals in the firms but not disseminated outside the firms, because of confidentiality. The one about Fortum was circulated within the organization and considered to be very useful; the one about Taylor Woodrow led to some consultancy exchanges with senior engineering department management; the one on British Steel was beginning to be similarly used when structural changes in the company intervened. A broader report on the construction industry, which formed the context of the project (see below), was in part based on these separate reports.

The industry context

1. The environment

Like most industries, construction is greatly affected, potentially at least, by massive changes in its business environment. Competition is intense and, for large contracts, increasingly international. Some clients are beginning to use sophisticated techniques, derived from manufacturing industry, to place increasing pressure on their contractors to reduce cost, speed construction, improve quality and manage buildings throughout their life-cycle. At the same time, delivery is more and more through complex networks of sub-contractors, rather than always using in-house resources. With the development of similar initiatives by a few sophisticated suppliers, construction companies run the risk of being "squeezed" and finding themselves in a weaker and weaker position. There is also much talk and a few examples of partnering. However, there is much evidence that more adversarial relationships persist: indeed, the increasing use of contract lawyers has intensified that trend in some respects.

This environment is richly represented by the set of partners involved in the ProCure project. Between them, they have all the characteristics described, so that the environment is present within the room whenever they meet. As in the outside world, relationships between them are both collaborative and, in some cases, competitive or even adversarial. A challenge for the project is therefore to manage interaction between them effectively. Part of our role is to try to help facilitate that process.

2. Business strategies

In general terms, the business strategies of the partners are moving towards more rationalized and proactive approaches. However, there is also recognition (particularly among the construction companies) that a more opportunistic stance, and close relationships with clients, is equally important to them.

The second major trend is that strategies can now be seen to be of at least three major types:

- contract-based approaches—essentially, the traditional model in the industry;
- process-based approaches, in which manufacturing systems engineering techniques are used to study, improve, and control

the entire workflow in construction. These involve the application of knowledge management, project management, and other techniques. Such processes can cope with quite a wide variety of changing demands for buildings;

● product-based approaches. Here, the rationalization of the design workflow is taken a step further. Distinctive expertise is capitalized by producing fairly standardized designs for a range of typical constructions relevant to a particular market. At the same time, much effort is devoted to understanding and serving the needs of that market. As with the process-based approach, this strategy allows some flexibility to modify standard designs to suit particular cases.

The two new approaches require a degree of centralization much greater than previously used in the industry. Far more effort must be devoted to capturing, analysing, recording, and using the accumulated experience derived from individual projects. Using this knowledge, management systems can then be developed to continue improving the management of design, purchasing, and construction. Instead of each project having its own systems, all projects are managed in the same fashion. It is no longer possible to "let a thousand flowers grow".

A third major trend is life-cycle costing and life-cycle management of buildings. This has a big impact on design activity, which must now take account of such factors as the cost of maintenance or even the demolition and disposal of buildings.

All of this leads to a situation in which the big companies in the industry are moving

from: work based upon a unique need, unique tender, unique design, unique components, unique construction process and so on;

to: some standardization at every stage.

There are obvious parallels here with the industrialization of simple service processes, as pioneered by Macdonald's. However, it has perhaps more in common with flexible manufacturing systems, where client needs are not so predictable and a range of possible responses is therefore necessary.

3. Tasks and workflows

The new business strategies lead to a fundamental redefinition of the primary tasks (missions) of the organizations. They are now moving into the business of managing and exploiting professional expertise. Such expertise is still used to manage the actual design, construction, and other workflow processes, but the latter are not necessarily carried out in-house. Indeed, the parties involved in the workflow also vary with the characteristics of the contract—in particular, the nature of the risk and benefits, the locus of control and ownership, and who does the work at each stage.

Another important factor that affects the nature of the business tasks is global operations. Today, work carried out for clients in other countries is often sub-contracted to local firms, who must use the prime contractor's methods and be integrated within an international network of other contributors. Thus, a key task is to integrate and co-ordinate the efforts of all involved.

4. Client and supplier relations

Relationships with clients can be seen as on a continuum ranging from domination to submission. In the construction industry, there is a long history of attempts by one party to a contract to dominate the other, and of corresponding resistance by the weaker one. In some cases, the relationships have become largely the province of lawyers.

There is a strong interaction between the content of business strategy and the nature of the relationships with the client. For some organizations, the business strategy can almost be described as aiming to get closer to the client in order to equalize the power relationship.

There have recently been several attempts to create collaborative relationships, or partnerships, in which both parties look after the interests of the other as well as their own. Among the ProCure partners, there is much talk of such arrangements. However, it seems that when an organization is dominated by (say) its client, then it tries in turn to dominate its suppliers. (And even within ProCure and other EC projects, collaboration is not always forthcoming.) The status of Preferred Supplier is the best that many construction companies hope for.

Goodwill is clearly not sufficient: Alter and Hage (1993) suggest a whole range of arrangements and actions that need to be taken. These deal explicitly with the kind of interorganizational relationships that are so common within the construction industry. In particular, the authors emphasize the importance of sharing risk, benefits, and profits; that relationships between partners of greatly unequal power rarely work; and that interorganizational institutions and other structural arrangements are necessary to make such systems work well. It seems that the very nature of contracting in the construction industry has to be addressed if real improvements are to be made.

Holti, Nicolini, and Smalley (1999), and others working within the industry, have developed innovative training approaches specifically for construction. Their work incorporates many of the principles outlined above.

It may be that the development of supply chain management and "relationship marketing" will make at least some of these innovations unnecessary. They have certainly brought big improvements to other industries previously dominated by exploitative and conflictual relationships. Any sustained attempt to get close and stay close to clients or suppliers broadens the interaction beyond formal contracting. [This section, pp. 194–197, is taken from Alan Dale's paper "Maximising the chances of successful technical innovation: corporate intentions and their relationship to human and organisational issues in the pilot deployment projects" (R 1102)]

Consultancy

Many of the general issues described were to crop up in specific form throughout the course of the project, and began to emerge during the preparatory phase. During this phase we were also acting as internal consultants to the consortium, facilitating Project Board meetings ("the social scientists spent a lot of time watching the rest squabble about technology"). Concepts of group relations were apposite here: none of the teams was dedicated to this project alone, all of them had other projects to look after, and all of them were under various kinds of pressure from their own home base/parent company. It was helpful to discuss this in terms of groups and how they function, using part of a model developed by Harold Bridger (Figure 8).

The arrow at A represents the group's task. Every single member of the group has a part of himself or herself inside the group, and a part not inside, and has the task of balancing and optimizing

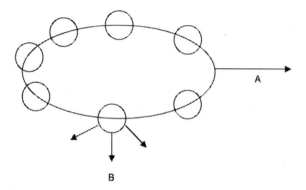

Figure 8.   A group and its task.

the relationship between them. The arrows at B represent the demands of the not-inside-the-group component, which may even point in a quite different direction from the group's task or project. This helps to explain much of what happens in a group. For example, in the case of this EC-funded project, with 50% funding, one obvious consequence was that only a proportion of individuals' time was allocated to the project, thus creating an obvious source of conflict, both for them and for the team. Just arranging meetings was very difficult. Taking part in such a project is not necessarily an expression of enthusiasm on the part of the companies. It is said that big companies tend to regard European Commission projects as "extras"—something that might turn out to be useful but with no immediate intention to adopt outcomes within the organization and no immediate link into company policy.

However, there were also many other and more subtle expressions of this tension, to do with internal company developments, the role of research and development within a company, its external economic environment, the career development of individuals, etc. Therefore, we also worked with some members and their colleagues on their own organization problems. Questions about the boundaries of ProCure began to be felt: how much time could one spend on such activity before it became more consultancy to the company concerned than consultancy to the project?

(The project also gave rise to some theoretical questions about this model of relations in groups—how is it affected when most members of the group bring their laptops, plug them in and work on them throughout, and no one knows what they are actually doing?)

Also during this phase, we developed a checklist of human and organizational aspects of technology design. This spelled out the broad topic into: (1) implementation issues (the changes in relation to individuals, the structure of the organization, the culture of the organization, relations between organizations, and patterns of risk); (2) methods for dealing with the implementation issues; and (3) implementing those methods. It is given in Appendix II. As part of their first project report, Taylor Woodrow tried it out against one of their other current projects.

The main phase

It is extraordinarily, and surprisingly, difficult to describe the three pilot projects themselves and especially to do this briefly; it was, indeed, difficult to understand them at the time! Obviously, this is partly because we were not technologists, but that was not the only reason.

It would have been helpful if the new technologies being developed could have been associated with specific new buildings. That was the original intention, but it turned out not to be possible, and the innovative elements remained curiously abstract.

In all the partner organizations, for various reasons to do with changes in the environment, the plans changed in the course of the project, in the UK pilot more than once. The changes in the environment were of different kinds: structural changes in the organizations within which the teams were working; economic changes in the environment of those organizations; and economic changes in the environment of their clients. The Finnish team lost its proposed pilot site, a power station in Poland, because the client had to retrench economically. The UK team lost its proposed pilot site twice. All the industrial partner teams had to cope with structural changes within their own organizations and the consequences of these changes during the course of the project, the biggest being that British Steel merged with Corus and that Daimler Benz merged with Chrysler.

Even without such major structural changes, it is a generic problem that the time scale of real construction projects is very different from the time scale of Research and Development. To get from a prototype to a full working system takes a good deal of effort and expense, and when one gets to the project it may be too late.

Social science workshops

The intention had been that at the end of the first year there would be a launch workshop combining technical training for staff working on the project and the beginning of the pilot-related social science activity. However, it turned out that technical training across the consortium was not felt to be appropriate, because their technologies were different and they were at different stages in their pilot activities. Without such a technical component, getting them all together for a social science workshop was not a realistic aim: they would not have attended, especially as there were at that stage disagreements within the consortium about the apportioning of funds. It was therefore agreed that there would be three separate workshops, and these took place in November 2000 in the UK and in February 2001 in Finland and Germany. To strengthen the connection between them, we suggested that each country-based workshop should also be attended by representatives from the other two. This happened in part: a Finnish colleague attended the UK workshop, two UK colleagues attended the Finnish workshop, and Finnish and UK colleagues attended the German workshop.

The aims of the social science workshops were:

- for the social scientists to learn more about the pilot projects;
- for the participants to learn more about relevant areas of social science;
- to start to identify the human and organizational issues within the pilots;
- to agree methods for monitoring and working with these.

A main function of the discussions in the workshops was to generate possibilities for engagement which could then be refined.

The three workshops turned out to be very different. This was due to the different nature and stage of the pilots, different size and composition of the groups, and different expectations/agendas of the participants. In the UK workshop there was greater emphasis on teaching aids and handouts, for instance about organization theory. This partly reflected the fact that the pilot was not clearly defined at this stage, so that it was difficult to draw the issues to be discussed from the pilot project itself. The German and the Finnish workshops focused more on the pilot projects themselves, letting accounts and discussion of these trigger accounts of research and experience from other situations, and using fewer handouts.

The members also brought with them different aspects of their environment: in the UK workshop, the provider of the proposed project website attended and gave a presentation; in Germany, a contractor attended and provided many examples of the consequences for contractors and their staff of the proposed technology; in Finland, both social scientists and engineers were surprised by how many people, from different parts of the company and including Board members, attended. It served as an opportunity for them to discuss the technical developments in the context of company developments.

Each workshop led to a report, which was fed back to the local partners, and the Finnish and German partners incorporated theirs as part of their own final project reports. The following are some brief comments about the workshops, followed by their practical outcomes.

The Finnish pilot

The workshop

In the preparatory phase we found that the workshop was being "sold" internally as a technical workshop, and the original social science aims at first had to be rather shoe-horned in.

By the time of the workshop, the proposed pilot site had been lost, and a decision had been made to test a "cost and resource library" instead of the simulation tool. This was a technology to manage a database of the cost of components and activities so that they could be accessed by salespeople out in the field to produce cost estimates and to revise them in the course of negotiations.

The pilot was therefore concerned with an internal method of exchanging information, though reflecting the external systems as well. One issue that emerged was that this was going to result in a heavy workload for some people—getting the data for the library, and not just getting data for themselves but for others to access. The current system referenced data from other cost libraries. A big issue for salesmen out in the field was a sense that they would have less freedom to negotiate and, above all, to make quick adjustments as negotiations proceeded.

In addition to providing a forum for issues of work organization to be discussed, this workshop also functioned as an opportunity for people from Fortum to meet each other to discuss general technical, implementation, and policy issues. They said that they only very rarely met in this way. The workshop, in fact, served to launch the first phase of the CostPower implementation, and a main outcome of the work done was a decision to test the technology in real tender cases rather than historical or hypothetical ones.

The pilot project

As the workshop proceeded, the main focus of the social science input and examples had turned more and more on the importance of the "messy realities" of implementation. The various examples we had presented from other situations and experience convinced the members of Fortum to use real situations for piloting and this, in our view, was the main achievement of the workshop. Two senior managers made a commitment to pilot the new software tool on live projects, instead of using retrospective data as had been previously planned. A third manager, who had already been using the software tool, agreed to write an evaluation report. In all three cases they would use the checklist provided by Bayswater.

The plan was that a report on these pilots would later be reviewed with Bayswater, and then help was to be provided as required with the implementation. The first of these happened, the second did not. One practical outcome arose from our comments and discussion of the draft report: it was that people were allowed to use the old tools in parallel with the new tool, which paved the way for more effective transition.

In fact, however, we had very little direct contact after the workshop, and the Finnish partners did not want Finnish social scientists involved either. The period after the workshop was dominated by structural changes and cuts within Fortum. We felt that one could not ask people whose lives were in turmoil and whose careers were under threat to pay much attention to these complex and unfamiliar things. Two key people who had been involved in the workshop left the company.

But shifting attention from historical and hypothetical cases to real ones was significant. After that, the reality has its own power. Data from real cases was used in the testing period, and users were interviewed in-house about their experiences. Experience was found to be different for the different functions; potential conflict was highlighted between expected benefits at company level and problems—for instance extra work—experienced at individual level. The data from real cases was used extensively for training.

The full findings and conclusions are given in the Fortum final report R3201b—"Cost power testing in real tender cases".

The UK Pilot

The report on the UK and German workshops, as well as the following edited account of the UK Pilot, were written by Emily Hutchinson. More detail is available about this pilot project than about the others, since a researcher was attached to it.

The workshop

Since the pilot was not yet clearly defined, it had been difficult to know for certain who should attend. It had been hoped that the workshop would consist of the people who would be involved in the pilot, both from a user perspective and from an "expert" perspective. However, it was impossible at that stage to know for certain who the users would be. Therefore, as well as the UK ProCure team members, people from Taylor Woodrow's design department and a member of Taylor Woodrow Construction also attended. Later experience confirmed that these had in fact been the relevant people, although it would have been useful to have the architect and structural engineer from the eventual (Christie Fields) UK pilot project as well.

Because the UK pilot was at such an early stage, the work was focused on thinking about what issues were likely to arise rather than what actual issues were. Below is a summary of an exercise to try and predict the kind of changes that might result from changing the way of working. The participants divided into two groups: the providers of the software system, and the users.

Table 2.   Summary of positives and negatives of the project website as seen by the providers.

Positives	Negatives
Improved security	Process training necessary (rather than system training)
Enhanced career prospects	Need to unlearn the old system
Higher self-fulfilment (as less admin)	
Quicker and increased communication	Less face-to-face communication
Better quality face-to-face communication	
More overview of the whole process	
Less stress long-term	More stress initially
Secretaries' role expanded to include document exchange	
QA and engineer roles likely to merge	
IT power will shift to users	
Less paperwork	
Easier access of data (worldwide)	
Accountability increases—everything can be monitored, traced and logged	
Information more transparent	
More equal power relations between organizations	
New types of contract	
Projects not so dependent on the architect and structural engineer—people in these roles will be freer to concentrate on professional work.	
More alliances and alignments of interests	
Costs reduced long-term	Some financial risks
Admin for health and safety easier	Some health and safety risks
Contract disputes easier to handle, as data transparent	
	Training needed for administrators

Table 3. Summary of positives and negatives of 3D modelling as seen by potential users.

Positives	Negatives
For consultants—should result in more detailed information earlier in the process	
Errors should be spotted earlier	Consultants—threat to their security, change of job—more thinking, less doing
Clients—greater security and better career prospects (as easier to attract buyers for the buildings)	
	Clients would need to re-train to use the technology
	Project managers—need to understand more about the design process. Suppliers would also need to improve their IT skills
Client can see the process more clearly	
Lead consultant has more control—owns the model	
More input from project manager to the design team as more information available	
Suppliers less face-to-face contact needed. Could have change of role to become supply and design function	
Clients—speed up the work, maybe result in more interest and variety	
Consultants—could make their work more interesting. Need breadth of knowledge	Consultants—could make their jobs worse—if lower level of knowledge
Project managers—make their work more interesting	
	May increase stress for clients—too much information?
	May increase stress for consultants as shorter timescales
	If not reliable may increase stress for project managers
Should be more delegation down the supply chain	
	Roles will change, departments may merge. Will need to train engineers, and change long-term recruitment strategies
Higher accountability	
Supplier—if their role changes to be more involved in design they will have more power and develop closer contract/legal relationships with others	
Contract/legal aspects might change	

Tables 2 and 3 above (out of four produced) show both positives and negatives. Points that could be seen as either positive or negative are shown across the two columns.

Some user comments on Table 2:

All this is too positive. Additional problem—seeing the complete document on screen.

Overall, this exercise showed that both users and providers thought that there would be major role changes along with changes in process, job content, power relationships, and communication, especially changes in process.

The workshop resulted in greater understanding and acknowledgement of the human and organizational issues. Methods for contributing to work on the pilot could not be agreed at this stage because of the uncertainty about the pilot itself. Instead, it was agreed that Bayswater would be invited to all UK pilot meetings; methods of engagement were expected to emerge from this.

The pilot project

As agreed at the workshop, and largely because in this case it was geographically possible, a researcher was attached to the pilot development, engaging with it as opportunity arose. She attended most pilot meetings, sharing the ups and downs and the optimism and pessimism as the situation fluctuated, and she instigated methods such as diaries for recording the experiences of the people involved and feeding this back.

Since we were present during the development of this pilot, this account will show more of its history and process than the others. It supplements the industrial partners' report on the UK Pilot Project (R3301) by adding some notes on:

1. the organizational context;
2. two "pre-pilots";
3. the brief life of the actual pilot and the issues that were experienced in relation to the project website and to 3D modelling.

1. THE ORGANIZATIONAL CONTEXT OF THE PILOT PROJECT

Many of the difficulties and frustrations experienced by the UK pilot project were the consequence of conducting a research project in an operational environment. There were a number of pressures from sources external to the project, in terms of the direction of the pilot, people's time, and workload.

The companies

Both Taylor Woodrow (TW) and Corus underwent major organizational and policy changes over the time-span of the project. Both organizations restructured to reflect changes in the market. This affected individuals in terms of disruption and threats to job security. It also had an impact at organizational level in terms of business strategies being revised. Taylor Woodrow were going through a process of redefining their internal IT strategy. One objective was to align the pilot with TW's internal IT, and there was some delay while this was being clarified.

Corus also underwent significant restructuring, aimed at changing its focus from being production-led to being more market- and customer-orientated. This led to major changes within the company and in the research that it carried out, and meant that key personnel were required to go offline from ProCure to carry out new corporate strategy.

Within each organization, ProCure was one of many projects being conducted, and also one of a number of projects that each team member was working on. To overcome the pull of other demands when people were not actually together in meetings, a system called *Net Meeting* was used between Corus, Taylor Woodrow, and the Bayswater Institute, for regular progress updates. Although this was useful to some extent, much of the time seemed to be spent in getting the connection to *Net Meeting* established. It did result in greater communication for a time (though this could have been partly because of the attraction of trying out *Net Meeting*).

The status of software

When the UK pilot was being planned at the proposal stage of ProCure, it was thought that data exchange standards would be far more advanced by the time the pilots started than turned out to be the case. This had an impact on the ambitions of the UK pilot. For example, it was planned that the Steel Construction Institute (SCI) would run a workshop to review the models and the transfer of information coming out of the Corus pre-pilot (see below). However, this did not take place, as the standard had not been developed to the stage needed for the software vendors to adopt it. Instead, the SCI related directly to vendors, using the models to get feedback and encourage the vendors to implement it.

2. THE PRE-PILOTS

It was planned to carry out two "pre-pilots", to allow initial exploration of the technology, before beginning the real one. This also had the function of maintaining momentum and enthusiasm during a time of organizational difficulty.

Yarm

The first pre-pilot, run by Taylor Woodrow, was based on a Tesco store being constructed at Yarm and aimed to trial and evaluate the use of design management software. A system called *Primavera Expedition* was piloted for project management. Some findings were as follows.

- To set up the system, the nature and structure of the project has first to be defined. This means that before the start of the project the organizations involved and the contractual relationships need to be identified, something that may not always be possible. Also, protocols need to be agreed, such as abbreviations for organizations, drawing conventions, review processes, and distribution lists.
- Training is needed to use the system—it has a different "style" and "feel" from other products. In particular, training is necessary to learn how to set up and configure reports.
- The type of software TW could use to some extent depended on the client. Even though they might have decided to use *Primavera Expedition*, they might in practice be obliged to use Microsoft *Project* or something else.

The project website was later used by the design team for about a month in the live project. A follow-up interview with the team was informative about the practicalities of using it as a way of exchanging information.

Egham Prima

The second pre-pilot, run by Corus, was based around an already complete office building, Egham Prima, and aimed to look at design development. The pre-pilot involved starting with the architectural drawings for that site, and using these to try and follow through on the basis of 3D modelling. It was apparent from this that changing to the use of 3D modelling would have a considerable impact on the way that the construction industry traditionally works. For example, using software such as *NavisWorks* meant that clash detection between models could be carried out in the design stage rather than problems only being discovered at the build stage.

This pre-pilot also highlighted a good deal of incompatibility between the different software packages, making it impractical to use them in the pilot. However, Corus managed to influence some of the vendors to progress developments to improve compatibility.

The 3D modelling aspect of the pilot consisted of the architect's and the structural engineer's designs being modelled by Taylor Woodrow and Corus. In terms of identifying human and organizational issues, it might have been better if the architect and the structural engineer had tried the 3D modelling themselves as "real" users, on a "real" project. The modellers from Taylor Woodrow were familiar with the software and so would have found it much easier to use than a novice user. They would also not have had the pressure of working in a design team on a live project.

It was planned that this modelling would be done in parallel with the live pilot project, and then at the end the old and new methods would be compared. However, as the eventual pilot (the Christie Fields project) was prematurely terminated, this could not happen. These problems, of course, limited the data emerging from the pilot. Diaries were kept by the modellers to record their experiences, but the information from them was limited as the work stopped at an early stage.

3. THE PILOT

This discussion is based on participating in meetings, diaries kept by the 3D modellers, and follow-up interviews.

The organizational context of the pilot

It might have been expected that a company such as Taylor Woodrow would easily find a suitable building for piloting the software, but this was not the case.

First, a building called Stamford House had been identified as the pilot project building, but during the social science workshop of November 2000 it emerged that this building project was cancelled. Around this time the possibility emerged of combining ProCure with the idea of a "Concept Office", which was being developed within Taylor Woodrow. This was a proposal to develop a set of standard units that could be combined to form a variety of types of office building. The possibility of combining it with ProCure was confirmed. However, there then arose some organizational problems.

Ownership issues. The Concept Office proposal was to be funded by TW's Property Division. It fitted well with the UK pilot, as both the Concept Office idea and the ProCure UK pilot were interested in developing the use of 3D modelling. Indeed, it was felt that ProCure had led to the Concept Office idea. An office building called Christie Fields 2 was identified as being a likely project for the pilot. It was thought that this would also be the first Concept Office building and so would combine the two initiatives well.

However, TW Property eventually decided to use another building project, not being built by TW Construction, as the first Concept Office, and this removed the possibility of combining the two projects. Since TW Property "owned" the Concept Office idea, TW Construction could not use it on non-TW Property projects. This internal separation between the Research and Development function of Taylor Woodrow, located within TW Construction, and the Property Division was a major structural problem for ProCure. They operated in effect as separate businesses, making co-operation difficult.

Business/economic issues. Despite the link with the Concept Office idea being broken, it still looked as if Christie Fields 2 (CF2) would be the construction project for the pilot. A kick-off meeting was held in January 2001 with the design team and project manager of Christie Fields 2. Progress began to be made: the project website was set up and the 3D modelling work started, shadowing the "live" design. There were delays due to planning permission, but this gave the modellers extra time to catch up with the live project. Then, at the end of July 2001, it emerged that the budget for CF2 was being cut significantly because of difficulty in letting office space in the already existing Christie Fields I building. In September, all work on CF2 was suspended indefinitely because of the general economic slow-down in office space requirements.

This was very disappointing for the UK pilot team, as there was no chance of starting again with another construction project at this late stage of the ProCure project. The best compromise was to finish the modelling and then simulate the process of communicating this to a steelwork fabricator, Quantrill, who agreed to take part in this process. Quantrill also agreed to use the project website.

Content issues of the pilot

During the short time that work was done on this pilot, some issues of content could begin to be identified. They will be discussed in terms of:

1.   the project website;
2.   3D modelling.

1. The website

Early doubts. At the initial meeting with the Christie Fields project manager, he expressed specific concerns about adopting the website for the project, expressed as the balance between costs and benefits. The costs were, in any case, easier to foresee than the benefits.

Costs:

● money;
● impact on the project team's work;
● protocols would need to be developed to use the website successfully, e.g., naming of documents (currently this was very informal), and the format of files when they were saved in the website.

Benefits:

● a quicker and more efficient way of communicating project information.

Also, at the beginning, there was some reluctance from the design team to put documents on the website. For example, the structural engineer was reluctant to issue information in a preliminary form before all changes were incorporated (and this was causing the project manager problems as it caused delays down the line).[3]

Early experiences. The structural engineer, architect, and project manager were interviewed at the end of 2001. They had used the website for three or four weeks during the detail design stage of Christie Fields. The issues that emerged were:

learning curve;
organization of documents;
layout of screens;
how the website is used;
accessibility of the website when away from the office;
e-mail notification;
paper *vs* electronic

The Christie Fields project, although referred to as just Christie Fields 2, actually consisted of several sub-projects. Four buildings had originally been planned (although the scope was then gradually reduced before the project was suspended altogether). Therefore, it would have been more useful if the documents on the website had been organized into separate groups, for each stage of the project.

The website chosen had been from a company called Sarcophagus. Websites set up for Tesco supermarket construction projects were found to be easier to use than the Sarcophagus website. This may be because the Tesco websites were designed by the contractors and so matched their requirements more closely. It was felt that in themselves the Tesco sites were more difficult; they were based on a hierarchy method, and to use this one needed to be familiar with how they should be ordered. However, the team was familiar with the Tesco method. So, because the Sarcophagus method, based on doing a keyword search, was intrinsically simpler, "we just threw people in . . . and they found it difficult."

Another consequence of the search method is that consistent terminology is needed. Since different people and organizations often use different terminology for the same thing, there is a need for protocols. Introducing protocols is difficult, as people may be working on several different projects with different protocols. The protocols also need to fit with each organization's protocols for document naming—the interface between the project website and the organization's document management needs to be handled. It was hoped that industry standards would develop.

Another related point was what happens if there is a search-based system and someone tries to find a document by using a keyword, but fails. The person will either assume it is not there, or try other keywords, or simply phone someone as the quickest way to get hold of it. The Sarcophagus website had no requirement that people provide document descriptions or keywords—there were no controls by the system.

Layout of screens. In terms of the human–computer interface, i.e., the layout of information on the screens, the format of the website was found not to be as easy to use as the Tesco websites.

How the website is used. The structural engineer and the architect were used to working together on projects and so had an estab-lished working practice. The structural engineer said that he would still like to work as they had done, but to use the website to commu-nicate the drawings when it was agreed that they were ready. He thought that this would be useful since subcontractors, who always need a lot of copies of drawings, could then access the information easily.

Also supporting this point was the fact that the architect and the structural engineer often exchanged documents that the project manager would not want to see. They could put them on the website and restrict access, but even so some end users did not see what added value that would give above the use of e-mail. (It was argued by the pilot project manager that the value would lie in the existence of an audit trail; this was one of a number of examples of long-term benefit not being relevant to short-term experience.)

The structural engineer felt that it would take time to use the website, and this would change the way they worked. Using e-mail is direct—when an e-mail is received all the information is there. A website needs to be checked every day, which is an extra step. (This issue was in fact addressed by the project website software vendor during the project, so that e-mail notifications were sent when documents were uploaded/amended on the website.)

The structural engineer pointed out that, even just using CAD drawings, procedures were needed to define how people should work with them to avoid confusion and mistakes. He felt that human checking of drawings was still needed.

Accessibility of the website when away from the office. The project manager had found that he had sometimes not been able to log in from other sites. Currently, he tended to carry files around. With the website he would, in theory, not have to do that—he could either download files to his laptop before leaving his workstation, or access the web remotely. One advantage of this was that he should be able to access any document at any time; with paper copies he could forget to take a file. However, he could be in a situation where he needed to make a quick decision based on a document but could not get access to the Internet.

E-mail notification. The architect had found it irritating that he was notified, along with all the relevant parties, even when he had put something on the web himself. Also, a balance needed to be found between making sure that people were aware of relevant material and not notifying them every time a document was uploaded. (Again, further enhancements to the e-mail notification system were later made to prevent this happening.)

Paper vs *electronic.* Given the present state of functionality:

- subcontractors were still driven by paper copies, they always want these in addition to electronic versions;
- the project manager said that he found it easier to process a stack of paper in an in-tray than electronic documents;
- all said that when they are sent information by e-mail, they just print it off;
- the project manager found that using the website was taking longer than using paper. Extracting information from the web takes far longer. For example, if you are not sure whether what you are looking for is within document a, b, c, or d, then to look on the website would involve downloading each document first to look in it. With paper files, you would just flick through them.

Main advantages. Having a central database of information.

Another possible advantage might be being able to provide the client with an as-built set of drawings. This is a requirement in all projects and currently was done via stacks of paper files. Providing a client access to a website removed storage space problems and could make it easier to find relevant information years after the build is complete. This could be used as a marketing tool—a real benefit to the client of using websites.[4]

2. 3D modelling

Early doubts. At the initial meeting with the architect and structural engineer on Christie Fields, it was apparent that they did not see advantages in 3D modelling. The main negative points raised in anticipation were:

- the architect thought that to use 3D he would have to design in 2D and then transfer that information to a 3D model. In fact, the idea behind the technology was that the designing would be done directly in 3D;
- the structural engineer and architect bear the costs but the benefits are gained further down the line, so why should they invest? For example, the fabricator currently worked in 3D and so receiving a 3D model would save him having to convert from 2D;
- the need for paper copies on site—how would this be done with 3D models?;
- even with 2D CAD, let alone with 3D, the project manager no longer gets rough sketches. People tend to do all the designs properly before sending them to him, so he has long periods in which he has no information and may become very anxious, and is then suddenly overwhelmed with information and documents.

Positive points raised were:

- changes only have to be made on one model rather than on several 2D diagrams;
- It saves time further down the line (e.g., for fabricators).

Early experiences. Points raised later, when experience had been gained, and from the 3D modellers:

- 3D models are generally used to produce 2D information on site rather than used as 3D; construction site workers do not have the technology to use 3D models to support their work;
- an effect of using 3D modelling might be budget changes—the structural engineer may demand a larger percentage of money, as they will be doing more of the work up front. This has various implications for budgets as well as for power relations within a design team;
- using 3D models can highlight problems more clearly and earlier than using 2D, but it cannot solve them—some people may have the expectation that it can;
- 3D models will also force the architects and structural engineers to be more "professional"—approximations will not be acceptable, so work will have to be of higher quality;
- it was thought that the architect also had concerns about quality issues—he was worried about others being able to alter his drawings;
- one of the 3D modellers from Corus explained that he still liked to print out drawings first before building the 3D model and that he found it difficult to see them on the computer ("you can't see the whole picture"). This is significant as it may apply more widely and therefore needs to be considered when proposing 3D modelling. It may be that people who were trained on a drawing board rather than a computer feel that they need to see a paper drawing to understand the design;
- some weeks into the work, one of the modellers reported that the architect had changed the design significantly, so the model had also needed significant changes. These changes had been much easier to make using 3D modelling than they would have been with 2D drawings. If, for example, a window needed to be moved by 500 mm, in 2D each separate line (and on several layers) would have had to be moved, but with a 3D model the whole object could just be repositioned;[5]
- the architect also said that previously relatively small changes to the building would require him to redraw all his drawings. The project manager was so concerned with the architect's problems in re-issuing drawings with amendments that he withheld some changes to the building that he would otherwise make (e.g.,

reducing the building height). This meant that the project manager would be bearing the costs of not making these changes, whereas with 3D modelling they would have been almost trivial.

Follow-up interview with the design team

About adopting 3D modelling, there was general agreement that whoever benefits should own the model and lead the project. The project manager felt that the ultimate beneficiary was the client, as it should mean that projects could be delivered cheaper or to better standard.

It was recognized that the model does not solve anomalies—it is still necessary to go back to each of the disciplines involved. However, it should certainly help to limit mistakes that occur on site. It was felt, on the other hand, that the number of mistakes and wastage on site was in any case much lower than it had been at the time of the Egan report (Construction Task Force, 1998). Processes had already improved since that time, so it was difficult to attribute causes. The level of wastage also depended upon the complexity of the build.

For 3D to work at the moment, particular processes and certain software packages are needed.

The structural engineer felt that 3D models would be more useful in certain complex projects such as a hospital, where a lot of mechanical and electrical services are designed in parallel rather than after the other design work.

The architect and the structural engineer did currently sometimes use 3D, but not for a whole job. They would only use it where there was real benefit for the client.

One advantage suggested by the project manager was that if they were repeating similar projects they could cut and paste parts of the model. This would enable them to make use of a far bigger proportion of similar data.

3D modelling forces one to think about the detail, and how it fits together, up-front of a project. There is a short-term cost for doing 3D modelling when it is first introduced, but over time this cost will disappear. The main barrier seems to be that it requires an investment rather than giving immediate returns.

It was felt that the main benefit was for the construction side rather than for design.

The German pilot

The workshop

INTRODUCTION—BACKGROUND AND OUTCOMES

The plans for the German pilot itself remained largely unchanged throughout the project, except in terms of scale. Two pilots had originally been planned, but as a result of reduced subcontract funding this had been reduced to one. The pilot was concerned with the more efficient management of CAD data (plans) by linking the document management systems of Daimler Chrysler and Ed Züblin to allow automatic transmission of data (Ed Züblin was the major construction contractor to Daimler-Chrysler).

One of the outcomes of the workshop was a decision to incorporate human and organizational issues in the contract documentation and the briefing meeting which is held between Daimler Chrysler and its contractors—together these determine the nature of their relationship and collaboration. It was also agreed to do some work within Ed Züblin and to conduct a literature review looking at error and new technology.

MEMBERSHIP

Eight people attended the workshop. It was our first encounter with a new head of the construction IT function in Daimler-Chrysler, responsible for factory planning in the IT Centre. He brought his operational colleague, the CAD Co-ordinator in the factory planning department, and he had also invited the managing director of a small construction company, STZ, who were regular contractors. In the course of the workshop, these three formed a view of how to take the work forward. Other participants were two from Ed Züblin, one from Haas and Partners, one visitor from Fortum Engineering in Finland and one from Corus in the UK. Two social scientists from The Bayswater Institute facilitated.

THE PROCESS

Throughout the two days, discussion of the pilot was interspersed with short presentations about relevant social science research and experience. For example, an analysis of what "human and organizational issues" means was in terms of concrete examples of human and organizational implementation problems from other projects. These illustrated the kind of effects that can result when new technology is introduced, and therefore also the possibility of considering them beforehand. In turn, the participants contributed examples where thinking about the people issues earlier would have been advantageous.

Another time there was discussion of different methods for dealing with implementation issues, and of transitional systems. The well-designed transitional system provides an opportunity to experiment with ways of relating to the new situation in an environment that is safe; it provides opportunities to try out more than one scenario, to contribute one's own experience and to make adjustments if necessary before adopting the new approach "live". The purpose of the pilots within ProCure should be to function as transitional systems.

DAY ONE

The pilot and Daimler-Chrysler's relationship with its contractors

The remountable car park having been dropped, the remaining pilot was concerned with linking the document management systems of Daimler Chrysler and Ed Züblin to allow automatic transmission of data. The current system involved exchanging data on floppy disks: EZ would phone DC to ask for the plans; DC would put them on disk and fill in forms to say who has asked for it and why they have given it to them; finally, someone from EZ would go to DC by car to pick up the disk (to satisfy security requirements they had to physically pass reception and complete their forms). During a project a lot of information has to be exchanged, and this was a very inefficient way of doing it. It could take up to four hours to exchange a set of documents.

One problem in moving towards exchanging data automatically was that the two organizations had different document management systems. DC had a system called *FAPLIS*, and EZ would have *WWB* to manage their documents (they currently had their own system, but this was limited). At the moment, when data was exchanged via floppy disk, each organization had to tell its own document management system where to store it. The aim of the pilot was to have this process carried out automatically by an intelligent software link.

There had been discussions with software companies and the link was being developed. EZ was already able to link in directly to DC, download the file, and also upload it. But the next stage would be trying to connect the two different EDMS systems. DC had given permission to cross some security levels. The pilot was using data from a building that had already been completed, so as to be able to compare the new way of working with the old in terms of cost, errors, time, etc.

When the new link was in place between DC and EZ, plans would be passed to EZ, but they are created in *Microstation* and EZ would have to modify them to add detail. To do this, they would first have to cut the plan up into smaller parts and then use their systems to add the detail. This would involve taking out a piece and redrawing it in *Zeicon* (their CAD package) with the new details. From this they would be able to see what the problems were, make the changes and then redraw it in *Microstation* to send to DC. A great benefit would be to do a direct translation.

When a new company wants to work with Daimler-Chrysler, they have to know about the data management systems from both the technical and the organizational side. The CAD Co-ordinator from Factory Planning sets up a meeting and explains the technical side (that they use *Microstation* etc.) and also the business side (the workflow, that they have to bring diskettes, that they have to sign contracts etc.). This process is called a "discussion", but DC is in a position to insist on what they require.

Three years before, DC had organized a "fair" for their contractors to inform them about the proposed new systems and found that the contractors were very interested in working in this new way. There is a benefit to small contractors in not having to drive back and forth with disks, and also in that the new system would be more flexible (they would be able to access the information outside standard working hours).

Human and organizational issues

Descriptions of the pilot and the participants' roles in relation to it triggered the beginning of discussing its effects. For instance, there might be great impact on people within contractor organizations who were currently responsible for dealing with the diskettes. A member of STZ called Beate, who was responsible for disks, came to be seen as exemplar, representing this issue.

At a general level, within DC, working with CAD was a political decision. Senior management liked to see 3D models, but had not considered the impact of changing the way of working to using CAD, so it was felt that there was a big gap between senior management ideas and the lower levels. In practice, although departments would produce the CAD data to show management, they still did the actual work in the old way. When models used to be made of wood, it was clear that this was only a model. With 3D models or "movies", it was not so clear and people assumed there was more behind it.

EZ was smaller than DC and there was not the same divide; in fact it tended to be the more junior people who wanted the more "way-out" technology. In both companies there was pressure to use 3D to win work.

Consequences for roles and tasks

At a specific level, roles likely to be affected by the change of working were as follows.

1. "Beate" (see above, p. 221)—not in the sense of an individual, but representing those whose current job was dealing with the fetching and sending of disks (sub-contractors).
2. In EZ's "Technical Office of Construction", all except the head of department.
3. All subcontractors of the DC factory planning department. Origins of problems will be unclear; the impact depends upon the size of company. Those who do not have their own IT departments will have to find support if they have problems, DC will not provide support for them.
4. All EZ's subcontractors.
5. The head of Construction IT will be affected personally if the system is not successful!
6. Technical operations services (who provide support) will have to support the new interfaces, encrypting across the web etc. This applies to both DC and EZ.

Also, the nature of problems would change. Where now there might be problems such as a disk not arriving, in future it was more likely to be problems with the data.

Consequences for organization

Within EZ, changes as a result of the new system will mainly affect the Technical Office for Construction.

Currently project managers have to sign off information before it is distributed, but with the new system they will not always do this. The engineers will be able to send documents out directly, so will have more responsibility. There was some concern that this could lead to more errors as there would be fewer checking stages—it would be up to the engineers to decide what the project managers have to see.

Other possible sources of misunderstanding could be from a reduction in informal communication—when everything is computerized there will be less opportunity to put informal notes on documents. Currently, when phone calls are made to check where the data are, other issues come up in the conversation, which might be problems that someone might not write down but that have been worrying them. When there is direct access to the data there will not be an explicit need for such phone calls. There may also be an increased chance of misunderstanding—a person might not realize that they need to know something or that they misunderstand something, but in an informal conversation this would come out. Another consequence of speeding up the processes is that there is less chance to talk to others—this is more efficient in that each person can work on more projects but means that there is less time for informal contact, or meetings. The people currently working at EZ realize that they need to go on talking to each other; however, when younger people come in who have not worked in the "old" way, they might not realize the value of the informal contact.

As an inherent effect of using computers, there would be more information available, but there was some concern as to whether there would be time to read it all or check it all. It was also felt to be harder to look at the information on a screen than on paper—on paper it is possible to see the whole diagram, whereas on a computer screen only a small section of the drawing is visible at one time.

Within DC, changes will occur in several departments.

The role of the technical support people will change. They used to have to deal with chasing up disks, or problems related to the data on the disks. The new system will create different technical problems. Other departments affected will be the IT department, the user department, and the care line.

For STC, the effect of the new way of working will be more time to work for other clients, as they will not be spending time travelling to exchange data. There is not a one-way dependency between STZ and DC: DC are also dependent on STZ, as the projects they work on are critical for DC. Both organizations learn from each other (DC learn from the small units as these are more flexible and so have more scope to try out new technology).

DAY TWO

On the second day the earlier discussions were revisited, to identify which issues were important, which ones could be addressed now, and what actions could be taken. It was suggested that some social content could be put into the briefing papers and meetings between DC and their contractors. However, this would be difficult as they do not have staff with the relevant knowledge; the general culture was one of being only interested in the technical aspects—whether something is working or not. It was suggested that the BI should help DC to modify contract documentation to include the social aspects and then to review it. This would then be used in the initial briefing meetings.

The analysis of who would be affected was revisited in some detail with a view to actions. It turned out that for DC the briefing meeting seemed to be central to many of the potential actions. For EZ the only action that emerged at this point was to increase the number of face-to-face meetings. This could be done as the changes, etc., would be quicker and they would not have to wait so long for something to be done before they met again. This might offset the reduction in informal information exchanges.

The implementation checklist (see Appendix II) was then used to work through the implications more systematically.

Errors

Concern had been voiced about the increased risk of errors when there are fewer review points and the increased speed means that there is less time to check for errors. People would be unlikely to spend time working to checklists (as in the aviation industry), since getting the work done quickly was seen as more important. It was agreed that BI would conduct a short literature review on the impact of speed on errors, and quality control in new technologies.[6]

Methods

After discussion about transitional systems, the head of Construction IT said that DC would be piloting the software with selected contractors before using it live; they were used to doing that. He accepted a suggestion from the social scientists of using different contractors for this each time, rather than always using the same ones, to avoid "hostage syndrome", where the hostage falls in love with their captor, i.e., the user identifies with the IT department and moves away from their role as a user.

CONCLUSIONS

Prior to this workshop, it appeared that the German group did not see the need to have any social science involvement with their pilot. Also at that stage, with the limited knowledge that BI had about the pilot and the people involved, it was not possible for the social scientists to provide the team with a list of likely issues that they might come up against. It had in any case been important that the German team identified such issues themselves.

As the workshop progressed, a number of human and organizational issues that would impact upon the success of the implementation of the new technology were identified by the German team. It was acknowledged that the traditional approach had been to concentrate on getting the technology right and only then to consider the impact upon the people and the organization. During the workshop an increased understanding of the types of issues that might arise developed, as well as acknowledgement that it might be advantageous to look at these at an earlier stage.

The pilot project

The head of Daimler-Chrysler's construction IT function and his colleague paid a two-day visit to the Bayswater Institute, in order to develop further the idea of adding concern for human and organizational implications to the company's "conversations" with prospective contractors. In the course of it, we simultaneously realized that to impose standards in such matters was a contradiction in terms. What potential contractors would need to demonstrate was that they were systematically reviewing human and organizational aspects of their work.

Similarly, a colleague from the main contractor, Ed Züblin, paid a two-day visit to plan following the work through within EZ.

ED ZÜBLIN

Züblin conducted an internal study of the anticipated effects on staff of the Central Planning Department of moving to the use of *PlanNet*. It consisted of asking the head of department, a project manager, a project engineer, a draughtsman, and a secretary:

(a) to describe the main categories into which their work was currently subdivided, and

(b) to estimate the percentage of work in each category carried out within different kinds and levels of control. They estimated this with regard to their current situation, before the introduction of *PlanNet*, and with regard to a likely future, when it would be in use. Social scientists were not involved, and experiences and attitudes were not included as categories.

DAIMLER-CHRYSLER

We had learned that Daimler-Chrysler normally begins every construction project necessitating data exchange with a "coordination meeting" or "conversation" between the parties involved— client, CAD representative, and contractor—to discuss, specify, and record in particular the organizational and technical rules that are to apply. It results in a "coordination meeting checklist", which is regarded as binding, although not necessarily in the form of a formal contract—all parties prefer to come to agreements that do not involve the bureaucratic and legalistic aspects of contracting (and the involvement with companies' legal departments which goes with that). The suggestion now was that it should become part of this coordination meeting, and of the checklist that follows it, that contractors should take certain measures to ensure that human and organizational issues are taken care of.

Daimler-Chrysler and 3D

Because this project needed to be reported, DC were asked for some description of what exactly people were being asked to implement, and this follows, with acknowledgements to DC staff:

> It is central to the philosophy of Daimler-Chrysler that the factory is an integral element in the manufacture of a product. Cars are now to a high degree being developed digitally. So that the factory can keep pace with the speed of car development and shorter product cycles, it has become necessary for the process of factory planning itself to be digital.
>
> It is for this reason that factory planning itself is being forcibly changed from 2D to 3D. Since 2000 the "digital factory" has become a policy and strategic goal of Daimler-Chrysler AG. The aim is that, from 2005 no plant will be built which has not undergone comprehensive virtual simulation in advance.
>
> The general aims for *Digital Factory Planning* are:
>
> - to arrive at high quality planning results in shorter times;
> - to reduce planning costs by digital networking of all relevant functions within the process and planning chain;
> - to avoid redundancy of planning and working;
> - the construction of a modular "3D factory unit construction system" to support efficient factory design and development;
> - 3D models for Virtual Factory prototyping.
>
> In parallel with the target of the "digital factory", a company-wide process of standardization has been set in train, the results of which flow into the "digital factory" project. The aim of this standardization process is comprehensive 3D factory planning, across all disciplines, based on planning with 3D standard modules. These standard modules are currently being defined in across-site working groups. The assumption for this is that 3D planning will be applied in all aspects of the factory planning process, i.e. architecture, facility planning, electrics, conveyor technology, layout, etc.
>
> To standardize the work within the 3D environment, agreements have been made across departments which lay down certain

planning standards concerning CAD. (N.B.: There is a need to differentiate between standard modules defined for the different departments and the general CAD standards which have to be kept.) The standardisation defines which elements of a building are represented, how, and in which data file. It is the basis for one of the targets of 3D planning, to provide a check for interference and collision between different planning disciplines. 3D does not mean that the factory planners generate an exact virtual model 1:1, but that they are able to make an interference check in the planning phase. This will enable them to work in a time-effective and above all cost-effective way.

The collaboration with Daimler-Chrysler

So, at a first follow-up meeting with the Daimler-Chrysler colleagues after the workshop, the original idea was modified: contractors would not be required to implement certain standards or procedures, but would be required to keep the human and organizational aspects under regular review. This fitted in better with the social scientists' values in that it was less in a control framework and more developmental than the first version, and also allowed for the possibility of unexpected consequences. From the DC point of view, it fitted in well with a company policy about "continuing improvement", and was therefore more likely to be accepted by management.

An instrument for such review was developed in iteration between the BI and DC, and translated into German (since the merger with Chrysler, senior DC staff were expected to work in English, but this could not be expected of building contractors). DC recruited three small contractor firms whose managers were willing to try this instrument out on a pilot basis. At that time, the new technologies being considered concerned the standardization of fonts and colours and the change to 3D planning. The experience of trying to standardize fonts and colours had alerted DC to the fact that contractors and their experiences had not been involved enough.

The instrument was discussed in draft with the three managers, who began to take an interest in questionnaire design, had some criticisms of the translation, and made some contributions to the design. By the time of that meeting, DC had decided to make the use of 3D planning compulsory from May 2002, and the exercise had become real and urgent. From then on the pilot exercise concentrated on 3D working.

The review instrument was then tried out by the three firms, and the answers (four responses from the three firms) were collated. For reporting, they had to be translated back into English.

While this was happening, DC tried the instrument out in two further companies. These results were more differentiated than the first three, and raised questions about the suitability of the instrument. In discussing the results of the pilot exercise with the first three firms, it also became clear that a questionnaire does not allow for enough expression of experience; to yield real understanding, there needs to be some interviewing as well.

These developments had started late in the ProCure time-scale. As the project was nearing its end, the head of construction IT requested an in-house budget that would enable the social science input to continue after the end of ProCure. It was felt to fit into company policy under the heading "continuous improvement", as well as "continual evaluation". The budget was not agreed, at least for the year 2003. However, some of the DC staff who conduct the co-ordination meetings continued to use the questionnaire. Moreover, the process had become iterative: review discussions between DC and its contractors during the course of projects and at the end of projects had been added to it.

I do not know whether this has lasted and how it has worked out in the long run. To be honest, I am afraid to find out.

Some reflections

The project provided an opportunity to explore adding an explicit contribution from the social sciences, about human and organizational aspects, to the agenda for technical change. It led to many reflections—listed below are some of them.

1. When new ICT systems are being developed and implemented, there are significant human and organizational issues that need to be addressed. In spite of many difficulties, it was possible for people to identify these issues at an early stage and to do some

work on anticipating them and planning how to deal with them; and it was possible for lay people to learn enough about the new technologies to be able to engage with the engineers in useful ways.

2. There has been much research about these issues. It is more important to find ways of working with what is known already than to instigate new research. That is why we proposed a model where social scientists would accompany a technical development long-term, with a view to making use of the methods, concepts and findings of the social sciences as and when issues arose.

    This model, of longitudinal accompanying research in an action research framework, seems to me to remain relevant. To the original reason, that the potential issues are many and varied and can arise at different times, must be added a second one in the light of the ProCure experience: it is that over time the context will change in unforeseeable ways.

3. Most of the difficulties experienced by ProCure were due to conducting a research project in an operational and business environment. Over the course of three years, nearly all the partners experienced major structural and policy changes. Research and funding frameworks and project plans need to assume that this is likely to happen, and build flexibility into their planning instruments.

    The UK pilot in particular illustrates the importance and relevance of context, as does to some extent the situation in the Finnish pilot. A research project within an operating company needs the systems around it more than those systems, at that stage, need the research project. The need to co-ordinate with those systems is likely to lead to unpredictable delays.

4. "Resistance" to a new technology should not be dismissed as "irrational":

    ● there may be no demonstrable link between long-term benefits and short-term experience;
    ● it may be that the benefits of the technology arise in a different place from the costs—at a different level of the organization, or in a different part of the supply chain. In such a case there may be a need to re-distribute the costs and benefits;

- the user may already have a good solution to the problem. If one finds out what benefits he is experiencing, it may be possible to incorporate them in the new system.

5. The usual methods of piloting new technologies, involving historical or hypothetical data for simulation, are unreliable. They depend on the limits of imagination and they permit the intrusion of wishful thinking. Simulations and pilot exercises must involve real data and real users, however "messy" the results appear. Such "messiness" may turn out to be the most useful outcome.

Notes

1. ESPRIT 29948. The final report on the project can be found online at http://cic.vtt.fi/projects/procure.
2. Daimler Chrysler not only manufacture cars, they build production and research facilities. Ed. Züblin AG, Stuttgart, is one of the largest German contractors in the field of building construction and civil engineering, and is DC's main building contractor.
3. This is very like the experience of the hospital staff in Chapter Six, who were unwilling to put information on the computer before it was certain or complete.
4. According to the ProCure project manager, this point has become even more important than it was at the time, as people increasingly want good information about their building.
5. This had been one of the prime reasons for undertaking the ProCure project.
6. This literature review later formed an additional deliverable (R3503 - "Using new technology in the German pilot: Implications for human error").

SECTION IV

THE BOUNDARIES WITH OTHER PROFESSIONS

The previous section has shown that the work people do gets designed almost indirectly, as a result of the work of many other professions. My experiences of research and action research inevitably brought a good deal of contact and collaboration with various parts of the engineering professions, system designers and ergonomists. That also brought with it taking part in some of their conferences and contributing to their publications. The papers in this section are a selection from that material. In these papers, experiences and findings from the research and action research described earlier are used to illustrate broader points. I have edited them to minimize repetition, but it is inevitable that some examples are used more than once, in different contexts and for different audiences.

There is also an element of proselytizing. Of course one tries to persuade! Engineers and system designers influence the design of jobs and the organization of work directly but implicitly, ergonomists contribute to it explicitly, politicians and administrators do it indirectly—over the years I seem to have had a go at all of them. But I have wanted to persuade with scientific justification. While I find the current mantra of "evidence-based" a bit cheesy, I believe there is a need to justify one's position, and hope that I managed it.

CHAPTER TWELVE

The production engineer's role in industrial relations

The 1970s were a time of difficult industrial relations in Britain. They were also a time of strong interest in questions of work satisfaction and job design throughout Europe. Having started in Norway in the 1960s, the ideas were most widely emulated and developed in Sweden. The car company, Volvo, designed and built a manufacturing plant for autonomous group working, and the publicity around this probably did more than anything to draw attention to the ideas. In the UK, a Work Research Unit was set up in the Department of Employment, and even the characters in *Coronation Street* talked the language of work satisfaction.

The professional engineering institutions became interested. This chapter gives the edited text of a lecture given in 1977 at a conference of production engineers, which was later published in their journal (Klein, 1978). Today, I would say for production engineer also read IT system designer.

*   *   *

Production process design

I want to discuss first some aspects of the design of production processes and later their connection with industrial relations.

Nowadays there are few people in the management professions who have not at least heard about some questions that are being asked about the nature of industrial jobs and some attempts that are being made to redesign them. It is difficult to know how much of such discussions or changes is familiar to this audience. You may have come across them in the context of theories of human motivation, or research about job satisfaction, or particular experiments, or the experience of particular companies like Volvo.

I have to make some assumptions about this audience, and I will assume that you have heard of these things, but mainly at the level of exhortation and propaganda. This is not a good position to be in, because all it does is make you feel uncomfortable and possibly resentful, without giving you anything tangible to get hold of.

Since there is nothing as practical as a good theory, let me begin with a brief reference to sociotechnical theory. This should get us out of the realm of mere exhortation. Sociotechnical theory makes explicit a simple fact, namely that the technology and the people in a production system are interdependent. Each affects the other. Technology affects the behaviour of people, and the behaviour of people affects the working of the technology. It is inevitable, it is a real part of the situation, and one needs therefore to take account of *how* they affect each other.

Production engineers know these things perfectly well, but they keep the knowledge in a separate compartment, as somehow less "real" than their knowledge about the behaviour of materials, and they therefore do not make use of it. Putting this another way, they generally define the systems they are dealing with in such a way as to exclude some relevant data. These data may be quite well known, but are regarded as an irritating interference with an otherwise beautiful rationality, rather than a part of the reality.

Let me illustrate this with a very small-scale example from recent experience. I am doing some work with a company that is building a new factory. The terms of reference are that they would like, for once, to get the human and social aspects of the work system taken account of at the design stage. As part of the preparatory work, I did a study in one of their older factories, where the product to be made in the new plant is already being produced. It is a food product. At one stage the finished items come sliding down a chute at the left of an operator, are carried from left to right along a belt on which they are shuffled into rows, before moving into a wrapping machine that wraps them as packets. The operator monitors this process, picks out any broken or jammed items, sees that the wrapping machine is supplied with paper, etc. There are eight of these arrangements spaced along the room, each one involving a chute, a moving belt, a wrapping machine and an operator.

During the preliminary study, an operator pointed out that it would be much better if the equipment was grouped together in pairs, four pairs of belts running parallel and attended by four pairs of operators, instead of eight single ones. "I'd have a mate, opposite me," she said. "We could talk. And we could help each other out. When I go to the toilet I wouldn't have to switch off, because she could watch mine for a bit." (What actually happens now is that, when the supervisor is not looking, operators switch off in order to visit each other for a chat.)

The suggestion constitutes a small, not very radical, improvement to take account of sociotechnical interdependence. When it was conveyed to management, they found that there was no chance of persuading the machine tool manufacturers to make the equipment so that some run from left to right and some from right to left, with the controls in the mirror position, which would have to be the case if operators were to face each other in pairs instead of looking at each other's backs.

Now, why on earth not? It is no kind of technical challenge. But it is a much bigger challenge than that—it is a challenge to seeing and acknowledging the operator and her role as a real part of the system. Production engineers see the operator's part in production systems as sets of disembodied tasks, with associated costs. They are not trained to see how such tasks and the experience of doing them combine into roles. So deeply ingrained is the traditional engineer's way of perceiving, that even in this company the engineer who went to see the manufacturers to try to persuade them to make the equipment to run in both directions thought he was doing so because it might then be possible to have one operator running two belts!

Two lessons from this example are, first, that there is no such thing as a "green field". There is no situation that does not have a history, and historically based constraints. If a project is serious, one has to penetrate back into equipment manufacturers and *their* designers. Second, it was quite salutary to discover that, even in a company that was making such explicit efforts, the message had not got through to all the staff.

I think the story really exemplifies most of the issues and it also anticipates, I believe rather obviously, the link between production engineering and industrial relations. But let me first say a little more about sociotechnical theory.

There is nothing new about the idea that people and work systems affect each other. Already in the 1920s there was research showing that, when people have a large number of things to process, for example, sweets to wrap, they tend to subdivide them into a number of smaller heaps, in order to experience achievement more often. Again, research in the 1920s showed that people do not work at the same pace throughout the working day, but vary their pace (Harding, 1931; Vernon, Wyatt, & Ogden, 1924; Wyatt & Fraser, 1928). This kind of knowledge about behaviour is not very subtle, and not very threatening. It does not go to the mysterious springs of human motivation. But it has never found its way into the design strategies of production engineering.

Sociotechnical concepts were first put forward in theoretical terms as a result of some studies of technical change in coal mining that were carried out by the Tavistock Institute in the late 1940s (Trist & Bamforth, 1951). In the coal-face studied, the cycle of coal-getting involved three operations:

- preparation, concerned with making the coal more accessible and workable;
- getting, in which the coal was loaded and transported away from the face;
- advancing, in which roof supports, gateway haulage roads, and conveyor equipment were advanced.

This cycle was carried out by small teams of miners who were (a) multi-skilled (i.e., each man could perform each of the tasks), and (b) self-regulating (i.e., what needed to be done was obvious from the situation, and they simply did it, without intervention from supervision).

With a higher level of mechanization, this cycle was split up over three shifts, each carrying out only one of the tasks. And it didn't work. Or rather, it worked, but the productivity increases predicted by the production engineers did not come off.

The new system required for its operation forty–fifty men, each working on a single task. The work organization that resulted was one in which the different teams were now working independently in shifts, each on different piece rates, but, by the nature of the task, dependent on one another to get their work done. Each of these teams of workers, optimizing conditions for itself, created and passed on poor conditions to the work groups responsible for subsequent tasks. Instead of enabling them to co-operate with one another, the new system created irresolvable conditions for inter-personal and intergroup conflict, resulting in competitive individualism, mutual scapegoating, and a high level of absenteeism, all of which contributed to the low level of productivity. At the same time all the controlling and co-ordinating activities now had to come from outside and above the teams, since no one at the workface knew the whole story.

It was this study that made clear how the technical and social systems need to be seen in relation to each other. Historically, what seems to have happened is this: first engineering, then production engineering, then work study and, in administrative work, Organization and Methods, have aimed at optimizing the technical system as if it were self-contained. In the process some other things were neglected, and that gave rise to a number of reactions. One of these, from the ranks of a particular kind of behavioural science, has been to try to optimize the social system as if this, in turn, were self-contained. We therefore get programmes and activities to do with communications, relationships, styles of management, participative leadership, which in their turn take no account of task or technology. Both approaches define inappropriately the boundaries of the system to be optimized. As a result, although a good deal has been said and indeed done to improve human relations in industry, it has remained a matter of separate compartments and what appears to be lip-service. It seems to be no easier than it ever was to integrate these concerns with the everyday working reality.

Allow me to make the point about interdependence once more, with an illustration from a different industry. It comes from an early study of human relations in the restaurant industry in America (Whyte, 1948). In some large restaurants, with several floors, a section of the process that was liable to much stress and friction was the service pantry. This was the stage where waitresses conveyed orders from the customers to countermen, who passed them to the kitchen and managed the flow of completed orders from the kitchen. The waitresses wrote out order slips and placed them on a spindle for the countermen to take off, or shouted their orders. The height and layout of the counter and, in particular, the existence of a spindle on which the orders were placed, played a significant part in the delicate and stressful relationship between the waitresses and the countermen.

What solutions does one look for in such a situation? If you love technical rationality and regard people as a messy, irrational nuisance, you will find a way to automate the system and eliminate human intervention. If you are merely fascinated by human relationships, you are likely to set up discussion processes between the two departments about their communications and relationships.

I find both approaches less than best. The exciting task—and this now takes us a long way beyond the simple example of the spindle—is to design technology so that it is congruent with human characteristics and good human relations.

What seems to me an important breakthrough has been made recently in Germany. The German government four years ago launched a programme called "Humanizing Life at Work". Companies that want to make changes in work organization can get large grants. They have to formulate what they want to do in agreement with the local works councils, estimate the costs, and, if the plans are approved, they can get up to three-quarters of the costs back from the Ministry of Research and Technology, on condition that they allow the work to be researched.

Two things about this programme are of particular interest in our context. One is that the sums involved have been rather large, permitting engineering research and development and engineering changes. The other is that the initiative in working out the changes has usually been taken by a company's engineers. German social scientists generally stick to research and do not, so far, get into consulting and advisory roles.

The changes have, in many cases, not been very radical or comprehensive, but they have got into the technology; i.e., they are more likely to be permanent and to be applicable on a large scale and not confined to local projects. For instance, some engineers have taken on board the need to free workers from machine-pacing, the idea that they and not it should determine pace. There is therefore a lot of work being done on the subject of buffer stocks.

The methodological break-through that I want to describe comes in the work of a group of production engineers in the University of Stuttgart (Metzger, Warnecke, & Zippe, 1975). They have been researching on alternatives in production design and strategies for selecting from them. In existing systems they are working on methods of costing that should include at least some of the human costs, like absenteeism and labour turnover, so that the real costs of a system may be known and more realistic choices made. In the design of new systems they have evolved a design strategy that goes like this.

They get together a design team, including two members of the elected works council. To this team they present about ten design criteria for the human aspects of the system. They did not take these criteria from the social science literature, but from their own thinking and introspection. They include such things as the opportunity to learn more than one task, the opportunity to move about in the course of the job, the opportunity to communicate with others, the opportunity to do one's own inspection. They get the design team to give these criteria an importance weighting, by doing paired comparisons: taking the first two criteria, is 1 more important than 2, 2 more important than 1, or are they equal? Then 2 and 3 as a pair, and so on.

The design team is then presented with a number of different ways of doing a job. In the example that I witnessed, and that concerned an assembly task, seven different layouts had been prepared. The members of the design team assess each of the layouts, giving it a score out of ten on each of the design criteria (opportunity to learn, to communicate, to move about, etc.) By taking these scores, and weighting them according to the results of the previous exercise, one arrives at a quantified "best buy", in human terms, *according to the values of that place*. This is then put up against the economic best buy, which has been arrived at by normal costing methods, and the outcome negotiated. In the example that I saw, the solution picked was the layout which had come second on the human side, because the highest-scoring one had been judged too costly.

This design strategy is already under criticism from a number of points of view. Some people say it is very mechanistic. Some are asking why there are two workers' representatives in the team, why not half the team? Others are asking why have representatives, why not the operators themselves? Or why these particular criteria, why not any number of others? Why these particular layouts, why not any number of possible others?

It is not necessary to make up one's mind on all these questions. The important thing is to grasp the essential core of the strategy: it is to find a way of making values explicit, which usually remain implicit in production design; of putting them on the table for discussion and if necessary negotiation; and then of incorporating them into production design.

The importance of this cannot be overstated. Some of you may be asking "why bother?" and that brings us to the other part of the question—what has all this to do with industrial relations?

The industrial relations aspect

For this, we need to go back for a while to the early days of the industrial revolution. We tend to think of them as a time when wicked employers exploited working people, and particularly children and women, under appalling conditions of work that are unthinkable today. We forget that this did not happen because the people of that time were unusually wicked. Child labour came to be used simply because machines were developed which were so simple that a child could tend them:

> Whenever a process requires peculiar dexterity and steadiness of hand, it is withdrawn, as soon as possible, from the cunning workman, who is prone to irregularities of many kinds, and it is placed in charge of a peculiar mechanism, so self-regulating that a child can superintend it. [Marx, 1958, pp. 432–433]

Women were employed and men put out of work because it is not rational to spend more strength or money than necessary. Hours of work were as long as human strength permitted because it is illogical to have costly machinery standing idle.

Not only working conditions, but working experience and roles were closely influenced by the nature of the technology. Here is one detailed contemporary description of this process.

In the English letter-press printing trade, for example, there existed formerly a system, corresponding to that in the old manufactures and handicrafts, of advancing the apprentices from easy to more and more difficult work. They went through a course of teaching till they were finished printers. To be able to read and write was for every one of them a requirement of their trade. All this was changed by the printing machine. It employs two sorts of labourers, one grown up, tenters, the other, boys mostly from 11 to 17 years of age whose sole business is either to spread the sheets of paper under the machine, or to take from it the printed sheets A great part of them cannot read, and they are, as a rule, utter savages and very extraordinary creatures. To qualify them for the work which they have to do, they require no intellectual training; there is little room in it for skill, and less for judgement; their wages, though rather high for boys, do not increase proportionately as they grow up, and the majority of them cannot look for advancement to the better paid and more responsible post of machine minder, because while each machine has but one minder it has at least two, and often four, boys attached to it. As soon as they get too old for such child's work, that is about 17 at the latest, they are discharged from the printing establishments. They become recruits of crime. Several attempts to procure them employment elsewhere were rendered of no avail by their ignorance and brutality. [*ibid.*, pp. 484–485]

Here is another, more general, description:

In handicrafts and manufacture, the workman makes use of a tool, in the factory, the machine makes use of him. There the movements of the instrument of labour proceed from him, here it is the movements of the machine that he must follow. In manufacture the workmen are parts of a living mechanism. In the factory we have a lifeless mechanism independent of the workman, who becomes its mere living appendage . . . The separation of the intellectual powers of production from the manual labour is, as we have already shown, finally completed by modern industry erected on the foundation of machinery. The special skill of each individual insignificant factory operative vanishes as an infinitesimal quantity before the science, the gigantic physical forces, and the mass of labour that are embodied in the factory mechanism. [*ibid.*, pp. 422–423]

You may be surprised to hear that all the quotations I have used come from Karl Marx's *Capital*. His book contains many fascinating analyses of the social consequences of technology. It took time to recognize and understand negative consequences and to tackle them, by legislation, by trade union combination, and by political action, and in the formation of attitudes and responses that time-lag has been all-important. Why are there, throughout Europe, political parties with the word "labour" or "worker" in their title? Because technology and the division of labour led to sections of the population being identifiable as "workers", whose experience of life was sufficiently homogeneous to give them interests in common.

The only thing wrong with Marx's analysis is that he jumped to the wrong conclusion. He attributed the problems of the industrial revolution to the greed of capitalist owners. We have seen that a change of ownership alone does not necessarily effect changes in the working experience of employees. The design of production processes is, of course, influenced by the wishes of owners and the need for profit; but we all know that companies do not necessarily maximize profits but have some other criteria as well, and how much directors in turn can be influenced by the sheer technical excitement of a new process and the persuasiveness of their technologists.

Where social consequences are considered at that stage, it is usually in terms of the short-term consequences, which are frequently called "resistance to change". It is at least as important to consider the long-term adaptations and adjustments that are likely to be made to any particular change. The industrial relations scene of today represents the long-term adjustment people have made to their working situation, and it is in this context of long-term adaptation that I invite you to consider the comment made to me recently by a young German trade unionist: "You mustn't do away with the mass-production assembly line, because the mass-production assembly line is the basis of collective organisation [*die Kollektive*]".

This is not a mere academic romp. In the most serious and real sense, the design philosophies and design strategies of today's production engineering play a large part in shaping the roles and conditions in which tomorrow's workers find themselves, and with them the attitudes and behaviour to which those experiences give rise. Show me your control system and I will tell you where the fiddles will arise. You are the people who influence who will have work, how closely and in what relation to each other they will work, what skills they will develop, how much control they will have over their own work situation, what decisions they will make, and therefore what practice in the making of decisions they will get. Marx and his followers have focused on ownership as the determining influence. I think it is production engineering that is the determining influence, and I believe it is in the training of production engineers that not only industrial relations but, to quite a large extent, social relations in a wider sense are shaped. As I said, Marx merely drew the wrong conclusion.

CHAPTER THIRTEEN

"Satisfactions in work design": some problems of theory and method

I have worked with ergonomists, learned from ergonomists, and argued with ergonomists. The learning has largely been about methods, and I have admired and envied the way they have confronted the need to get into design and the way their contributions to design have become institutionalized. The arguments, on the other hand, have been about the boundaries of the subject, questions of measurement, and whether only human aspects that are susceptible to quantification are important in the design of jobs.

This chapter presents a paper that was addressed to a conference of the International Ergonomics Association entitled "Satisfactions in work design" in 1977 (Klein, 1979). It was partly a response to an attack on the "softer" social sciences and their use of value judgement.

* * *

I am glad and interested to see ergonomists exploring outside their traditional boundaries, but sorry that they have chosen to focus on "job satisfaction".

Job satisfaction is not a design goal. As far as I know, it has never been the goal of serious researchers and action researchers working empirically in the field of job design. It may be an indicator that one is reaching or failing to reach a goal, but even then it is not a very reliable one. National surveys consistently show something like 75% to 80% of people as being fairly well satisfied with their current work situation—but I don't know what that means. I can interpret comments indicating dissatisfaction because they are usually about specific issues. I can sometimes interpret comments about specific items on the positive side. But I don't know what to do with general aggregate measures of satisfaction except, very occasionally, as indicators of trend, and I know of no one who uses them as anything else.

The work of the Tavistock Institute of Human Relations has been one of the main influences in opening the door to the possibility of choosing from among alternative forms of work organization, or alternative job designs, according to criteria to do with people; and in that work you will not find job satisfaction mentioned. What you will find mentioned are roles (as distinct from tasks), role relationships, interdependence, and criteria for the design of jobs that are to do with learning, development, and growth.

What this is about seems to me to be very simple and not to require all those tortured little models. Because a large part of people's waking life is spent at work, work should have some characteristics and provide some experiences that are helpful to their development. This suggests that the design of jobs should incorporate design criteria such as the opportunity to continue learning, to relate to and communicate with others, to contribute to the setting of standards, to have feed-back on one's performance, to have some control over one's own work situation, at least over such things as pace and movement, to use and develop skills.

Certainly, criteria such as these are based on value judgement. I cannot ask clients to share this value judgement, but I can offer it to them to accept or reject, and I can offer them strategies for making their own values explicit. The problem is that you cannot ask someone whether he wants an apple if he has no previous experience of apples. You have to provide an opportunity to try apples before deciding whether to accept or reject them. Since any client population is in any case unlikely to be homogeneous, the challenge to the designer is to provide for opportunities which do not have to be taken up, or which can be taken up differentially. That is not beyond the bounds of ingenuity and that is what one's work is about.

I also cannot ask the ergonomist as a job designer to share my values, but I can ask as a scientist that he or she should make their own values explicit. Every job design has values implicit in it and ergonomists, no less than people working in the "softer" human sciences, have a responsibility to make their values manifest and to let their clients choose whether they share them, and not to pretend that they come from some realm where choices do not have to be made.

Let me change frames of reference for a moment from individual psychology to sociology and structure. If you separate the setting of standards from the meeting of standards and allocate these functions to different roles in the system, then I can predict that those who are being controlled will try to find ways to regain control. In any specific control system I can predict where the fiddles will be. If you set things up so that one set of people makes decisions and a different set of people is required to carry them out, there will be structural division in the institution concerned. The people involved may or may not express satisfaction; I don't know. I do know that conflict will have been designed into the system and that the response will be either overt conflict or some form of withdrawal.

It may be that, in terms of psychological health, conflict is preferable to passivity. There are, in fact, many people now who believe that structural division in industry is an entirely satisfactory state of affairs and should not be interfered with. How you react to this is a political choice; in any case, design choices are followed by adaptations and adjustments. They have long-term behavioural consequences and professionals have a responsibility to take that seriously and not to play academic parlour games.

A non-political way of putting what I have just been saying is that people make adjustments and adaptations to the work situations in which they find themselves. When you redesign a job (and we are not often in a green-field situation, working with new jobs), you are not only attacking the structure of that job, you are also attacking the adjustment and adaptations that people have already made to it. And that is the dilemma—we are working in a context.

It is not only an ethical and political dilemma, but a scientific one. Context is the problem surrounding the validity of findings in the social sciences. From the social science world come ideas with varying degrees of verification. Maslow's hierarchy of needs concept and Herzberg's two-factor theory of motivation are examples of ideas that, in parts of the social science community, are regarded as inadequately verified, while in parts of the user community they are regarded as useful products of social science. There are probably no findings so respectable as to remain completely unchallenged.

Absence of consensus about what are valid findings is partly due to the politics and career structure of academic life To some extent, the identity and worth of one's own work, or that of one's team or school, are established by challenging the work of others, and this may not necessarily be done by replicating the work but by using different methods that, in any case, are likely to lead to different findings. However, there is another consideration, which is more intrinsic to the subject matter: the distinction between an idea and a valid finding is, in principle, less fundamental in the social sciences than in the natural sciences because of the greater influence of differences in context. Even in the same historical period, different ideas which are not apparently compatible are put forward simultaneously, but concerning which one can find evidence if one looks carefully enough. Even more, a different geographical or historical context will affect the evidence for the same idea. Differences in context mean that some investigations are not repeatable, or not repeatable in the same form. Differences in context and time probably constitute the greatest problem in establishing any fundamental parallels between the social and the natural sciences.

However, this does not imply chaos, and total relativism. There are underlying generalities over which different concrete manifestations cluster. In the field that is generally called behaviour in organizations—although this is a phrase I dislike—I can suggest three examples of such underlying generalities that probably have a more than temporary validity.

First, the structural characteristics implied by time, market, technology, and control systems in an organization will have behavioural consequences. Second, within narrower systems boundaries, the structural characteristics of jobs and work roles have some psychological consequences for the people doing them; in turn, people can influence the structure of their environment to some extent. The technical and social systems are interdependent. Third, process as well as content is relevant. This implies, first, that how things are done (for instance, how changes are introduced) will be relevant to outcomes a well as the content of what is done. And it implies, second, that groups and organizations can learn to review themselves and treat the processes by which they work as subjects for explicit consideration.

When it comes to application, context again makes replication and comparison difficult: whether an organization is the first pioneer to try out a new concept, or the twentieth follower, or whether it is compelled into application by policy or by law, will make a substantial difference to the result, and this really complicates our work tremendously. The enthusiasm with which something is being introduced may be the most influential factor around. On the other hand, sophisticated subjects may become immune to the Hawthorne effect and some change strategies may not be effective when tried repeatedly.

Now, I have been in the habit of thinking that these are problems of social psychology and sociology, and that psychology is relatively free of them. But my attention was drawn to the 1977 presidential address to the British Psychological Association, which I found quite surprising. This is Dr May Davidson speaking, having taken application in psychology as her theme:

> It is a common experience of applied psychologists that more is expected of them by some other human beings than they can in fact deliver. The psychologists, in turn, expect their discipline to provide better solutions to many problems than it can produce.

She ascribes the discomforts and conflicts currently experienced by many applied psychologists to the fact that they were forced to emerge from a "safe and sterile" psychometric tradition by three things: (a) longitudinal studies which took into account the influence on behaviour of situational and environmental variables and emphasized the dynamism in human affairs; (b) the growing evidence of experimenter effects on behavioural research and the tendency to create situations leading to self-fulfilling prophesies; and (c) an explosive growth in behaviour therapy and behaviour modification, which turned the applied psychologist into an interventionist.

These dilemmas sound to me remarkably similar to the ones in my own field—it seems to me we are in not dissimilar positions.

Because of these dilemmas, and because the reality we are dealing with is so complicated, the concepts that have emerged to deal with it have been inadequate, in two distinct ways. They have either been concepts that deal with only a part of the reality, so that one will always find some part of the data that they have not accounted for, or they have been formulated at such a high level of generality that they are not operationally very useful. Among the first I would include the Herzberg theory and the hierarchy-of-needs concept. They can be criticized; they do not account for everything. But they do make sense of some experience, of some of the data. There "is something in" the idea of a hierarchy of needs— even the most objective design criteria will have different salience, different degrees of importance, in different economic circumstances. There is an area of usefulness between taking an idea literally and rejecting it altogether.

Systems concepts, including the concept of the sociotechnical system, I take at the moment to be formulated at such a high level of generality as not to be, by themselves, operationally very useful. A great deal still has to be done to make them operational and, in the meantime, the attractiveness of systems concepts in theory should not delude us into thinking that we have the tools to deal comprehensively with the problems of job design in practice. Ambiguity remains part of our work situation whether we like it or not, so we might as well lie back and enjoy it.

Finally, I want to put forward two methodological problems, which I take to be key ones at the moment, and which present very exciting methodological challenges to us. The first is the problem of combining quality with quantity. At a conference last year, a Swedish researcher gave a paper on the consequences of a job design project. The whole paper was concerned with the responses of two women in the project. One of them had flourished and developed in the course of it, the other had experienced difficulties, and the researcher discussed the work that had been done with her, the adjustments that had been made, and so on. That is, if you like, the "ideal type" of one tradition—in the British and Scandinavian context we are familiar with projects where great care is taken to work with a particular group, a department, etc. How does one do that on a large scale? For example, I do some work with one of the clearing banks in England. I know how to work with a branch of the bank and I know how to work with a district in which there are a number of branches. But I have great difficulty in knowing how to work with something that has three and a half thousand branches and over 50,000 employees.

The German government programme on "humanizing work" is very much in the other direction: it is about diffusion, about application on a large scale. Partly because public funds are being spent, and partly because of a particular scientific tradition, they are looking for knowledge that has general application and that can be incorporated into design strategies or administered via the law, via structure, and via technology. And because of that—this is of course very much over-simplified—there is some tendency for individuals in the projects to be the rather passive recipients of design and research attention. I do not know how one handles both levels simultaneously, and I think it would be very exciting if we were to focus our attention on this problem.

The second methodological problem is about relating different frames of reference to each other. I have mentioned the complexities of context. The only person who incorporates comprehensively all aspects of the context of a job is the person doing it. That is why design strategies involving the job-holders themselves are a greater safeguard than reliance on specialists and experts to ensure that important things will not be left out. It is not merely a matter of the ideology of participation. In so far as professionals are involved, it is quite clear by now that there are a number of distinct frames of reference, all of which are relevant. Ease of operation, safety, personal development, interest groups; one could list quite a number. The challenge is how to relate them to each other. It is easy to say "multi-disciplinary work", but I know of no really satisfactory way to do it. One must not create a mere mish-mash, one cannot simply "unify". There is much work still to be done, possibly painful, in learning how to relate frames of reference to each other. In the meantime, once ergonomists venture outside their traditional boundaries, it is not all unbridled intuition, philosophy, and politics. There are empirical research findings, there are disciplined methods and there is experience, outside the boundaries of ergonomics as well as within them.

CHAPTER FOURTEEN

The management of innovation: from platitudes to reality in job design

This chapter is part of a paper given in 1980 at a conference on robotics, with the overall title "The management of automation".

The keynote speaker at the conference was the Chairman of British Steel. His speech was intended to be light-hearted, and he drew a happy, futuristic picture of how robots would relieve housewives of mundane tasks like cooking. In the discussion, I suggested that cooking might actually be experienced as enjoyable: I had recently, for the first time, made an apple strudel. The task had taken two hours, had been exhausting, and had given enormous pleasure. After that, much of the conference discussion centred on the question of apple strudel, and I began my own talk with "You take half a pound of flour . . ."

* * *

L adies and gentlemen, I would like you to help me celebrate an anniversary. In January 1981 it will be twenty-five years since I joined, as a junior research assistant, a research project on the Human Implications of Work Study, which was carried out in the then Department of Scientific and Industrial Research. The assumptions behind the project were: productivity was low; work study helps productivity; people on the shop floor tend to resist work study; if you understand more about that resistance, you may be able to overcome it.

In the course of the research we came to see work study, above all, as a form of social control. It was an attempt to control people's behaviour, sometimes down to the most minute second-by-second detail. People responded to this by reasserting controls of their own: in the short run, when work study was being newly introduced, they disliked being controlled in this way and this was called "resistance". In the long run, where work study had been going on for a long time, people found ways of coping, of rediscovering areas where they could exert controls of their own. In management language, this was called either "fiddling" or "restrictive practice". There was a time when I thought I was probably an international expert on fiddling; and indeed once, when I gave a lecture on this topic before a German trade union audience, their reaction was to roll in the aisles with laughter and say, "How did you know?"

At that time there were a lot of appreciation courses, training courses, and conferences on work study. Very often these would include a session on "human implications", usually on the last afternoon, and one would be "wheeled on", as it were, to do the "human implications bit". It was too late to influence the main content, but at the same time it satisfied the requirement that something about people should be included. What one tended to say, of course, was that to understand and deal with resistance it was necessary to re-examine the underlying assumptions on which the practice of work study was based in the first place.

A few years later it was the turn of operational research. In the mid-1960s there was a good deal of discussion about collaboration between operational research and the social sciences; conferences were held and people talked about "human aspects". However, what many OR practitioners understood by co-operation between OR and the social sciences was that social scientists should help to make their projects more acceptable. Requests took the form of "we have devised a rational system, and the irrational people won't wear it". With patience one could then persuade them that, if people consistently would not "wear" an idea, there might be some relevant data that had not been taken into account. On that kind of basis, one could then work collaboratively. To give an example: I was at Esso at that time and did quite a lot of joint work with OR people, on distribution systems. The company has distribution terminals around the country, where product is stored and from which it is trucked outside to customers. These might be garages or central heating installations, etc. That kind of operation seems to lend itself very readily to OR applications. Our collaboration began with an OR man proposing a system that included the idea that a truck driver should arrive at work in the morning, find his instructions and route in the cab of his truck, get in and drive off, without any kind of overlap with the activities or work systems of the terminal, or between his role and other roles in the terminal. There would not even be any contact with the order clerk, normally a very frequent occurrence during which, although there were problems, at least some information was exchanged and some understanding developed. Most of the rest of the company—or so it sometimes seemed—was worried about why drivers did not seem to be identified with the company, its problems, and its interests. There really is a connection between the overlap and contact an operator has with other activities in the organization and the extent to which he or she will be identified with it; once such connections are understood, more appropriate systems can be worked on, and these need to recognize conflicts of interest.

You will by now be getting the drift of this introduction: in the course of twenty-five years, the things at the end of which one gets "wheeled on" to "do the human relations bit" have been getting more sophisticated, and today it is robots. But the message is essentially the same: whenever you design a piece of equipment or a system you are, implicitly or explicitly, designing the consequences. If the consequences are to be taken seriously, then the time to take account of them is at the design stage. In twenty-five years this message has, on the whole, had very little impact on designers of systems and equipment. Compared with resistance to change of that calibre, I think shop-floor operators who resist change are a bunch of amateurs.

The role of human and social criteria in design

If you are concerned about the human implications of technology design, I think there is a hierarchy of problems. The first one is whether people care at all, and this problem I am not concerned with here. It cannot be solved by persuasion, manipulation, or the imposition of ideas from outside. To be of real value, the commitment or interest must come from within.

The next problem in the hierarchy, I am afraid, is a veneer of sophistication that is by now very widespread. Many people have learned the language of "job satisfaction", "job enrichment", etc., and one quite often finds things done in the name of such concepts without any real enquiry as to what exactly it is that is being done. In one of the films shown in this conference yesterday the commentator kept saying that his machine would do away with "rotten" jobs. He is, of course, entitled to be enthusiastic about his machine, but he should not need to justify that enthusiasm by assuming "rottenness" in jobs which he has not actually investigated.

Having got through the rather facile lip-service, we come next to the real problems of how to work with design criteria. I should like to illustrate these with an example.

It comes from a company that had built a new factory. The company's plant engineer had read a good deal of the literature on new forms of work organization and had a strong and genuine commitment to improving people's work experience. Before showing me round the plant he admitted to some embarrassment, saying, "We still have some terrible jobs here." He said he would show the worst jobs first, and took me to the packaging room. The product (a food item) was moved from a central conveyor along a number of spurs, at the end of each of which a man stood, shovelling it rapidly into boxes. "That's no job for a grown-up man," the engineer said, "We shall have to automate it". (This seems to be the only alternative engineers are trained to think of.)

I suggested that there were some things that could be done to improve the job, short of automation. For instance, it could become a two-man station, so that operators would have someone to talk to and could have some experience of co-operation as well as the experience of pushing product into boxes. It would also help if the product went into a buffer zone, from which the operator could call off the material and therefore control the pace instead of being controlled by it. However, this worried the engineer because "buffer stock means investment".

He then took me on the basic factory tour, from raw material delivery to the finished product, until we were back in the packaging room. The first operation there was that the product was wrapped in paper by a sensitive, high-speed wrapping machine: "To make sure this doesn't go wrong, we built in five metres of buffer." I didn't say anything, my eyebrows just went up a little, and he said, "Oh, my God!" When buffer stock was required to ensure the good working of a machine, it was not questioned; when it was required to improve the working situation of a human operator, it was "investment" and debatable; the engineer realized the discrepancy as soon as he had voiced it. What he would have needed—and had not received in time—was not a challenge to his values but help in making his values operational.

In this story the problem has been about the internalizing and operationalizing of values. I would like to give another instance to show that, even when that has happened, there is then still a need to make appropriate institutional arrangements.

This incident happened while I was in Esso, where we had done a lot of work on these concepts with industrial engineers and management service people, some of whom had really internalized them. One day, the chief engineer in charge of construction projects came to see me. He had to extend a distribution terminal. A new pipeline was being laid from one of the refineries, and capacity at the terminal had to be increased. He was not sure whether to build a new control room at the entrance to the site, so that a driver would hand in his documents as he drove in and receive his instructions on driving out, or whether to increase the size of the existing control room in the centre of the site. His question was, "What difference would it make in terms of the motivation and social organization of the drivers?" Now, that was a fantastic question for an engineer to ask. It shows how well he had internalized what this is about. I asked for about three weeks to produce an answer. But the engineer was locked into a timetable that had to do with the opening of the new pipeline, and he just could not wait. That was a very sad episode—despite all that sophistication and good will, on that occasion nothing could be done. Time has to be allowed for the necessary research; most answers do not come off the shelf.

Finally, I would like to mention very briefly two design strategies through which the integration of social values with technical

and economic ones can be pursued. The first is about the systematic testing of alternatives. Again in Esso, we did a project concerning the refuelling of aircraft at London Airport. Very briefly: at that
time Esso did about forty per cent of the refuelling of aircraft there.
For this purpose the company had a building with a control centre,
and space for product, trucks, and drivers in the airport. With the
increase of traffic through the airport, the job of the controller of the
operation had become increasingly difficult, and the whole question of redesigning it had arisen. We brought in a team that, after
very detailed studies of the operation, made a number of redesign
suggestions and built a simulated control room in their laboratory.
It was a very detailed (and therefore quite expensive) simulation,
with analysis of the ticker tape from the control tower, students
playing the roles of truck drivers, etc., and the actual controllers
came to sit at redesigned desks to work the simulation. The point
of the story is that they tried four different methods before deciding which one to use, and the criteria on which the eventual method
was selected from the four included human criteria (Shackel &
Klein, 1976).

Thus one possible way of making human values operational is
the systematic testing of alternatives, early enough, with human
criteria playing a part in the selection. And, of course, the time to
do this is when you are about to invest in plant. It is a fairly expensive exercise, but when you are about to spend several millions on
plant, a small percentage spent on the roles of the operators would
seem to be a good investment.

The second design strategy has been developed by a group of
young production engineers in the University of Stuttgart. It was
developed in more conventional production assembly situations,
not high level automation of the kind you are considering, but the
same principles apply. The strategy is as follows: they get together
a design team, which includes two of the elected works committee
representatives. They then present the design team with a number
of human criteria in job design (which, incidentally, came not from
the social science literature but out of their own thinking). These
include such things as "Does the job provide the opportunity to
communicate with others?" (They interpret communication in a
very pragmatic way: for example, to be able to communicate you
must be able to make eye contact; noise levels must be such that

you can hear a human voice.) "Does it provide the opportunity to do some of your own inspection?" There are about ten of these items. They then ask the design team to give an importance weighting to these criteria, by doing a paired comparison: given criterion 1 and 2, is 1 more important than 2, 2 more important than 1, or are they equal? And so on.

Having done this importance-weighting exercise, they put it aside and then present the design team with a number of different layouts for doing a job. One particular example was an assembly job, for which they had produced seven different layouts. They then ask the design team to score each layout on each criterion: taking layout A, give it a score out of ten for opportunity to move, opportunity to communicate, opportunity to learn, etc. Then layout B, layout C, and so on. If you weight the result of that exercise with the result of the previous exercise, you arrive at a quantified "best buy," in human terms, *according to the values of that team*. *Not* according to some abstract philosophy, or what social scientists say, but according to local values. At the same time they also do the normal economic costing of the different layouts. They then put the most economic up against the most "humane" and negotiate, using the normal sort of negotiating procedure. In the example that I witnessed, the final selection was the layout which had come out second on the "human" side because the top one had been considered too costly (Metzger, Warnecke, & Zippe, 1975).

That method is already under considerable criticism in Germany. Some people say it is very mechanistic, and of course it is, rather. Some people say, "Rather than those particular criteria, why not any others that it might have been?" Trade Unions are saying, "Why two members of the works council on the team? Why not fifty per cent?" Some people are saying, "Why those particular seven layouts, why not any number of others that it might have been?" All of these are serious questions that need to be dealt with. However, one can extract from this strategy two very important principles:

1. Values can be made explicit. They can be put on the table, discussed, and, if necessary, negotiated.
2. Values can be built explicitly into systems and equipment.

Whatever your values are—and it is not for me to tell you what they should be—ways can be found of making them explicit and incorporating them into design. That is the real message. If you ask me why it is important, the reason is not really about being "nice" to people, it is about being consistent. In terms of mental health, it seems to me to be dangerous and damaging that we express one set of values in our private, social, and political lives and a different set of values in our working arrangements, without really intending to. And we need to be more proactive in the way we design these things.

CHAPTER FIFTEEN

On the collaboration between social scientists and engineers

This chapter presents a paper that arose out of involvement in a project about the design of advanced manufacturing technology, called "Designing human-centred technology".

Howard Rosenbrock was Professor of Control Engineering at the University of Manchester Institute of Science and Technology (UMIST). He was rare among senior engineers in being interested in sociotechnical ideas and in job design, and in 1982 he obtained a research grant from the Science and Engineering Research Council to design a "Flexible manufacturing system in which operators are not subordinate to machines". (An FMS is an automated system incorporating several manufacturing operations that would previously have been done on separate machines.) He put together a steering group for the project, which he asked me to join.

It was a stimulating group, which engaged in long philosophical discussions about the nature of work and of manufacturing. But Howard wanted the steering group to make a major contribution to the research itself, and in this he found me disappointing. I need to get some understanding of the technology I am dealing with before I can make a serious contribution, and for that a few steering group meetings per year were not enough. There were in fact two technologies to understand:

the technology of metal-cutting, and computer technology. On the first, I asked UMIST to give me some concentrated teaching, treating me like a first-year engineering undergraduate. In this way I learned at least enough to understand what the researchers were dealing with. But I did not, at that stage, master the computing side well enough. It was my first serious contact with computing, and the project constituted too deep a deep end to be thrown into without some systematic training.

One outcome of the project was that Howard and Mike Cooley, a fellow member of the steering group, obtained a grant from the European Commission to develop a "human-centred" manufacturing system. And a main outcome of *that* was that the European Commission felt it had done its duty by human aspects of technology. For many years it became impossible to get human considerations taken account of in any of its other projects.

The paper has been edited from my chapter in the book to which the researchers and members of the steering group of the project all made contributions (Rosenbrock, 1989). It touches on some of the ambivalence between the professions.

*   *   *

Introduction—the dynamics

There is a dynamic that psychologists call "splitting". It is a process of psychic economy, whereby people tend to simplify a complex situation for themselves by attributing all its x characteristics to one of a pair, and all its y characteristics to the other. The goodies are all-good and wear white hats, and the baddies are all-bad and wear black hats, and possibly also black moustaches. Splitting means that one is most unlikely to see a black moustache under a white hat.

Splitting is very pervasive—people identify one football team, one political party, one nation as all-good, and (with a strong tendency to see only two even where there are more) another as all-bad. Scientists are supposed to be all-rational, and artists all-intuitive; industrialists concerned only with money (and nothing else), academics only with knowledge (and nothing else). And, although many people know with a part of their mind that things are really not like that, once splitting is established and becomes institutionalized, those involved get caught up in it and it becomes very hard to break out of. Companies have to encapsulate their "soft" aspects in personnel departments or donations to ballet companies, in order to maintain their required "toughness" intact. Politicians are unable to say *anything* good about policies of their opponents. In turn, people begin to live up to what is apparently expected of them.

Something like this has happened in relation to technology and its inputs and outputs. Clearly, they are interdependent: on the one hand, the inputs to design decisions in manufacturing systems are not only knowledge about the properties of materials and the dynamics of machining. They are also, first, factors affecting the individual designer, such as values and assumptions about how people function and about what is really economic, and, second, organizational factors affecting design processes, such as pressures on the team from outside, status differences when alternatives have to be selected, career development issues, etc.

On the other hand, the outputs from design decisions in manufacturing systems include effects on the perceptions, attitudes, skill repertoire, and behaviour of individuals, on organization and therefore also, in aggregate, on society. The consequences for the people who work with and around the technology mean, in turn, that technology is often not operated in the ways in which its designers, from a split position that blanks out the human and social aspects, intended. A split position would then lead one to conclude from this that people should be eliminated from the system, not that they should be taken into account more realistically.

The *raison d'être* of the UMIST project was the profound effects of technology design on the work experience, and therefore on the development and autonomy, of the individuals and groups who work with it, and thus on society. A shared acceptance of the importance of this held together a very diverse steering committee.

What needs pointing out, however, is that the social and technical aspects of technology are not only split off, but that the splitting against which attempts to work in an integrated way now take place is deeply institutionalized. It permeates education, research, and the professional institutions and their literature. There are populations whose horizons are dominated by the one, and populations whose horizons are dominated by the other. Social scientists read what social scientists have written, engineers read what engineers have written.

One anecdote may serve to illustrate how this institutionalization in turn perpetuates the splitting: after some time as a member of the steering committee of the project, I considered that I was not being as useful as I might be because I did not understand the technology well enough. I asked for some teaching, and for a week was treated like an engineering undergraduate learning about metalcutting. Among other things I was shown a video that is used in teaching first-year students. It was an excellent teaching aid, but within the first five minutes two things had happened:

1. The operator was referred to as a constraint, a cost, and was never mentioned again.
2. The content itself—the engineering—was very fascinating and absorbing.

These two things together would, of course, help to set a student's attitude for life and be very difficult to counteract later.

Engineers and social scientists in the present age are therefore, to a considerable extent, products of this deeply institutionalized splitting. So powerful is it that large parts of both professions see no relevance in collaborating with the other at all. A feature of the situation is that some social scientists are afraid of technology and some engineers are afraid of getting into the human area. These fears are difficult to acknowledge and, from such fears, the human aspect may get turned into pseudo-mechanical form, like "the man–machine interface" or "the human factor". On the other side, the term sociotechnical has recently become popular, but activities going on under that label are frequently still confined to working only with the social system. "We are not here to discuss technology", said a consultant introducing a training course on sociotechnical systems.

There is also a substantial history of mutual criticism. On the side of the social sciences, more precisely of sociology, criticism has its roots in studies of the human and social consequences of production technology, and was originally not directed at engineering design but at the economic framework within which it was taking place. Marx's original analysis of the societal consequences of trends in manufacturing technology contained much of what a present-day social scientist would call sociotechnical understanding; that is, understanding of the interplay between human and technical aspects of technology.

However, Marx did not draw sociotechnical conclusions, i.e., he did not conclude that social aspects should therefore feature in engineering design. He attributed the problems he saw to the ownership of private capital and the drive to create surplus value. He did not take seriously, as an independent contributing factor, the simple need to reduce complexity and the resulting models of man in the minds of engineering designers; in other words, splitting. Since designers were generally working for the owners of capital the omission is understandable, and indeed there is some connection. But we know today that trends in design do not automatically change when ownership changes, as in nationalized industries or in socialist societies, or when the need for economy abates, during phases of subsidy. Splitting and its consequences are powerful independent contributing factors.

In the 1920s, 1930s, and 1950s in Britain, a range of researches and other activities of social scientists began to elucidate specific rather than global problems. For example, empirical research showed that, given the opportunity, people varied their working pace in the course of the day, without loss of output (Harding, 1931). This has never found its way into the kind of "knowledge" that is explicitly used in design. Quite recently, the managing director of a company in the domestic electrical appliance industry reported that he was "amazed" at how miraculously their industrial relations improved when they took the mechanical drive off their assembly line.

What happened instead was a split development. Production engineers continued to work on the assumption that controllability and predictability required evenly spaced, i.e., mechanical, pacing. Then, in the 1950s, when standards of living were recovering from the war, the motor industry began to suffer from waves of strikes, many of which were unofficial and short. No one recognized that an important function of a short strike is simply to create a break, an interruption from work, and that they were happening in situations where work was machine-paced.

Again, early research showed that, if the work system did not provide feedback (knowledge of results), people would insert a way to obtain such feedback informally (Wyatt & Fraser, 1928). And again, empirical research showed that, if people's actions were closely controlled as in work study systems, they would react by inserting controls of their own. Fiddling in work-studied incentive schemes had the function of exercising creativity and regaining control over one's work situation, which the formal system did not permit (Klein, 1964).

The study that conceptualized much of the earlier research in a cumulative way was one that showed that, given experience of a job and some flexibility, people would find the optimum way of doing it for themselves. Conversely, if a new technology did not take account of their experience, its productivity potential was not realized: the technical system and the social system were truly interdependent (Trist, Higgin, Murray, & Pollock, 1963).

Some engineers and their institutions began to be interested in the findings of this kind of empirical social research. With increasing frequency, social scientists were invited to take part in the conferences of engineering institutions. However, before a move towards integration in design could get very far, a second trend within the social sciences was making itself felt. The expansion of social science teaching and writing in the 1960s brought with it the re-emergence of critique as the dominant mode. This time it tended to be *mere* critique, on the basis of a pre-existing formal theoretical framework, rather than empirical and grounded investigation as had been the case before. Given that the frame of reference for critique was well established, and frames of reference for synthesis and contribution only beginning to be worked out, critique was simply an easier option, and many social scientists chose it. The two trends—sociological critique and sociotechnical design—to some extent came into conflict. The difference is a fundamental one.

At the same time, public awareness of a need to bring social science and engineering together was growing. But it turned out that, where arrangements were made for social scientists to make a contribution to the education of engineers, they have tended to do it from a split position, i.e., they have tended to teach elements of social or psychological theory, not to help engineers incorporate human and social factors into their engineering. I personally regard this as one of the tragedies of the century.

There is little point in speculating about whether values developed as result of the habit of critique, or the habit of critique was a consequence of values. It is in any case a fact, significant in the context of the UMIST project, that when we advertised for a social scientist to work with engineers in the UMIST team on the design of a technology, there were very few applications for the post, in spite of substantial unemployment among social science graduates. It was not the kind of job their teachers, in the late 1970s, had prepared them to want—or, indeed, to be able to tackle. Twenty-five years earlier, young social scientists would have given their eye-teeth for such an opportunity.

Engineers, in turn, in so far as they have been aware at all of what social scientists were doing, have resented being forever criticized. They notice that social scientists are not given to studying the ways in which human life has been made easier by the products of engineering. They consider that the social sciences have little in the way of positive contribution and find social scientists unwilling to try to help instead of criticizing. And, if they experience resentment, engineers can get their own back. It is easy to trap a social scientist with questions that are not only unanswerable, but that serve to block the contribution that might be made. The following are two real examples, from experience.

The first concerned the design of a new plant. "We want to design this plant so that the operators will be happy. What we need from you is advice on what colour to paint the walls to achieve this."

The second concerned the design of equipment.

Social scientist: "We need to keep options open for the operator." Engineer (after doing a quick calculation): "I reckon there are about four billion options. Which ones do you mean?"

This combination of recognizing the value of the other and resentment of the other is the dynamic that psychologists call ambivalence. And both the habit of critique and the habit of resentment are sufficiently well established to have some of the characteristics of cultures, affecting to some extent even those, in both professions, who do wish to collaborate. It is against this background that attempts to work together take place.

Models of science

As this discussion now moves on to the practical aspects of collaboration, it will confine itself to the concepts, methods, and experience of those social scientists and those engineers who do wish to engage in collaborative work. For even where there is a wish to collaborate, there are still considerable handicaps. The phrase "multi-disciplinary work" trips from the tongue more easily than it is realized in practice, and that does not apply only to these particular disciplines.

It is possible to postulate two models of science in approaching the topic of job design and work organization: in one, there is a high value placed on measurement and quantification in the search for precise guidelines. The other accepts ambiguity and conflict of interest as part of the reality being dealt with. (It is salutary to remember that "scientific management" was to a large extent motivated by a wish to take conflict out of the situation by developing "objective" standards that would be self-evidently correct and that would therefore be accepted by both management and workers. It has been one of the main causes of conflict ever since.)

It would, however, certainly not be true to say that engineers necessarily adhere to the first model, and social scientists to the second. On the one hand, it was surprising to discover, in the course of the UMIST project, how much of engineering is still empirical (though that "still" shows the power of the stereotype) and how much room for debate there is among engineers. On the other hand, a good deal of social science research is conducted within the natural science model.

There are also cultural influences at play. In Germany, for example, there is a clause in the Company Law of 1972 which requires that "proven scientific findings about the workplace must be applied". This sounds strange to British ears, where research involving people at work has been very context-specific and where the emphasis in application has been on cases and experiments rather than on the broad application of generalized "knowledge". The clause in Company Law in turn has had considerable influence, both on the sponsorship and on the nature of research carried out, since it was passed.

The disciplines in relation to values

There is considerable confusion about the connection between values, human needs, and the professional contribution to joint design. Social scientists do not have a monopoly on "human values". Nor do the social sciences represent some kind of authoritative statement about what human values are. What social scientists do have is, first, some understanding of what human beings need for their development. Values about job design and work organization may then be expressed in terms of which of these needs has primacy. Second, they have some methods that help to articulate and make explicit the values and priorities held by people in a particular situation. And third, they have some methods for operationalizing these.

The first attempt to formulate needs to obtain meaning and self-development in the course of work into criteria for the design of work situations was made by Emery and Thorsrud (1969). While various attempts at catalogues of this kind have been put forward since then, and emphasis and interpretation may vary, the basic needs that are being articulated in that list remain constant: the need for autonomy, the need to use one's skills, the need for opportunities to learn and go on learning to limits set by oneself, the need for feedback as an aid to autonomy and learning, the need for purpose, and the need for interaction with others in purposeful activity.

In what follows, these will be discussed not in terms of priority but in relation to the UMIST project. Purpose, in a flexible manufacturing system, is fairly clear. The meaning given to the term "human-centred" in the project turned out to be in the areas of autonomy and the use of skill. The basis of the UMIST project was a recognition on the part of engineers that Taylorism had been (or rather, is) about minimizing autonomy and the use of skill on the part of operators, and the central focus of the design activity was in these two areas. However, that left two more: interaction with others and development through learning. Interaction with others and group aspects cannot be designed into a piece of equipment, they are a matter of how that equipment is then installed and used by its purchaser. This problem, which concerns the boundaries of the system that the designer can influence, was discussed a number of times during the project but not resolved. We learned of a design group in Germany that entered into negotiation with potential purchasers about how their product was to be installed and used, but that does not seem a very realistic strategy. The best thing I could think of was something equivalent to a maintenance manual, designed not only to protect the features that are designed in (some of which could be counteracted in installation) but to extend them, on the lines of "To use this equipment in the sense in which it was designed, you should . . ."

That leaves the need to go on developing through learning, and this was an area of controversy within the project. The engineers approached the "human-centred design" task specifically from a wish to counter the effect of Taylorism, with which they were familiar, and this led them to emphasize autonomy and valuing the operator's use of skills, particularly tacit skills. The social scientists started, not from Taylorism specifically, but from human development needs in general, and that included the importance of learning as well as the other factors.

In the project, this issue found expression in the "blank table debate": briefly, initial suggestions stressed that values for speeds, feeds, and depths of cut should be calculated by the software and displayed for evaluation and possible editing by the operator. The alternative suggestion was that the operator should be able, if desired, to fill in his or her own values in a blank table without first seeing the computed values, and then, again if desired, call up the latter for comparison. For the ramifications of this debate, see Rosenbrock, 1989, Chapter Three.

The disciplines in relation to outputs

As a group of professions, engineers have, of course, been evolving their methods and developing their products for much longer than social scientists. Social reflection about the output of technology is as old as technology itself (certainly the authors of Genesis had a view about the condition of man once he had to labour, and saw even God as needing a rest). But, as disciplines that attempt to aggregate the outputs at a societal level or study them systematically at individual level, and thus to verify social reflection empirically and systematically, the social sciences are young by comparison. And as professions that attempt to contribute the resulting knowledge and methods in a variety of spheres and in the design of plant and equipment, very much younger still. The very process of studying and commenting, by bringing gaps to light, has led them into critique and contributed to splitting, and thus hindered the development of the contribution.

Nor do the social sciences have much to show in the way of products, at least as products are seen by engineers. By definition, where an idea or a finding in social science is accepted as valid, it becomes incorporated into the general common sense. The idea of unconscious motivation is now part of the general view of human behaviour, featuring in literature, journalism, and general conversation quite naturally, and without any need to refer explicitly to the body of psychoanalytic theory and practice that gave rise to it. Mothers are now encouraged to stay in hospital with their small children as a matter of common sense, not as a consequence of research that demonstrated the effects of not allowing it (Bowlby, Robertson, & Rosenbluth, 1952). Thus, the useful products of social science are likely to be understanding, methods, practices, and institutions. Sometimes they may be standards, but where standards are applied the processes of developing them, which social scientists may sometimes consider more valuable than the outcomes because of the learning involved, will have been bypassed. Engineers, on the other hand, are likely to want outputs in engineering terms, i.e., at least in the form of standards.

Standards that social scientists can formulate with confidence and without an empirical "research loop" are likely to concern processes, not outcomes. "No installation without a transitional system involving prototyping", rather than "No cycle time less than x seconds"; "Operators should have some say in shaping their environment", rather than "The walls should be blue". This kind of advice may be experienced as especially irritating when the particular population of operators is not yet available.

The disciplines in relation to methods

Where the social sciences are particularly strong at present is, first, in the concepts and methods for making values explicit and, second, in operationalizing them.

If space is provided for this, it can in fact be a fundamental contribution. Given the long-standing and deep tradition of splitting, being "human centred" in attitude and assertion is not enough. Methodologies are needed for operationalizing it, but this may not be what engineers expect. I have been surprised in more than one situation that people who would not dream of making decisions about materials, or temperatures, or surface finishes without some kind of systematic trials, insist on making or asking for decisions about people by inspired guesswork.

One is somehow reminded of how Italians describe the behaviour of foreign tourists in the face of Rome traffic. It is said that some foreigners, no doubt otherwise quite rational people, faced with the need to cross a busy street, put up one hand to stop the traffic, hold the other tightly over their eyes, and plunge. Like manufacturing design, it quite often works.

Take this example: in a shipping organization, a number of policies including "integrated crewing" were introduced, designed to encourage seafarers to identify with the particular employer rather than with seafaring as a whole. It seemed at least possible that people who go to sea do not want to identify with a particular organization; but when questioned about why he was so sure that they would want to if given the opportunity, the manager concerned put his hand on his heart and said, "Because I feel it here."

Another member of the Steering Committee, John Fox, made a similar point in an interal committee paper, in the context of a discussion on intelligent knowledge-based systems (IKBS):

> Few complete systems are ever evaluated objectively. Consequently wishful thinking about the virtues of particular computer systems is rampant. It is not uncommon for systems that are described as user-friendly to be rejected as unusable. Sometimes software design ideologies are formulated on the basis of fragmentary implementations or even pure intuition. The consequence of this lack of objectivity is that practical designers can't know what to believe—which IKBS ideas really are good ones ready for application and which are not. Part of the problem is the lack of an empirical attitude. AI (artificial intelligence) workers do not seem to be expected to measure the performance of their techniques. Also there is a lack of training in evaluation methods . . .

Third, the social sciences have a methodological concern for the links between process and outcome. This has given rise to the concept of the "double task". Any organization, team, committee, board, working party, has in effect two tasks: the primary task for which it was set up (sometimes referred to as task 1), and the task of designing, implementing, maintaining and reviewing the institutions, processes and mechanisms needed to carry it out (sometimes referred to as task 2). When task 1 is simple, or the people involved intuitively very skilled in these things, it may not be necessary to attend to task 2 in a very explicit way. Most often, however, it is necessary to deal with task 2 explicitly, and sometimes even to suspend business and pay attention to it, for a time, to the exclusion of other matters. The dynamics at the input end of design have direct consequences for the output end; in fact, that is often where the origins of poor design decisions are to be found. If design decisions are made for reasons other than design needs, the outcome is bound to be problematic. For example, a fierce argument about which of two layouts to adopt in a new plant was conducted on cost grounds (which were considered to be acceptable grounds for debate—see Chapter Nine). It was, in fact, about the competition between the company's and its parent company's engineering departments (which was not acceptable). The costs could not be assessed in their own right unless the dynamics could be worked through.

"Working through" is a process of dealing with such issues that may be very hard work for those concerned, but that often leads to an apparently intractable problem being reformulated.

The fragment that follows is an example of working through. Reference has been made to a difference in orientation between two views of what is meant by "human-centred", with particular reference to the role of learning opportunities. In the project, the difference had emerged as a debate about whether the operator should instruct the computer or whether the computer should make suggestions that the operator, from his or her experience, could override. Towards the end of the project, an attempt was made to recapitulate that debate, with a view to trying to understand it and learn from it. The framework now was not conducting the argument, but working through the difference. Because of this, the problem got reformulated in the process:

Social scientist: From the point of view of human development, there is a high value on learning.

Engineer: But why learn what the computer thinks it knows?

Social scientist: If we do it your way, there will be so many occasions when the operator accepts what he is given that the assumption will be "the computer knows".

Engineer: If we do it your way, the operator is encouraged to enter a learning situation with the computer which is false.

Social scientist: The same is true if we do it your way. Also the operator will learn more and more what is in the computer and that will reinforce passivity. In my way he is making the *first* step.

Engineer: But his first step will increasingly be like the computer. He should be learning to laugh at the computer.

Social scientist: My fear is that, since the computer will not be wrong all that often, and since designers are also learning, he is unlikely to reach that position.

Engineer: Your way would encourage him to learn from the computer. My picture of you is that you think *all* learning situations are good.

Social scientist: I think he first needs to know how the computer does it before he has the confidence to disagree.

Engineer: He needs induction training on that, including that there are uncertainties. Something like "in these situations be suspicious".

At this point the discussion changed to the nature of the induction training that would be needed. The reader should note the shift that has taken place.

There is now joint recognition that there is an area where two desirable objectives cannot both have priority and the nature of the mix needs to be clarified.

There is joint recognition that the problem cannot be solved through the software design alone.

The mode has changed from debate to separate contributions around joint problem definition.

Since the boundary—the nature of the mix to be taught—was not clear, it was felt that operators should be invited to the discussion, that analogous situations should be sought and examined, and that practical examples should be included in the induction training. Induction training would also have the great advantage of introducing some human support and not relying on the man–machine interface for everything. Once formulated, it might be extended to a handbook. In other words, once the framework shifts from debate to joint problem-solving, some of the other problems begin to be less intractable.

There then took place a redefinition of the central task, as it emerged from the need to formulate induction training and the need to clarify the relationship between the computer's knowledge and the operator's knowledge. It was to design the "centre of gravity" for learning.

To illustrate how contact and joint work facilitate the internalizing of concepts, it was now the engineer who formulated this as a *double task*, with two things having to go on simultaneously, thus:

Design the "centre of gravity for learning"	
Design the "centre of gravity"	Facilitate the learning of the design team

Operational issues

Considering how long the concept of sociotechnical interdependence has been around, critical mass for these ideas remains a long way off. One of the reasons for this seems likely to be that discussion and development have focused too exclusively on the values and paradigms, to the neglect of the operational issues involved in turning them into practice, and to the neglect of institutionalization.

The joining of the two perspectives can take many forms. Engineers may internalize the concepts. In one such case, the project engineer began to write job descriptions in terms of the experiences and relationships involved as well as the activities to be carried out. Human aspects that are predictable, such as selection and training, may be incorporated in planning systems such as Critical Path Methods. But many issues cannot be anticipated in such a structured way. The design of transitional systems such as prototyping, simulation, and the systematic testing of alternatives may be a particularly fruitful area for collaboration.

The following are some of the issues that arise in the course of operationalizing integrated working.

Phasing

Once engineers and social scientists are working together, many of the issues that have been discussed often emerge operationally as problems of phasing. Putting the disciplines and their concerns together does not automatically lead to integration, the consequences of the original splitting still have to be dealt with. Otherwise, if a project or development process has been designed with the assumptions of one discipline, the contributions of the other may appear as things that will hold us up.

The following are three examples of problems of phasing, from experience.

1. *Company A* was an oil company, engaged in building a new fuel-oil pipeline from one of its refineries to a major distribution terminal. Fuel-oil facilities would need to be built at the terminal, which until then had been engaged in the storage and distribution of other products.

One decision that had to be taken concerned the site of the control room. One alternative was to build a new control centre at the entrance to the site, so that truck drivers would be given instructions as they drove out, and hand in documents as they drove in. This would have the effect of geographically separating the control of loading from the physical operation of loading. The alternative was to extend the existing loading and transport control room at the centre of the site. The engineer in charge of the construction came to ask what the difference would be in terms of the social organization and attitudes of the drivers. It was an unusually perceptive question; finding an answer would involve doing some work with the drivers.

I estimated that I could have an answer for him in three weeks, but he could not wait. Major consequences for work roles and group relations were, of course, implied in the decision, and the engineer realized this. But he was locked into a schedule linking the design and construction of the new building with the opening of the pipeline and could not create a three-week delay. He had assumed that an answer might be available ready-made (Klein, 1976b).

2. *Company B* was engaged in building a new plant, for the manufacture of confectionery. Much of the production machinery was to be transferred from their existing older building and the job design contribution concerned the organization of work around existing equipment rather than the design of new equipment.[1]

When I first met the company's Project Group, a site for the new factory had been acquired and planning permission obtained, and they were beginning to discuss architects and the general shape of the building. Within ten minutes of joining one of their meetings for the first time, I discovered the problem of phasing. Although I had been involved as early in the process as one may reasonably expect, from some points of view it was already too late.

The prospect of an entirely new factory, an opportunity that people have only very rarely, was acting as a focus for a powerful vein of idealism in the company. Not only did they want the jobs in the new factory to be satisfying for the people working there, they wanted the architecture to be innovative, to be human in scale, and to make a distinct contribution to the environment. This had involved a good deal of discussion about company philosophy. Two concepts for the new factory were being debated: on one hand the concept of a large, hangar-like structure, within which there would be freedom and flexibility to arrange and rearrange things; and on the other hand the concept of a village street, with small production units, as well as social facilities such as a tea bar, a bank, possibly one or two shops, adding up to give the feel of a varied and small scale village-like environment where people moving from one unit to another would inevitably meet each other. This would be far removed from the conventional idea of a factory.

Within a few minutes of joining the group I was confronted with the question: "What do you think—large hangar or village street?" I had, of course, no basis for an opinion and realised the dilemma we were in. The concept with which I intended to work was that of the production system as a sociotechnical system. To translate this concept into practical reality, one needs to understand the manufacturing process and its technology in some detail.

The company felt that they could not even begin to talk to architects until they had some idea of the basic shape of the building they wanted; one could not sensibly discuss the shape of the building without some idea of the production layout; and I could not contribute to discussion about the layout from the job design point of view without some sociotechnical analysis of the production process. At that stage I had not even seen the production process.

3. *Company C* was also engaged in building a new plant, this time a high-speed canning plant. It was to be built on a site where the company already had some other operations so that, while the operators who would be manning the plant were not yet available, there was a trade union organization. A Job Design Committee was established for a time, including representatives from three unions, to consider the nature of the jobs being created in the cannery.[2]

Two control systems engineers were involved in the planning of the cannery. They became interested in the idea of job design and, after some preliminary induction to the topic, one of them gave a presentation to the Job Design Committee. He said that, at that stage, the control systems could still be designed in almost any way the Committee wanted. He liked the idea of working as a service to the operators who would later be doing the jobs. But he pointed out that, once the floors were laid, with channels for the cables, it would be very difficult to change. The trade union representatives at that stage did not have enough knowledge of the process to be able to be very specific about what they would want. The technology was very new and advanced, and the engineers had about two years' start on them in thinking and learning.

The problem of participants, or social science professionals, being out of phase with engineering designers in their absorption of the necessary know-how is very general (Eason, 1982). Unless arrangements can be made for it to be dealt with, contributions are likely to be limited to general-level statements and "participation" is likely to be superficial and unreal.

Systems boundaries: the meaning of "human-centred"

Within the human and social sciences there is a long-standing debate about how criteria that make a piece of equipment easy to use relate to criteria that make the work being done meaningful and that are conducive to the development of the person doing the work. In some instances they are identical, e.g., safety and health.

In some instances they are different; e.g., the operator's autonomy does not generally feature among the usability criteria which human factors professionals apply. In some instances they can even be in opposition; e.g., usability criteria usually include short learning times, while developmental criteria put a high value on continuing opportunities for learning.

These differences are sometimes debated as differences in values, but may also be discussed as differences about system boundaries, i.e., about what is considered to be within the system, and therefore susceptible to design change, and what is outside the system and part of the environment, i.e., to be taken as given. The issue is likely to crop up within multi-disciplinary design teams as well. It has two facets: on the one hand, how far responsibility goes for the impact that a technology will have, and, on the other, parameters to include in design considerations.

It may be useful to think of this problem in terms of a typology of outputs. Where an output is a *tool* as a means of doing something else, or creates a task that is only a part of a role so that the configuration of the role itself is out of the hands of the designer, the aims of good integrated design may properly be in the direction of "usable". Where a product or system creates *roles*, and where the configuration of the role is therefore in the hands of the product or system designer, usability should be a minimum baseline, and the aim of good integrated design must be more in the direction of "developmental". At any rate, in such a situation the issue cannot be ignored. The product or systems designer cannot help influencing long-term consequences such as future personal development or organization, or industrial relations, whether he or she wants to or not.

One can, in fact, postulate more than one such scale, and the boundary will not be in the same place on all of them. It may be useful to draw a profile across them for a particular product, such as:

From	To
Affects task	Affects role
Tool	System

Where an output profile is near to the left-hand column, it is not unreasonable to restrict "human-centredness" to usability criteria. The nearer it is to the right, the more do developmental criteria need to feature as well. This approach would by no means elimi-nate value-based debates, for instance on the question of when to treat people as responsible in matters of safety and when to elimi-nate "the human factor"; but it may help to contain them.

Making it happen: institutions and infrastructure

Where the idea of the collaboration between social scientists and engineers is new to people, they are likely to be preoccupied with what this will actually mean in practice and how to set about it; they are not so likely to worry about longer-term considerations. How-ever, this kind of work has now been going on for long enough for some long-term issues to become clear—not so much how to make it start, as how to make it stick. The issue is institutionalization.

To institutionalize something is to build it in; it was pointed out at the beginning of this chapter that the problem is not so much that the technical and social aspects of engineering design have become split off from each other, as that the split is deeply institutionalized.

The general idea may be illustrated by an example: society has made a decision, crystallized in law, to restrict driving to one side of the road. This apparently simple decision is supported by a surprising number and range of institutions: the assumption that it must happen is built into the *design* of vehicles. It is built into the *training* of drivers, as well as into their *legitimization* (licensing). It is built into the formulation of *codes* and *standards* (the Highway Code, standards about the width and layout of roads, etc.). Then there is the *continual reinforcement* of seeing that others do it and, finally, *sanctions* (punishment) if it does not happen. These institu-tions, in turn, are supported by *funds, training establishments, staffing,* and *monitoring* (traffic police).

It is the combination that makes these institutions, together, powerful and effective. In addition, a breach of the decision is generally clearly visible and unambiguous. As a result of all that, the decision is mostly carried out; drivers are not continually having to decide on which side of the road to drive.

Social aspects of work systems are, of course, not generally so unambiguous, and some of these institutions would be inappropri-ate. But it must be remembered that this is partly a matter of local tradition. In Germany, as we have seen, it is the law, with its accompanying sanctions, that says that "scientific findings about the workplace must be applied". In Germany, too, human factors methods and findings form part of the substance of some trade union agreements.

Where something can be formulated as a standard, that is a form of institutionalization. Where it can be integrated into the technology, such as dialogues that provide genuine options, or indicators on a machine that provide feedback, or buffers that mitigate pacing, that is a more powerful form.

But to ensure that such structural influences are taken seriously in the first place, and for situations that cannot be formulated in these ways, the need is to achieve a degree of culture change. To attain this, it is not a matter of one or more social scientists joining a team; the sociotechnical viewpoint must be represented powerfully enough, early enough, and consistently as a matter of routine. It must feature in the syllabuses of engineering students, in the appropriation for capital investments, in R & D budgets, in the qualifications and emoluments of technical directors.

It has taken me a long time to recognize what a mistake it is to appear to be solo when going into this activity, rather than institutional. First, a social scientist working solo as a member of an engineering activity is likely to be at the receiving end of all the ambivalence, the hopes and anxieties and resentments that have accumulated in relation to the social sciences. If the things he or she says are unwelcome, they are likely to be seen as personal rather than professional contributions. Second, he or she will not have at his/her fingertips all the substantive and methodological contributions of all the social sciences. And third, the number of things he or she has time to deal with will be very limited.

This is so even within a small team working on the development of a piece of equipment. It is much more so in the design and development of large-scale plant, where there are so many things going on at the same time that it is hopelessly optimistic to see them all as consistent and rational tributaries of the mainstream. So, for example:

- there may be market changes during the design and building process that influence the production capacity that is needed, leading to decisions outside the design teams;

- equipment will be purchased off-the-shelf and therefore cannot be influenced unless this influence is exerted long before actual orders are placed, i.e., unless the culture of the equipment manufacturers can be influenced as well;
- engineers move out of teams and are replaced by others who have not shared the history of collaboration. The social scientist is likely to have put the main effort of developing collaboration in at the beginning and may not recognize the need, or have the time, to start again from scratch.

All these instances illustrate that the system that is carrying the design and development processes is an open and not a closed one. In these circumstances, mere collaboration between social scientists and engineers is not enough. Mere collaboration, however well it may be working, is too weak a mechanism to cope with open systems characteristics. On the other hand, mere infrastructure is not enough either, and formal guidelines circumvent the necessary processes of development and mutual learning. What is needed is collaboration supported by institutions and infrastructure.

Notes

1. A fuller description of the case in which this example features is given in Chapter Eight.
2. A fuller description of the case in which this example features is given in Chapter Nine.

SECTION V

AND FINALLY . . .

Of course, there is no "finally". But, looking back over all this material, I do have some reflections. There is also the boundary with policy and institutions. I have occasionally, over the years, discussed questions of policy, and will give some indications of these here. This chapter partly draws on various discussion documents written at different times.

CHAPTER SIXTEEN

And finally—some reflections on institutions and policy

Without reiterating all the arguments, there seems no reason to doubt that work remains central to human existence. The legacy of the idea that "the job" is an out-of date concept (about which, in any case, one hears much less today) is that we know employment today to be highly diverse, not that people's need for meaning has changed. What varies is how available work is, where and how it is carried out, the degree of protection available to those who do it, how it is rewarded, the technologies and laws and practices that shape its nature—in other words, the political, economic, managerial and technical contexts that shape both people's overall work experience and the actual tasks that they carry out. Within these varying contexts it is possible to influence the nature of work in directions that help rather than hinder human development and the satisfaction that people can gain from their work. Quite often this happens by chance in any case—satisfaction and development may be found in many jobs. But enough is known for this not to have to be a matter of chance. It is not more knowledge that is needed, but institutional will.

One needs to remember that this is not just a matter of how people feel subjectively about their work but, as was seen in

Chapter Five, how it affects their perceptions, attitudes and behaviour. One also needs to remember that people like to be part of something that functions well and get very frustrated if it does not. In many IT systems, if the human aspects are not taken care of, the system does not work well. This is not so true of older production technologies where, in purely economic terms, Taylorism could work well.

The subject remains vitally important. And, while some of the original problems of working experience may have, at least for the time being, been exported to Far Eastern countries represented by the collective noun "China", working people in those countries are also likely to express needs beyond their immediate economic ones, sooner rather than later.

Whatever present or future changes there may be in the content of work, researchers and action researchers cannot go far wrong if they remain grounded—in the details of individuals' experience, and in the operational realities of work systems. For me personally, emphasis has shifted at times back and forth between the job and the job in context and infrastructure. That brings with it the unresolved question at the end of the chapter on Luddism—how to link them. But what I find has not changed, from the early Fabian pamphlet to the most recent project activity, is an implacable commitment to the empirical details and realities.

Reflecting on the experience represented by these papers, it seems to me that an important research question now looks like this:

1. What aspects of work that are helpful to people in their development can be designed and built into products, plant, office environments, and technologies?
2. What aspects can be built into institutions and processes?
3. What really does, like democracy, need to be discovered again by every generation?

There has been quite a lot of discussion in these papers about the first of these, and there is more in the literature. I would like to say a little about the others, and about some institutions and processes where a more fundamental and enduring consideration of the human and organizational issues could be built in.

Funding structures for transitional systems

Where organizations are willing to engage in development activities, it should be possible to fund these in such a way that the field site pays a proportion of the costs, for the value that is obtained, and the research community pays a proportion, for a research output. This is different from the present practice of making industry pay a proportion of their costs when they are involved in research activities. It is an attempt to put development activities themselves in a research frame and learn from them.

The funding of research itself needs to include a place that recognizes the function of transition. I believe that the model we tried in the ProCure project—accompanying a technical development in a longitudinal way in an action research frame—provided a useful transitional system. It needs to be explored further, and others devised.

In terms of conventional research, this carries some risks: there would not be many case studies for purposes of comparison, and the activities in the case studies would be concerned not only with studying problems but with developing solutions. This goes against some of the tenets of the classical research model, according to which research carried out leads to knowledge of a general kind, which is then applied. In the field of the human implications of technology the classical model has conspicuously not worked, because the feedback loop is too long and ineffective, so that there are different populations involved. One reason for suggesting an action component is precisely that much knowledge and many research findings simply do not find their way into practice. A second reason is that the social sciences should provide a contribution and not merely *post hoc* analysis and critique. And third, the range of potential issues is great and they change over the course of an innovation or development.

Grounded research in real situations has implications for the format of research administration. The process of formulating a grant proposal forces people to postulate a logic and linearity that do not reflect the real world. In such a model all the tasks are clearly outlined, and there is a logical order in which B follows A, and C will happen in month X. But, as we saw in ProCure, three years is a long time in a world where markets change, organizational

structures change, and technologies change. In fact, each organization had its own business going on at the same time, which affected
the project; in most cases the project was one of many that people
were working on; and there were also factors within the organizations (such as decisions on IT strategy) and outside the organizations (such as industry standards development) that prevented
progress being made as planned.

The links between work and technology

My aim, indeed the aim of all sociotechnical approaches, was all
along to get the consideration of human and organizational factors
integrated with the work of technology development and implementation. It took a long time to understand why this was so consistently difficult: "Projects" in which social scientists made a
contribution to engineering developments were simply too weak a
mechanism to counteract institutionalized splitting. It began to
seem more important to tackle the roots of the splitting and search
for strategies of integration, than to place all the emphasis on collaborative design and development projects, even though these had
always been a source of interest and learning. Engineers wonder
why implementing new technologies is so difficult. Social scientists
wonder why the wheel of human and organizational issues has to
be continually reinvented. The answer to both questions lies in the
fact that technical, human, and organizational aspects are not only
split off from each other, but that this splitting is deeply institutionalized. It follows that to reverse this trend requires not only
integrated working but the institutionalizing of integrated working.

In the field, integrated working is not so difficult, as several of
the projects show. An important outcome of the ProCure project was
that some engineers in the project originally tended to categorize
issues or problems as "technical" on the one hand, and "human/
organizational" on the other; the contact with social scientists led,
at least in some cases, to issues being seen more in terms of the interplay of technical and human/organizational factors leading to
operational problems.

However, relevant changes in institutions and processes would
amount to a culture change. This would, by definition, be slow and

not come as a result of single, ostentatious bursts of pressure. Shoe-string budgets are a recipe for failure. Designated amounts of money for research, demonstration projects, or publicity campaigns, have had little effect in the past and may even be counter-productive in lulling people into thinking that the issue has been dealt with. Thus, short-term and long-term strategies may in some instances come into conflict. There is a need to put in place long-term mechanisms aimed at a shift in emphasis. Some factors contributing to this are as follows.

The organization of training

Physical and human scientists are typically trained within university departments whose central thrust is towards their own discipline. In enlightened departments, computer scientists may have a course of lectures by a social scientist or a human–computer inter-action (HCI) specialist from outside, or psychologists may be taught a programming language. But this is not adequate, and the HCI specialists or social scientists who do such service teaching may teach only the theories of their subjects, not how to integrate them with engineering or computer science. In turn, social scientists need teaching and training in development and application of their disciplines. Especially, social scientists who may be involved in the education of engineers and designers should not be regarded as qualified to do this from a merely academic and research back-ground.

An important criterion for what constitutes a science is that knowledge should be cumulative. In this the career structure in universities, the insistence on novelty, and the pressure to publish present serious problems for social scientists. Continuing to develop a promising line of enquiry carries nothing like the respect and prestige of starting a new one, and it is easier to commission new research than to work out how to use what exists already.

Among professionals, it would be important to stop using the term "soft" to describe the human aspects of work systems. It is a way of avoiding their reality, as if human reactions are somehow ephemeral, intangible, impossible to confront. They are not. What is true is that human and social systems are very adaptable, can adjust to many situations, and therefore do not appear to demand early attention as clearly as economic or technical or green factors demand it. The nature of the adjustments they make may then later be felt to be undesirable, without the causal links being recognized.

Teaching and learning materials

For some time I tried to get funding to collaborate with authors in annotating engineering textbooks and other learning materials. While everyone thought it was a good idea, it got batted between the Economic and Social and the Engineering and Physical Sciences Research Councils until it died of exhaustion. Institutionalized splitting, of course, extends to the research councils. They have had some joint initiatives, but never on a permanent basis.

Questions of regulation and standards

This is a political, cultural, and scientific hot potato. At the macro level, the leaders of the European Union are currently (2007) debating whether a new treaty should be about the open market, or about a social market with regulation, aiming at full employment. At the micro level, there is a question about what may be lost in terms of learning and personal growth when matters are dealt with by regulation and standards, and what is risked and lost when they are not.

It is a question that applies at many levels. In many instances there is a discernible shift from open-ended, grounded diagnosis and action formulation to a more prescriptive and formalized approach to the same problem. Of course, it seems natural that, having invested heavily in a learning and development activity in the first place, one should want to disseminate the outcomes by formalizing them and not repeat what may have been an expensive and laborious process. Project experience or research findings may be encoded in a set of standards for others to follow.

But there are dangers in this approach. If a standard, or even a process, is applied automatically, without understanding the circumstances in which it was developed and without a diagnostic approach to the circumstances in which it is to be applied, this is likely to result in inappropriate application. There are also dynamics involved, which concern the autonomy of those who develop and those who follow such "rules". First, it is one thing to try to make sense of the overwhelming complexity of the environment for oneself by encapsulating it in categories and rules; it is quite another then to reify those categories and rules as if they had some kind of absolute quality. Second, there is a power relationship involved: on the whole people want to devise their own solutions, not follow the solutions of others.

There are some cultural differences involved in this debate, which I believe to have their roots in the different legal systems of the British and continental countries: on the one hand a legal tradition based on case law, and on the other hand one based on the Napoleonic Code.

But there are also some over-arching trends, to which sociotechnical thinking itself has become prey. In a culture of acronyms, bullet points, and executive summaries, "STS" has, in some circles, joined TQM, BPR, EC, TPM, JIT, CI in the succession of global visions and total, comprehensive solutions to all problems. The reality is more sober, harder work, less inspirational and more worthwhile than "movements".

It is not impossible to think of enabling, rather than prescriptive, legislation: for example, health and safety legislation can be extended, to include "psychosocial health". Here, too, however, the dilemma reappears: prescriptive regulations tend to be applicable to narrower aspects of work organization; broader aspects are difficult to capture in regulations, and may in fact be damaged if treated in a prescriptive way. Pursuing the theme of an enabling rather than a prescriptive framework, one might be able to make it mandatory, in the design of new plant and equipment, rather than doing certain prescribed things, to devote a percentage of new capital investment to design and development activities concerned with the nature and content of the work being created.

In 1986, an opportunity to further the enabling of integrated working presented itself. I was invited to give evidence to a Committee of the European Parliament and included in this evidence a suggestion that should go some way toward dealing with the splitting. It was that technologists applying for development grants should be required, as part of their grant applications, to say what effects they expected their project to have on a number of human and organizational categories. Not that one could expect accurate predictions, but applicants would be forced to give thought to these matters and that, in turn, might feed back into the education system where the splitting has its roots. Some of the members of the European Parliament liked this idea. They modified the categories to include some others they considered important, and in November 1986 the Parliament passed a resolution stating:

> [The European Parliament] believes that applicants for financial support under Community technology and research schemes should be required to state what effect they expect the new technology to have on employment, the nature of the work, skills, health and safety at work and older workers for whom retraining is no longer possible. [Doc A2–142/86]

I really thought I had achieved something, and it wasn't even a self-interested pitch for the social sciences—in such a framework an explicit contribution from the social sciences would become redundant. What I did not realize was that the European Commission is not obliged to take any notice of the Parliament.

Management practice and training

One has to remember that people's experience at work comes from how they are treated as well as from the nature of their task.

With the current rapid change in the structures and boundaries of employment, many people find themselves in positions of managing, where they have influence over the lives of others, with little preparation. There are the sophisticated management theories of the business schools and MBA programmes, but in terms of the actual day-to-day practice of managing, and for people who do not go to the business schools, there is a yawning gap. The need to say good morning to people, to thank them for their efforts, to understand where they are coming from, to think ahead and consult them, or at least keep them in the picture about what is going to happen, to let them make a contribution and have a say in how work is done or is organized—things of this kind are considered too primitive for the lofty accreditation procedures of management development and training. Management training also does not usually include things like how tasks may be combined into meaningful jobs and how people can arrive at solutions for themselves. These are among the things that seem to need to be discovered by every generation, but their discovery could be made easier.

How the three questions interact

Thus, the three parts of the research question which I suggested at the beginning (What aspects of work that are helpful to people can be designed and built into products, plant, environments and technologies? What aspects can be built into institutions and processes? And what really does, like democracy, need to be discovered again by every generation?) obviously interact. The second one is the independent variable: the more that is built into institutions, such as the training of technologists and managers, the more can then be built into plant, technologies, and working arrangements, and the less has to be rediscovered. The less that is built into institutions, the less will be built into technologies and structures, and the more has to be rediscovered. There is, in any case, an irreducible core that really does have to be rediscovered, not only by every generation but by every individual.

But there is also a great deal of rediscovery that owes more to the stimulus of discovering than to real changes in the situation. If I was more given to interpreting unconscious motivations of behaviour than I generally dare, I might suggest that the fun of discovery is partly what prevents us from dealing with the problem. Changes in the nature of work have been used as the justification for needing to find out what seem to me to be the same things, again and again. I believe that the reason lies more in the dynamics of putting knowledge into practice: it is the process of discovery, both on the part of researchers and on the part of others involved, that provides the impetus, not the changing nature of the work itself.

About the half-filled glass

I am sometimes criticized for seeing only the empty half of the glass, and it is true that I tend to see more potential in a situation than is eventually achieved. This sometimes irritates clients, who may think that quite a lot has actually been achieved. (Ah, but are they not perhaps rationalizing the fact that they themselves could have done more?) Although I recognize this in my own makeup (thirty-two sub-managers of the bank branches in Chapter Ten had a valuable experience; it is my fate to worry about the other three thousand), it is also a wider phenomenon. When Ken Eason and I collected case studies in applied social science during the 1980s, every one of the practitioners we interviewed expressed some disappointment, and talked about more that could have been done, in projects that to us, as outsiders, seemed to have been good and successful.

Much of this is a question of where your perception draws the line that defines a piece of work: round that part of the population that gained some benefit? At the point where the project is going well, or the point where it has run into obstacles or out of steam? Round the aspects that were dealt with or the aspects that were not dealt with? At the point where the lessons learned emerge in some other form? Or simply at the point where the funding ended? In so far as knowledge of results is an important factor in work satisfaction, it is one that social scientists have to manage without.

Work: its rewards and discontents

(An Arno Press collection)

Anderson, V.V. (1929). *Psychiatry in Industry.*

Archibald, K. (1947). *Wartime Shipyard.*

Argyris, C. (1954). *Organization of a Bank.*

Baetjer, A. M. (1946). *Women in Industry.*

Baker, E. F. (1933). *Displacement of Men by Machines.*

Barnes, C. B. (1915). *The Longshoremen.*

Carr, L. J., & Stermer, J. E. (1952). *Willow Run.*

Chenery, W. L. (1922). *Industry and Human Welfare.*

Clark, H. F. (1931). *Economic Theory and Correct Occupational Distribution.*

Collis, E. L., & Major Greenwood (1921). *The Health of the Industrial Worker.*

de Man, H. (1929). *Joy in Work.*

Dreyfuss, C. (1938). *Occupation and Ideology of the Salaried Employee.*

Dubreuil, H. (1930). *Robots or Men?*

Ellsworth Jr., J. S. (1952). *Factory Folkways.*

Floyd, W. F., & Welford, A. T. (Eds.) (1953–1954). *Symposium on Fatigue and Symposium on Human Factors in Equipment Design.*

Friedmann, E. A., & Havighurst, R. J. (1954). *The Meaning of Work and Retirement.*

Friedmann, G. (1955). *Industrial Society.* Edited by H. L. Sheppard.

Goldmark, J., & Hopkins, M. D. (1920). *Comparison of an Eight-Hour Plant and a Ten Hour Plant.*

Goodrich, C. (1925). *The Miner's Freedom.*

Great Britain Industrial Health Research Board, Medical Research Council (1977). *British Work Studies.*

Haggard, H. W., & Greenberg, L. A. (1935). *Diet and Physical Efficiency.*

Hannay, A. (1936). *A Chronicle of Industry on the Mill River.*

Hartmann, G. W., & Newcomb, T. (Eds.) (1939). *Industrial Conflict.*

Heron, A. R. (1948). *Why Men Work.*

Hersey, R. B. (1932). *Workers' Emotions in Shop and Home.*

Hoppock, R. (1935). *Job Satisfaction.*

Hughes, G. S. (1925). *Mothers in Industry.*

Husband, J. (1911). *A Year in a Coal-Mine.*

Kornhauser, A., Dubin, R., & Ross, A. M. (Eds.) (1954). *Industrial Conflict.*

Levasseur, E. (1900). *The American Workman.*

Lincoln, J. T. (1909). *The City of the Dinner-Pail.*

Marot, H. (1918). *Creative Impulse in Industry.*

Mayo, E. (1933). *The Human Problems of an Industrial Civilization.*

Mayo, E. (1945). *The Social Problems of an Industrial Civilization.*

Moore, W. E. (1951). *Industrial Relations and the Social Order.*

Morse, N. C. (1953). *Satisfactions in the White-Collar Job.*

Myers, C. S. (1925). *Industrial Psychology.*

Noland, E. W., & Wight Bakke, E. (1949).*Workers Wanted.*

Oakley, C. A. (1946). *Men at Work.*

Odencrantz, L. C. (1919). *Italian Women in Industry.*

Purcell, T. V. (1960). *Blue Collar Man.*

Reiss Jr., A. J. et al. (1961). *Occupations and Social Status.*

Reynolds, L. G., & and Shister, J. (1949). *Job Horizons.*

Rhyne, J. J. (1930). *Some Southern Cotton Mill Workers and Their Villages.*

Richardson, F. L. W., & Walker, C. R. (1948). *Human Relations in an Expanding Company.*

Roe, A. (1956). *The Psychology of Occupations.*

Sayles, L. R. (1958). *Behavior of Industrial Work Groups.*

Seashore, S. E. (1954). *Group Cohesiveness in the Industrial Work Group.*

Shepard, W. P. (1961). *The Physician in Industry.*

Smith, E. D. (1939). *Technology and Labor.*

Soule, G. (1956). *What Automation Does to Human Beings.*

Spofford, H. P. (1881). *The Servant Girl Question.*

Staley, E. (Ed.) (1952). *Creating an Industrial Civilization.*

Stein, L. (Ed.) (1977). *Work or Labor.*

Tead, O. (1929). *Human Nature and Management.*

Tilgher, A. (1930). *Work: What it has Meant to Men Through the Ages.*

Todd, A. J. (1933). *Industry and Society.*

Tugwell, R. G. (1933). *The Industrial Discipline and the Governmental Arts.*

US House of Representatives, Committee on Labor (1914). *The Stop Watch and Bonus System in Government Work.*

Vernon, H. M. (1921). *Industrial Fatigue and Efficiency.*

Walker, C. R. (1922). *Steel: The Diary of a Furnace Worker.*

Whitehead, T. N. (1938). *The Industrial Worker.*

Whitehead, T. N. (1936). *Leadership in a Free Society.*

Whyte, W. F. (1948). *Human Relations in the Restaurant Industry.*

Checklist for implementation issues

Implementation issues

I t will be essential to incorporate questions about the human, social and organizational aspects, and methodologies concerning these aspects, with the development of the pilots as this proceeds, and not leave them to be discovered afterwards. While practical measures to deal with these questions will be needed at different stages of the development, the parties need to be aware of them even at the earliest stages, since they may affect strategic decisions. The questions are presented here as a checklist and are intended as a stimulus for analysis. They are drawn from research in other settings and are therefore a starting point for your own organization: add any others that you think are needed.

The changes in relation to individuals

Who (what categories of people) will be affected by this technology? For each category of persons:

(a) Do they have a satisfactory system already? Have they had the chance to tweak that system to their needs which they won't have with the new one?

(b) How will the new system affect their future?
    (i) Security—greater, or less, or unchanged?
    (ii) Career prospects—better or worse prospects? Different career path or unchanged?
(c) How will the new system affect their skills?
    (i) What do they need to learn?
    (ii) What do they need to unlearn?
    (iii) Is the effort worthwhile?
    (iv) No change?
(d) How will it affect their working relationships?
    (i) Is it likely to lead to support and co-operation?
    (ii) Is it likely to create conflict and competition?
    (iii) Will there be appropriate face-to-face interaction?
(e) How will it affect the content of their work?
    (i) More interesting, or less?
    (ii) More varied, or less?
    (iii) More freedom, or less?
    (iv) More overview of the whole process, or less?
    (v) More control over their work, or less?
    (vi) No change?
(f) Effects on stress levels?

Is there likely to be a difference between short-term and long-term effects in any of these areas?

The changes in relation to the structure of the organization:

(a) Will new roles or departments be needed?
(b) What will happen to the old ones?
(c) Merged departments?
(d) New power relations between departments?
(e) What sources of misunderstanding or conflict are possible between them?
(f) Who gains and who loses from such changes?
(g) What effect on accountability?
(h) Will inspection and control of work be more local or more remote?
(i) Will decisions be more centralized, more local, or the same?

The changes in relation to organizational culture.

(a) What values will it tend to emphasize?
(b) Will there be changes in the locus of control and what effects will these have?
(c) What norms (unwritten rules) is it likely to produce?
(d) What effects is speedier development likely to have?

How will changes affect relations between organizations?

(a) New power relations between organizations?
(b) New types of contract?
(c) New types of dependencies?
(d) New types of groupings?
(e) New alignment of interests?
(f) No change.

How will the patterns of risk change, for organizations and for individuals?

Who owns the solution?
Who maintains the solution?

Methods for dealing with implementation issues

For any of these issues listed (or others, not listed here), decisions need to be made about how to approach it. Some possibilities are:

1. Do nothing: there is no need or it will look after itself.
2. Involve the affected parties with the implementation team.
   (a) At what stage?
   (b) The actual parties or representatives?
   (c) Briefed at what stage (people cannot contribute without preparation)?
3. Training
4. Teaching or presentations
5. Workshops
6. Working parties

7. Simulations (that include "soft" aspects)
8. Pilot exercise (that includes "soft" aspects)
9. A research loop
10. A literature review

Implementing the methods

1. Who is responsible for initiating/doing?
   (a) Experts.
   (b) Users.
   (c) Managers.
2. At what stage?
3. With what budget?
4. With what other support?
5. Within what time scale?
6. Responsible to whom?

REFERENCES

Alter, K., & Hage, J. (1993). *Organizations Working Together*. Newbury Park, CA: Sage.

Anthony, R. N. (1960). The trouble with profit maximisation. *Harvard Business Review*, 3(6).

Bailes, K. (1977). Alexei Gastev and the Soviet controversy over Taylorism, 1918–24. *Soviet Studies*, 92(3): 373–394.

Bailyn, L. (1993). *Breaking The Mold: Women, Men, and Time In The New Corporate World*. New York: Free Press.

Beck, U. (2000). *The Brave New World of Work*. Oxford: Polity Press.

Bell, D. (1956). *Work and Its Discontents: The Cult of Efficiency in America*. Boston, MA: Beacon Press.

Bowlby, J., Robertson, J., & Rosenbluth, D. (1952). A two-year old goes to hospital. *Psychoanalytic Study of the Child*, 7: 82–94.

Bridges, W. (1994). *Jobshift: How To Prosper in a Workplace without Jobs*. New York: Perseus.

Brown, W. (1960). *Exploration in Management*. London: Heinemann.

Burns, T., & Stalker, G. M. (1961). *The Management of Innovation*. London: Tavistock.

Bullinger, H.-J., Rieth, D., & Euler, H. P. (1993). *Planung entkoppelter Montagesysteme: Puffer in der Montage*. Stuttgart: Teubner.

Cherns, A. (1976). The principles of sociotechnical design. *Human Relations, 29*(8): 783–792.

Cherns, A. (1987). Principles of sociotechnical design revisited. *Human Relations, 40*(3): 153–162.

Construction Task Force (1998). *Rethinking Construction: The Report of the Construction Task Force to the Deputy Prime Minister, John Prescott, on the Scope for Improving the Quality and Efficiency of UK Construction.* London: Department of the Environment, Transport and the Regions.

Crossman, E. R. G. W. (1960). *Automation and Skill. DSIR Problems of Progress in Industry, No. 9.* London: HMSO.

Dalziel, S. J., & Klein, L. (1960). *The Human Implications of Work Study: The Case of Pakitt Ltd. Human Sciences Unit, Warren Spring Laboratory.* London: Department of Scientific and Industrial Research.

Darvall, F. O. (1934). *Popular Disturbances and Public Order in Regency England.* Oxford: Oxford University Press.

de Man, H. (1977). *Joy in Work.* New York: Arno Press.

Donaldson, L. (1996). The normal science of structural contingency theory. In: S. R. Clegg, C. Hardy, & W. R. Nord (Eds.), *Handbook of Organization Studies* (pp. 57–76). London: Sage.

Drucker, P. (1969). *The Age of Discontinuity: Guidelines to our Changing Society.* New York: Harper and Row.

Eason, K. (1982). The process of introducing new technology. *Behaviour and Information Technology, 1*(2): 197–213.

Eason, K. D. (1988). *Information Technology and Organisational Change.* London: Taylor and Francis.

Eason, K. D. (2002). People and computers: emerging work practice in the information age. In: P. B. Warr (Ed.), *Psychology at Work* (5th edn). London: Penguin.

Eilon, S. (1959). The industrial engineering revolution. *Journal of the Institute of Production Engineering,* August.

Emery, F. E., & Thorsrud, E. (1969). *Form and Content in Industrial Democracy: Some Experiences from Norway and other European Countries.* London: Tavistock.

Emery, F. E., & Trist, E. L. (1965). The causal texture of organizational environments. *Human Relations, 18*: 21–32.

Euler, H. P. (1977). Zur empirischen Kritik von Konzepten der Arbeitsstrukturierung. *Fortschrittliche Betriebsführung und Industrial Engineering, 26*(5): 303–312.

Euler, H. P. (1987). Neue Arbeitsstrukturen in der Elektroindustrie – Ergebnisse sozialwissenschaftlicher Untersuchungen. *Der Bundes-*

minister für Forschung und Technologie. Series "Humanisierung des Arbeitslebens" (vol. 83). Frankfurt: Campus-Verlag.

Freud, S. (1930a). *Civilisation and Its Discontents. S. E., 21*: 64–145. London: Hogarth.

Fricke, W. (2003). Thirty years of work life programmes in Germany. P. F. Wood (Trans.). *Concepts and Transformation, 8*(1): 43–68.

Glaser, B. G., & Strauss, A. L. (1968). *The Discovery of Grounded Theory: Strategies for Qualitative Research*. London: Weidenfeld and Nicolson.

Goldthorpe, J. H., Lockwood, D., Bechhofer F., & Platt, J. (1968). *The Affluent Worker*. Cambridge: Cambridge University Press.

Gorz, A. (1999). *Reclaiming Work: Beyond The Wage-based Society*. Cambridge: Polity Press.

Handy, C. (1994). *The Empty Raincoat: Making Sense of the Future*. London: Hutchinson.

Harding, D. W. (1931). A note on the sub-division of assembly work. *Journal of the National Institute of Industrial Psychology, 5*: 261–264.

Herzberg, F., Mausner, B., & Snyderman, B. B. (1959). *The Motivation to Work*. New York: Wiley.

Higgin, G. (1973). *Symptoms of Tomorrow*. London: Ward Lock/Pluine Press.

Hill, P. (1971). *Towards a New Philosophy of Management*. London: Gower Press.

Hobsbawm, E. J. (1952). The machine breakers. *Past and Present*, Feb: 57–70.

Holti, R., Nicolini, D., & Smalley, M. (1999). *Building Down Barriers*. The Tavistock Institute Interim Evaluation Report.

Hoxie, R. F. (1915). *Scientific Management and Labor*. New York: D. Appleton.

Hulin, C. L., & Blood, M. R. (1968). Job enlargement, individual differences, and worker responses. *Psychological Bulletin, 69*: 41–55.

Huws, U. (2003). *The Making of a Cybertariat*. New York: Monthly Review Press.

Jahoda, M. (1966). Notes on work. In: R. M. Loewenstein, L. M. Newman, M. Schur, & A. J. Solnit (Eds.), *Psychoanalysis: A General Psychology* (pp. 622–633). New York: International Universities Press.

Jahoda, M., Lazarsfeld, P. F., & Zeisel, H. (1933). Die Arbeitslosen von Marienthal. Österreichische Wirtschaftspsychologische Forschungsstelle. Leipzig: Hirzel. English edition (1971): *Marienthal: The Sociography of An Unemployed Community*. New York: Aldine-Atherton.

King, D. (1960). *Vocational Training in View of Technical Change.* European Productivity Agency, Project No. 418.

Klein, L. (1963). *The Meaning of Work.* Fabian Tract 349. London: Fabian Society.

Klein, L. (1964). *Multiproducts Ltd. A Case Study in the Social Effects of Rationalised Production.* London, HSMO.

Klein, L. (1975). *Neue Formen der Arbeitsorganisation.* Göttingen: Verlag Otto Schwartz.

Klein, L. (1976a). *New Forms of Work Organisation.* Cambridge: Cambridge University Press.

Klein, L. (1976b). *A Social Scientist in Industry.* London: Gower.

Klein, L. (1978). The production engineer's role in industrial relations. *Production Engineer, 57*(12).

Klein, L. (1979). Some problems of theory and method. In: R. G. Sell & P. Shipley (Eds.), *Satisfactions in Work Design: Ergonomics and Other Approaches.* London: Taylor and Francis.

Klein, L. (1989). On the collaboration between social scientists and engineers. In: H. H. Rosenbrock (Ed.), *Designing Human-Centered Technology: A Cross-Disciplinary Project in Computer-Aided Manufacturing* (pp. 81–97). London: Springer-Verlag.

Klein, L. (2001). Luddism for the twenty-first century. *International Journal of Human–Computer Studies, 55*: 727–737.

Klein, L. (2005). *Working Across the Gap.* London: Karnac

Klein, L., & Eason, K. (1991). *Putting Social Science to Work: The Ground Between Theory and Use Explored Through Case Studies in Organisations.* Cambridge: Cambridge University Press.

Kleinberg, A., & Blatny, F. (1937). *Das Denkmal der unbekannten Proletarierin.* Karlsbad: Druck- und Verlagsanstalt "Graphia".

Kohorn, E. I. (1996). Decision making for chemotherapy administration in patients with low risk gestational trophoblastic neoplasia. *International Journal of Gynecological Cancer, 6*: 279–285.

Lawrence, P. R., & Lorsch, J. W. (1967). *Organization and Environment: Managing Differentiation and Integration.* Cambridge, MA: Harvard University Press.

Leadbeater, C. (1999). *Living on Thin Air: The New Economy.* London: Penguin.

Levy, F., & Murnane, R. J. (2004). *The New Division of Labor: How Computers Are Creating the Next Job Market.* Princeton, NJ: Princeton University Press.

Lewin, K. (1920). *Die Sozialisierung des Taylorsystems. Praktischer Sozialismus,* no. 4. Berlin: Verlag Gesellschaft und Erziehung..

Lindholm, R., & Norstedt, J. P. (1975). *The Volvo Report*. Stockholm: Swedish Employers' Confederation.

Lupton, T. (1963). *On the Shop Floor*. Oxford: Pergamon.

Manchester Centre for Healthcare Management, University of Manchester, The Bayswater Institute, London, Medical Informatics Group, University of Manchester, & School of Postgraduate Studies in Medical and Health Care, Swansea. (2001). Research evaluation of NHS EPR/ICWS Pilot Sites. Available online: www.disco.port. ac.uk/ictri/projects/EPR_pilot_eval.htm.

Marchington, M., Grimshaw, D., Rubery J., & Wilmott, H. (Eds.) (2004). *Fragmenting Work: Blurring Organizational Boundaries and Disordering Hierarchies*. Oxford: Oxford University Press.

Marx, K. (1958). *Capital* (English translation). London: Lawrence and Wishart.

Merrifield, J., & Mackay, L. (1999). Junior doctors and the hospital computer information system. *NHS Executive EPR Programme*, Occasional Paper 2.

Metzger, H., Warnecke, H. J., & Zippe, H. (1975). Neue Formen der Arbeitsstrukturierung im Produktionsbereich. *Z. ind Fertig*, 65: 665–670.

Moynagh, M., & Worsley, R. (2005). *Working in the Twenty-first Century*. Leeds and Norfolk, Economic and Social Research Council and The Tomorrow Project.

Mumford, E. (2003). *Redesigning Human Systems*. Hershey, PA: IRM Press.

Mumford, E., & Weir, M. (1979). *Computer Systems in Work Design—the ETHICS Method*. London: Associated Business Press.

Neff, W. S. (1965). Psychoanalytic conceptions of the meaning of work. *Psychiatry*, 28: 324–333.

Perrow, C. (1970). *Complex Organizations*. Chicago, IL: Scott, Foresman.

Pugh, D. S., Hickson, D. J., Hinings, C. R., & Turner, C. (1969). The context of organisational structures. *Administrative Science Quarterly*, 14: 91–114.

Rapoport, R., Bailyn, L., Fletcher, J. K., & Pruitt, B. H. (2002). *Beyond Work–Family Balance: Advancing Gender Equity and Workplace Performance*. San Francisco, CA: Jossey-Bass.

Rifkind, J. (1995). *The End of Work—The Decline of the Global Labor Force and the Dawn of the Post-market Era*. New York: Tarcher/Putman.

Rosenbrock, H. H. (Ed.) (1989). *Designing Human-Centred Technology: A Cross-Disciplinary Project in Computer-Aided Manufacturing*. London: Springer-Verlag.

Rudé, G. (1964). *The Crowd in History, 1730–1848.* New York: Wiley.

Sale, K. (1999). The achievements of 'General Ludd'; a brief history of the Luddites. *The Ecologist, 29*(5).

Schön, D. A. (1971). *Beyond the Stable State.* New York: Basic Books.

Scott, S., & Buckingham, J. (1994). *Life and Work in Greenwich District Hospital Before and After HISS.* NHSME Information Management Group, Reference IMGME D4008.

Sennett, R. (1998). *The Corrosion of Character — The Personal Consequences of Work in the New Capitalism.* New York: Norton.

Shackel, B. (2000). People and computers—some recent highlights. *Applied Ergonomics, 31*(6): 595–608.

Shackel, B., & Klein L. (1976). Esso London Airport refuelling control centre redesign—an ergonomics case study. *Applied Ergonomics, 7*(1): 37–45.

Sochor, Z. A. (1981). Soviet Taylorism revisited. *Soviet Studies, 33*(2): 246–264.

Taylor, F. W. (1911). *The Principles of Scientific Management.* New York: Harper.

Trist, E. L. (1981). The evolution of socio-technical systems. In: A. H. Van de Ven & W. F. Joyce (Eds.), *Perspectives on Organization Design and Behaviour.* New York: Wiley.

Trist, E. L. (1989). Psychoanalytic issues in organisational research and consultation. In: L. Klein (Ed.), *Working with Organisations; Papers to Celebrate the 80th Birthday of Harold Bridger* (pp. 50–57). Private publication: ISBN 0 901882321.

Trist, E. L., & Bamforth, K. W. (1951). Some social and psychological consequences of the longwall method of coal getting. *Human Relations, 4*: 3–38.

Trist, E., & Murray, H. (Eds.) (1993). *The Social Engagement of Social Science; a Tavistock Anthology. Vol II: The Socio-technical Perspective.* Philadelphia, PA: University of Pennsylvania Press.

Trist, E. L., Higgin, G. W., Murray, H., & Pollock, A. B. (1963). *Organizational Choice: Capabilities of Groups at the Coal Face under Changing Technologies: The Loss, Rediscovery and Transformation of a Work Tradition.* London: Tavistock.

Turner, A. N., & Lawrence, P. R. (1965). *Industrial Jobs and the Worker.* Cambridge, MA: Harvard University Graduate School of Business Administration.

Vaill, B. P. (1982). The purposing of high-performing systems. *Organisational Dynamics,* Autumn: 23–39.

Vernon, H. M., Wyatt, S., & Ogden, A. D. (1924). *On the Extent and Effects of Variety in Repetitive Work*. Industrial Fatigue Research Board, Report No.26. London: HMSO.

Walker, C. R., & Guest, R. H. (1952). *The Man on the Assembly Line*. Cambridge, MA: Harvard University Press.

Wall, T. D., Kemp, N. J., Jackson, P. R., & Clegg, C. W. (1986). Outcomes of autonomous workgroups: a long-term field experiment. *Academy of Management Journal, 29*(2): 280–304.

White, M., Hill, S., Mills, C., & Smeaton, D. (2004). *Managing to Change? British Workplaces and the Future of Work*. ESRC, London: Palgrave Macmillan.

Whyte, W. F. (1948). *Human Relations in the Restaurant Industry*. New York: McGraw Hill.

Whyte, W. H. (1956). *The Organization Man*. New York: Simon and Schuster.

Woodward, J. (1958). *Management and Technology*. DSIR Problems of Progress in Industry, No. 3. London: HMSO.

Woodward, J. (1965). *Industrial Organisation: Theory and Practice*. Oxford: Oxford University Press.

Woodward, J. (Ed.) (1970). *Industrial Organisation: Behaviour and Control*. Oxford: Oxford University Press.

Wright Mills, C. (1956). *White Collar: The American Middle Classes*. New York: Oxford University Press.

Wyatt, S., & Fraser, J. A., assisted by Stock, F. G. L. (1928). *The Comparative Effects of Variety and Uniformity in Work*. Industrial Fatigue Research Board, Report No. 52. London: HMSO.

INDEX